Graphic

# STEVEN HELLER & SEYMOUR CHWAST

# Graphic Styles

## FROM VICTORIAN TO POST-MODERN

## HARRY N. ABRAMS, INC., PUBLISHERS

**ACKNOWLEDGMENTS**

For Louise and Paula

Pushpin Editions:

Producer: Steven Heller
Designer: Seymour Chwast
Associate Designer: Roxanne Slimak
Researcher: Barbara Dominowski

Harry N. Abrams, Inc.:

Editor: Margaret Donovan
Art Director: Samuel N. Antupit
Cover design by Seymour Chwast © 1988

Unless otherwise stated, illustrations are from the authors' collections.

Library of Congress Cataloging-in-Publication Data

Heller, Steven.
    Graphic Style.

    Bibliography: p.
    Includes index.
    1. Graphic arts—History—19th century—
Themes, motives. 2. Graphic arts—History—20th
century—Themes, motives. 3. Commercial art—
History—19th century—Themes, motives. 4. Commercial art—History—20th century—Themes,
motives. I. Chwast, Seymour.
II. Title.
NC998.2.H45   1988   741.6'09'034   88–3287
ISBN 0–8109–1033–0 (cloth)
ISBN 0–8109–2588–5 (pbk.)

Paperback edition published in 1994 by
Harry N. Abrams, Incorporated, New York.

Clothbound edition published in 1988 by
Harry N. Abrams, Inc.

Printed and bound in Japan

The authors wish to thank Barbara Dominowski for her tireless research, efficient identification and organization of materials, and continued loyalty and good humor. Roxanne Slimak for her production expertise and unfaltering patience. Margaret Donovan, our editor at Harry N. Abrams, for her invaluable editing and unflagging enthusiasm. Sam Antupit, our art director at Harry N. Abrams, for his encouragement. Paul Gottlieb, our publisher at Harry N. Abrams, for his support. Martina Schmitz for her research in the early stages of this project. Jeff Powers for his fine production assistance. Ed Spiro for his much-needed photography. And Sarah Jane Freymann, our agent, for her staunch efforts on our behalf.

This book would not have been possible without the cooperation of numerous people who were generous sources of material. Thanks to: Elaine Lustig Cohen, at Ex Libris, New York, for kindly making available her photographic records. Chris Mullen for his generosity and intelligence in locating, explaining, and securing materials from the United Kingdom. James Fraser, director of the Library at Fairleigh Dickinson University, Florham-Madison Campus, for his wisdom and for providing us with our single most important resource. Renée Weber, Librarian, Special Collections, Fairleigh Dickinson, for handling our countless requests for materials and bibliographic information. Robert Brown, of the Reinhold Brown Gallery, for his many contributions. Barry Friedman, of Barry Friedman Fine Arts, for opening his files to us. Stephen Greenglass and Mercedes Quioga at the Mitchell Wolfson Jr. Collection of Decorative and Propaganda Arts, who lent us some of our most prized rarities. Alexandra Corn and Jack Rennert at Posters Please, who allowed us access to some remarkable posters.

And our sincere appreciation to all the public and private collections from whom we received assistance: Karl Wobmann, Kunstgewerbemuseum, Zurich; Rolf Thalmann, Gewerbemuseum, Basel; W. A. L. Beeren, Stedelijk Museum, Amsterdam; Dr. Marie-Luise Sternath, Graphische Sammlung Albertina, Vienna; Lucio Santoro, Santoro Graphics, London; Georgia Barnhill, American Antiquarian Society, Worcester, Mass.; Pamela Robertson, Hunterian Art Gallery, University of Glasgow; Freda Matassa, Goldie Paley Gallery, Moore College of Art, Philadelphia; Elena Millie, Library of Congress, Washington, D. C.; Alicyn Warren, Graphic Arts Collection, Princeton University Library; Melody Ennis, Museum of Art, Rhode Island School of Design, Providence; Thomas Grischkowsky, The Museum of Modern Art, New York; Miss C. M. Parry, Walker Art Gallery, National Museums and Galleries on Merseyside, Liverpool; Sheila Taylor, London Transport Museum; Bauhaus-Archiv Museum für Gestaltung, Berlin; Memphis Milano, Italy; Musée de la Publicité, Paris; The Everson Museum of Art, Syracuse, N. Y.; Collection Michael Pabst, Verlag Silke Schreiber, Munich; Angewandte Kunst Museum, Vienna; Bildarchiv Preussischer Kulturbesitz, Kunstbibliothek mit Museum für Architektur, Modebild und Grafik-Design, West Berlin; The National Art Library, Victoria and Albert Museum, London; Museo Depero, Rovereto, Italy; Civici Musei di Udine, Italy; New York Public Library; Cooper-Hewitt Library, New York; Pierpont Morgan Library; Cammie Naylor, New-York Historical Society.

Thanks also to those private collectors and artists who lent material: Steven Guarnaccia, Margaret and John Martinez, Eric Baker, Nathan Gluck, Szymon Bojko, Tony DiSpigna, F. H. K. Henrion, Tom Eckersley, Abram Games, Gyorgy Kepes, Alex Steinweiss, Paul Rand, Leo Lionni, John Follis, Josef Müller-Brockmann, Armin Hofmann, Gene Federico, Rudolph de Harak, Lou Dorfsman, Saul Bass, David Lance Goines, Paul Davis, Barry Zaid, Milton Glaser, James McMullan, Robert Crumb, Michael Salisbury, Colin Forbes, Henry Wolf, Willi Fleckhaus, Franciszek Starowieyski, Jan Lenica, Roman Cieslewicz, Andrzej Czeczot, Edward Dwurnik, Mieczyslaw Gorowski, Leszek Drzewinski, Jerzy Czerniawski, Andrej Pagowski, Krystyna Hofmann, Victor Moscoso, John Van Hamersveld, Rick Griffin, Wes Wilson, Keisuke Nagatomo, Shigeo Okamoto, Kenji Itoh, Tadanori Yokoo, Yusaku Kamekura, Shigeo Fukuda, Kazumasa Nagai, Ikko Tanaka, George Hardie, Wolfgang Weingart, Siegfried Odermatt, Rosmarie Tissi, Hans-U. Allemann, Michael Zender, Dan Friedman, Inge Druckrey, April Greiman, William Longhauser, Nancy Skolos, John Jay, Joe Duffy, Charles Spencer Anderson, Jane Kosstrin, David Sterling, Warren Leherer, Art Chantry, Christopher Garland, Louis Fishauf, Mark Marek, Seth Jaben, Sussman/Prejza & Company, Inc., Michael Manwaring, Woody Pirtle, Alan Colvin, Michael Vanderbyl, Stephen Snider, John Casado, Susan Johnson, Alexander Jordan, Garald-Paris Clavel, Pierre Bernard, Alain Le Quernec, Gert Dumbar, Joost Swarte, Paul Wearing, Chermayeff & Geismar Associates, Louis Silverstein, Rudy Vanderlans, Michael R. Orr, Donna Bagley, Rachel Schreiber Levitan.

Further thanks for their generous support: Bloomingdale's, New York; Fiorucci, New York; Victoria Guirado, Artemide Inc., New York; Keiko Kubota, Editor-in-Chief of Rikuyo-sha Publishing, Inc., Tokyo; Diana Edkins, The Condé Nast Publications Inc., New York; Anne Su, Swatch Watch USA Inc., New York; Tom Goss, Associate Editor of *Print* magazine; Marisa Bulzone, Editor of *Graphis U.S.*; Charles Helmken; Phil Meggs; Sharon Stern.

# CONTENTS

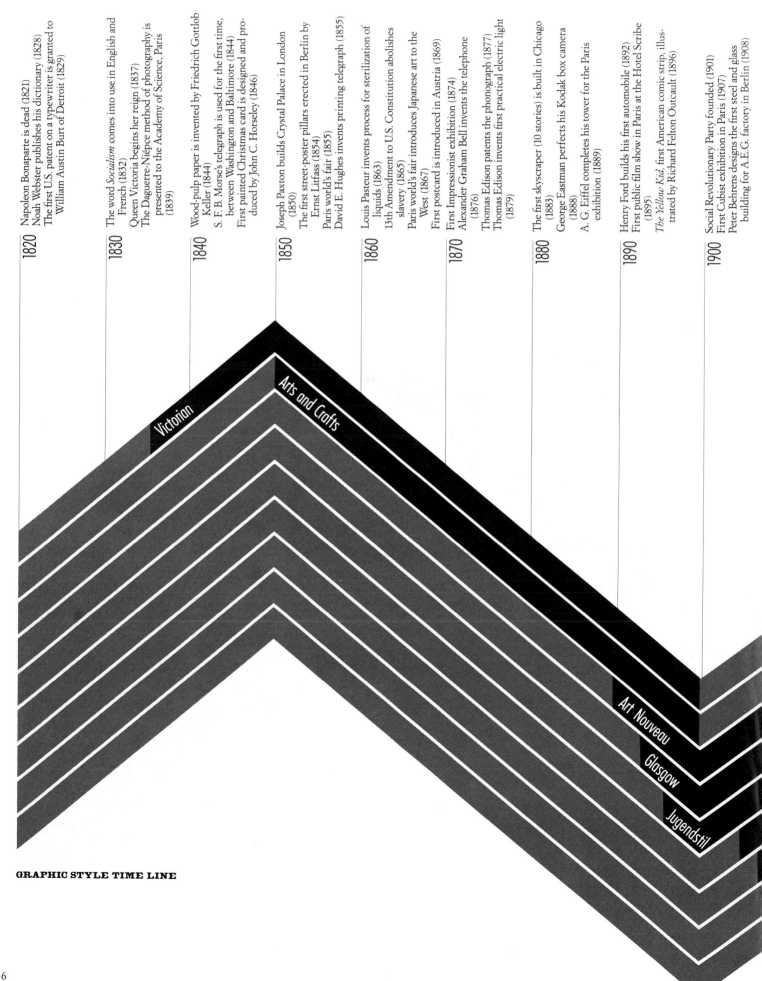

Napoleon Bonaparte is dead (1821)
Noah Webster publishes his dictionary (1828)
The first U.S. patent on a typewriter is granted to William Austin Burt of Detroit (1829)

The word *Socialism* comes into use in English and French (1832)
Queen Victoria begins her reign (1837)
The Daguerre-Niépce method of photography is presented to the Academy of Science, Paris (1839)

Wood-pulp paper is invented by Friedrich Gottlob Keller (1844)
S. F. B. Morse's telegraph is used for the first time, between Washington and Baltimore (1844)
First painted Christmas card is designed and produced by John C. Horseley (1846)

Joseph Paxton builds Crystal Palace in London (1850)
The first street-poster pillars erected in Berlin by Ernst Litfass (1854)
Paris world's fair (1855)
David E. Hughes invents printing telegraph (1855)

Louis Pasteur invents process for sterilization of liquids (1863)
13th Amendment to U.S. Constitution abolishes slavery (1865)
Paris world's fair introduces Japanese art to the West (1867)
First postcard is introduced in Austria (1869)

First Impressionist exhibition (1874)
Alexander Graham Bell invents the telephone (1876)
Thomas Edison patents the phonograph (1877)
Thomas Edison invents first practical electric light (1879)

The first skyscraper (10 stories) is built in Chicago (1883)
George Eastman perfects his Kodak box camera (1888)
A. G. Eiffel completes his tower for the Paris exhibition (1889)

Henry Ford builds his first automobile (1892)
First public film show in Paris at the Hotel Scribe (1895)
*The Yellow Kid*, first American comic strip, illustrated by Richard Felton Outcault (1896)

Social Revolutionary Party founded (1901)
First Cubist exhibition in Paris (1907)
Peter Behrens designs the first steel and glass building for A.E.G. factory in Berlin (1908)

1820
1830
1840
1850
1860
1870
1880
1890
1900

Victorian

Arts and Crafts

Art Nouveau

Glasgow

Jugendstil

**GRAPHIC STYLE TIME LINE**

**1910**
- Armory Show introduces modern art to New York (1913)
- World War I (1914–18)
- The first jazz record is issued by the Original Dixieland Jazz Band (1917)
- Russian Revolution (1917)

**1920**
- Benito Mussolini becomes Italian Prime Minister (1922)
- Al Jolson appears in *The Jazz Singer*, the first full-length talking film (1927)
- Kodak develops 16mm color film (1929)
- Wall Street crash initiates a world economic crisis (1929)

**1930**
- Adolf Hitler is first appointed German chancellor (1933), then Führer (1934)
- Spanish Civil War begins (1936)
- Henry Luce begins publication of *Life* magazine (1936)
- World War II begins (1939)

**1940**
- The first automatic computer, or electronic brain, is developed in the U.S. (1944)
- Atomic bomb is employed in war; World War II ends (1945)
- The transistor is invented at Bell Labs (1948)

**1950**
- Korean War begins (1950)
- Color television is first introduced in the U.S. (1950)
- Elvis Presley has his first rock 'n' roll hit (1956)
- Soviets launch Sputnik I, first earth satellite (1957)

**1960**
- U.S. scientists develop laser (1960)
- President Kennedy assassinated (1963)
- U.S. bombing of North Vietnam (1965)
- Apollo 11, first manned lunar landing (1969)

**1970**
- U.S.–South Vietnam and North Vietnam sign a cease-fire agreement (1973)
- First test tube baby born, in England (1978)
- Anwar Sadat and Menachem Begin sign Camp David accords (1978)

**1980**
- Space shuttle flights begin with the *Columbia* (1981)
- Relatively high temperature superconductors developed (1986)
- *Glasnost* policy is implemented by Russian Communist Party Chairman Gorbachev (1987)

Swiss International Style

Revivalism and Eclecticism

Polish Style

Art Deco

Dada

Vorticism

Bauhaus

Constructivism

New Typography

Late Modern

British Modern

Japanese Modern

De Stijl

Streamline

Basel

Psychedelia

Post-Modern

Punk

Wiener Werkstätte

Expressionism

Plakatstil

Futurism

Memphis

*All art is at once surface and symbol.*
Oscar Wilde, *The Picture of Dorian Gray,* 1891

*The humblest as well as the most exalted ornaments may one day become elements in that revealing whole,* the decorative style of an epoch.
Emile Gallé, Nancy, France, 1900

*Style is the signal of a civilization. Historians can date any artifact by its style, be it Egyptian, Grecian, Gothic, Renaissance, Colonial, American or Art Nouveau. It is impossible for man to produce objects without reflecting the society of which he is a part and the moment in history when the product concept developed in his mind.... In this sense everything produced by man has style.*
Sir Micha Black,
The Tiffany/Wharton Lectures, 1975

Style, in its most general sense, is a specific or characteristic manner of expression, design, construction, or execution. As it relates to graphic design, style suggests the dominant visual aesthetic of a particular time and place. The word has also been used to refer to a specific graphic designer's signature: his or her preference for a certain typeface or family of faces, for a characteristic color palette, and for either a decorative or a functional approach. Style is further defined by the material being designed and the audience for whom it is being produced: corporate style differs from editorial, news style from advertising, polemical style from commercial, and so on.

The graphic designer is basically organizing and communicating messages—to establish the nature of a product or idea, to set the appropriate stage on which to present its virtues, and to announce and publicize such information in the most effective way. Within this process, style is a transmission code, a means of signaling that a certain message is intended for a specific audience. By manipulating visual forms into an appropriate style, the designer can attract the right audience for a product or idea. In 1969 strategists in the reelection campaign of New York Mayor John Lindsay commissioned Peter Max, then guru of the commercial youth style, to design a psychedelic poster to attract the newly enfranchised baby-boomers. Likewise, in 1972, the promoters of George McGovern's presidential campaign used a Larry Rivers poster to lure a similar group; in the opposing camp, Nixon's publicity men came up with their own version of a youthful-looking poster. While the two presidential candidates proffered distinctly different points of view, their posters thus had similar graphic styles.

Simply defined, *graphic style* is the surface manifestation or the "look" of graphic design. This book is concerned with how that look has evolved and been reapplied since commercial art had its beginnings as a result of the revolutions in industry and commerce during the nineteenth century. Yet, even with such a narrow focus, a linear examination of style is still complicated by the fact that artists and designers do not always dutifully follow the arbiters of taste in their respective periods. What we call the Victorian style, for example, covers a period of seventy-five years and has countless nuances and variations; Art Deco, the decorative arts movement dominant between the two world wars, also is an amalgam of distinctly different methodologies. Upon close examination, however, there are enough visual characteristics common to most products of each period to justify the use of the *Victorian* or *Deco* umbrella.

In studying and analyzing style through the ages, historians have developed a system of classification that commonly focuses on painting, sculpture, architecture, furniture, and clothing and pays only scant attention to graphic design. Nevertheless, the advertising, posters, packages, and typefaces of a period, as well as its illustrations and cartoons, are equally, if not more, indicative of the society in which they were produced. As mass communication, commercial art is often a synthesis of other arts and technologies, demystified and made accessible to a broad audience. In fact, a vernacular graphic style usually indicates popular acceptance of visual philosophies that were once inaccessible, avant-garde, or elitist.

The farther one backtracks in history, the more singularly representative of its epoch a style appears to be (partly, of course, because lack of documentation tends to force generalization). Our relatively recent past is notable for a myriad of styles that occupy comparatively brief, concurrent periods and come and go with such speed that a kind of cultural detonation results when one collides with another. The question that now concerns graphic style is whether today's new technologies, like those of the Industrial Revolution, will change the substance, and not merely the surface, of graphic communications. While designers hope for a more

1. Will Bradley. *The Masqueraders.* Poster, c. 1894.
The Metropolitan Museum of Art, New York. Gift of Fern Bradley Dufner

coherent future, the buzzword that best sums up contemporary graphic style is "life-style." Design itself has become a commodity: more than ever before, decorative graphic design is assigned the task of seducing the customer into buying products.

From the Victorian era to the present, graphic design has had to serve various economic and cultural masters, and thus there have been numerous ways in which graphic styles have evolved. Certain styles were developed for aesthetic reasons (Art Nouveau), while others were politically motivated (Dada). There are those based on the need for corporate identity (Swiss International), on commercial requisites (Post-Modern), and on moral and philosophical foundations (the Bauhaus). Some were influenced by the fine arts (Art Deco), others by industry (Plakatstil). Some national styles became international movements (Futurism). A few styles enjoyed long duration—two or three (Constructivism, Expressionism, Surrealism) exert influence even today—though most were comparatively short-lived. And many historical styles have been revived, reinterpreted, and misused by succeeding generations.

Graphic designers today freely rummage through a big closet of historical styles looking for ones that are adaptable for their purposes. Sometimes, as they reprise a vintage graphic style, it will be an appropriate and graceful use—the product image is enhanced by being linked to another place and time. More often, designers without distinctive visual characters of their own attempt to adopt a once viable style without regard for the factors that brought it about in the first place.

As early as 1856, in an essay titled "The True and False in the Decorative Arts," Owen Jones condemned the contemporary practice of trying to make "the art which faithfully represents the wants, the faculties and the feelings of one people represent those of another people under totally different conditions." In the sixties a revival of French Art Deco gave rise to a hybrid decorative manner in American design. While creative practitioners took

2. Vassily Komardenkov. *Storm Cavalry*. Cubo/Futurist design for a book of poems, 1920. Courtesy Ex Libris, New York

the time to understand Deco's formal aspects, to make them unique and even expressive, most designers carelessly mimicked Deco's lightning bolts, raybands, and display typefaces. At best they produced a nostalgic conceit that said little about the time in which it was produced and less about the product or idea being newly presented. More recently, the radical form language of Russian Constructivism endured a similar "reappreciation." Instead of using the style to influence and shape a new vision—in the way Constructivism inspired the Swiss rationalist design of the forties and fifties—contemporary designers employed Constructivism's dynamic asymmetry and primary colors as casual toys, copying the surface qualities without regard for original intent. This tendency, however lamentable, may be regarded in one way as a logical and inevitable response. Although style divorced from its *raison d'être* by time and circumstance is just an empty shell, some designers may see it as a tempting refuge when faced with the necessity for original thinking.

Of course, this kind of appropriation is not unknown in art history, which is marked by periods of innovation and

then—years, decades, even centuries later—of reappreciation or revival. Along with the revivals that are merely shallow borrowings and those that honestly attempt to reestablish forgotten standards, there are still others that prove to be gateways to new discovery. The Pre-Raphaelite Brotherhood of English painters, for example, sought in the nineteenth century to emulate the purity of Italian religious painting during the Early Renaissance. To a period of predominantly realist art, the Brotherhood brought back the important and virtually neglected element of the imagination and thus was able to make a meaningful historical contribution. About the Pre-Raphaelites' direct influence on Surrealism, Marcel Duchamp said that they "lit a small flame which is still burning despite everything." Hermann Broch, on the other hand, argues that a preponderance of neo-this and neo-that in any period of art really signifies that the false or fraudulent is pervasive. Broch applies such a judgment to the Neo-Gothic and Neo-Baroque of the late nineteenth century, despite their impact on architecture, fashion, and applied arts. Such stylistic contrivances, he says, are nonstyles, because they do not truthfully represent their time and place.

Although Art Nouveau was, in fact, the first true modern international style, the term *Modernist* is commonly reserved for the antibourgeois, utopian art movements of the early twentieth century. The design innovations of the Modernist movement were the ones most obviously woven from whole cloth rather than patched together from imitations of the past. The unprecedented Cubist experiments of Picasso and Braque from 1908 to 1913 stimulated painters, fashion designers, and graphic artists for decades to follow. For designers the Cubist letter/image collages, in which word fragments were made by juxtaposing unrelated letter forms, suggested an original and expressive method of typographical communication. Employed for poetry, manifestoes, and exhibition announcements, these types were essentially advertising tools, their ultimate purpose the propagation of a new vision. Their marriage of word and image eventually helped bridge the gap between the fine and applied arts that had grown ever since the early days of printing.

From the Modernist tree grew many branches, each more or less supported by a formal design language and a philosophical underpinning disseminated through an official periodical. Though Theo van Doesburg's unadorned De Stijl typography differs visually from Solomon Telingater's Constructivist lettering, both adhered to the basic tenets of reductionism: ornament was a sin (as Viennese architect Adolf Loos declared); simple linear and geometric forms were virtues; and asymmetry was everywhere dominant. In Germany, Paul Renner's geometric sans-serif type, Futura, offered an exciting alternative to the antiquated and fussy blackletter Fraktur; in Russia, typographers

3. El Lissitzky. *Die Kunstismen.* Book cover, 1924. Courtesy Ex Libris, New York

used dynamic type arrangements to powerfully symbolize the Productivist age.

Such innovations were not without their critics. In speeches before design organizations in the twenties, Thomas Maitland Cleland, a renowned American typographer and advertising designer in the classical tradition, zealously decried the New Typography. Its "alluring short-cuts and seductive philosophies—a disturbing Babel of undigested ideas and indigestible objectives" were, Cleland

stated, the result of "the relentless craving for something new.... Typography is a servant of thought and language to which it gives visible existence. When there are new ways of thinking and a new language, it will be time enough for a new typography." Such critics refused to believe that a new way of designing, free from the shackles of formality, could be effective for conventional advertising purposes or that their classical approach, though beautiful in the right hands, represented past, not present, achievements. The New Typography, like most Modernist innovations, wasn't simply a matter of style for its own sake but rather style resulting from necessity.

Among those answering such charges was the German Jan Tschichold, who codified the Constructivist-influenced, asymmetrical typographic approach into a form language in his "Elementare Typographie" of 1925. Tschichold declared, "The rules of the old typography contradict the principles of fitness for purpose in design. Unsymmetrical arrangements are more flexible and better suited to the practical and aesthetic needs of today." Championing these forces of graphic innovation and criticizing those who copied past styles, Wassily Kandinsky said, "Such imitation resembles the antics of apes."

Of course, the virtues of any style, like those of any typography, are determined by how and to what purpose it is applied. In the wrong hands an otherwise beautiful stylistic mannerism can be made trivial and ugly. For example, the elegant typefaces developed in the eighteenth century by François Ambroise Didot and Giambattista Bodini were bastardized two centuries later by tasteless Victorian commercial job printers. While a few serious typographers tried at the time to maintain standards, they were undercut by the increased need for fast and economical commercial printing and by the proliferation of craftsmen without aesthetic training. Thus, graceful classical forms were made to serve the cluttered visual look of the age.

Even in its own time, the widespread use of a style by untutored practitioners

usually degrades the style, although it may increase its visibility and public acceptance. To fill his famous retail store with expensive inventory, Arthur L. Liberty shamelessly stole and altered original Art Nouveau designs. He did create an unprecedented market for the style but also contributed to its demise through overexposure. A few decades later the Bauhaus encountered a similar problem. Displeased with the irresponsible execution of Bauhaus-like wares by commercial firms, the school's director, Walter Gropius, railed against "imitators who prostituted our fundamental precepts into modish trivialities."

Yet it is inevitable that the moment a unique creation becomes a style, the great leavener called fashion comes into play. Some of the styles discussed here began as honest individual efforts with distinct purposes that ultimately became officially or universally adopted. In some cases, the individuals originally responsible for the styles were willing participants in their popularization; in others, they believed that to be true to their ideals required abandoning the popularized styles for purer forms.

Vanguard art has often been transmuted into commercial style, despite the best intentions of artistic pioneers to keep it out of the mainstream. German Expressionism was avowedly radical—in its aesthetic before World War I and in its pacifist polemic during the war. For years, its artists were criticized and rejected by the art establishment. Eventually, however, Expressionist works came to be perceived and honored as Germany's first contributions to Modernism; after the war Expressionism virtually became Germany's national style. Its emblematic hard-edged woodcuts formed the basis for much of the stylization in modern advertising and printing, a fact that quickly led to its obsolescence as an avant-garde form.

Even Dada—which in Germany rejected the artistic pretensions and emotional excesses of Expressionism and asserted an antiart position—could not escape being usurped by stylists. Through its distribution of mass-produced advertisements, periodicals, books, and posters,

Dada propagated a distinctive collage, montage, and typographic style that has been borrowed by less politically committed designers, then and now. Today the Dada style, as reflected in Punk and Neo-Expressionist design, is an effective code for conveying the tempests of contemporary youth.

Some of the most significant twentieth-century avant-garde art movements were successful in propagating their ideas through the popular commercial media, only to find their radical visions overexposed and trivialized. Italian Futurism was formulated in 1908 by F. T. Marinetti as a striking contrast to the Neoclassical Novocento Italiano style, but it was also wed to Benito Mussolini's emerging Fascist party. The influence of Futurism's forceful interpretation of the Machine Age grew as did Mussolini; it flourished as both a national and a commercial style after his power was secured. Yet the obvious requisites of an authoritarian regime—especially once Italy entered the war—ultimately caused Futurism's subordination to party needs. What remained of the original graphic style was merely a decorative Futurist veneer.

The past half-century has witnessed a proliferation of design styles, some enduring, others short-lived. The rise of the Nazi party and later the beginning of World War II had a direct impact on many design forms. Though many Modernists were forced to flee Europe or go into hiding, the disbanding of the dominant art and design movements only briefly interrupted the stylistic continuum of graphic design. Indeed, during the war, many significant designers developed individual styles consistent with Modernist thought, among them the Americans Paul Rand and Lester Beall and the European immigrants Herbert Matter, Alexey Brodovitch, and Herbert Bayer. Others, like the Swiss Max Bill, Josef Müller-Brockmann, and Armin Hofmann, built a new form language from the legacy of the Constructivists and the Bauhaus.

Various postwar graphic styles grew up around the efforts of such innovative stylists, many of whom were prolific writers on the theory and process of their vision.

4. Paul Rand. *Modern Art USA*. Book cover, 1956

From the ashes of war sprang new industrial states, with distinct communications needs. No longer simply an offshoot of other disciplines and media, graphic design served a primary role in establishing and maintaining the identity of business. Within the dominantly rationalist ethic exemplified by the Swiss, design in the fifties also saw a flowering of eclecticism and revivalism. No single style dominated: rationalist design found a home within the expanding corporate universe; eclecticism was ideal for certain advertising, publishing, and merchandising needs; and, later, the Psychedelic style, an original synthesis of Secessionist, Symbolist, and East Indian motifs, expressed the vibrant but brief life of the youth culture.

Through Punk, New Wave, Japanese, and the Basel School, we have arrived at Post-Modern, a resurfacing of classical forms clothed in updated traditional ones. At once symbolizing respect for the past, obsession with the present, and perhaps fear of the future, Post-Modern has replaced Art Deco as the latest international style.

Graphic design has come full circle in the eighties. It has evolved from the primordial clutter of Victorian Neo-Gothic, through the austere functionalism of Modernism, and back again into a mélange of Neoclassical layering. Although analysis of art history from this perspective reveals interesting cultural data, *Graphic Style* does not aim to offer new, scholarly methods for the study of popular culture. Rather, it is the first book to present an annotated chronology of the most significant stylistic movements, schools, and trends in printed communications from the nineteenth century to the present. Neither an inclusive nor conclusive history, it is more a map with which to navigate the continually changing topography of graphic design.

As such, *Graphic Style* is primarily concerned with the image, not the image-maker. Rarely is one man's or woman's genius solely responsible for the development or popularity of a significant style. While we discuss some individuals who provided prototypes for a style, we consistently emphasize the formal, emblematic visual characteristics of a design period. Thus, for instance, a designer who worked in several stylistic periods may be represented only in the one in which his or her work first appeared. Some of the work illustrated is attributable to a specific designer, but there is an equal number produced by unknowns. Graphic design is first a service, not an art, and most quotidian printed matter is unsigned and often anonymous. The apprentice and journeyman designers of any period followed the dominant forms and standards set down by established printers or in manuals, and this is the work that has most frequently survived.

*Graphic Style* therefore addresses how and why elements of Arts and Crafts, Jugendstil, Constructivism, Expressionism, and the other significant methodologies became conventions used by printers, layout artists, and advertising designers for commercial and business purposes. By tracing the roots and development of style, we aim to show how graphic design has interacted with the material culture, how it has served both as an adjunct to and as the vanguard in the development of broader period styles. In effect, we are tracing nothing less than the evolution of the popular tastes of a period.

Steven Heller

**GRAPHIC STYLE**

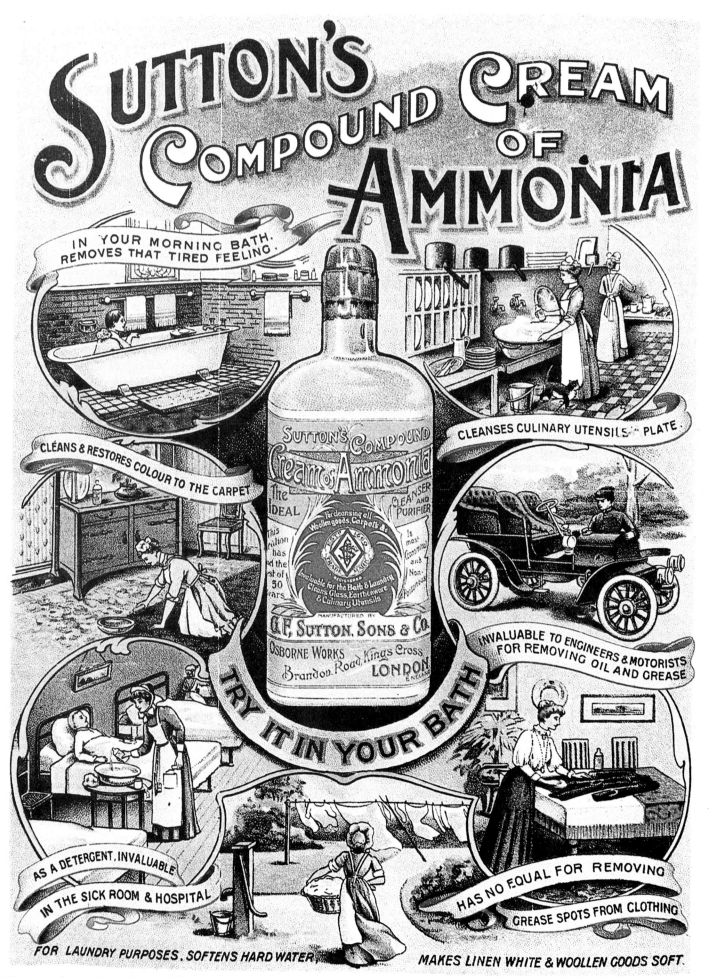

5. Designer unknown. *Sutton's Compound Cream of Ammonia.* Advertisement, 1907. Courtesy Chris Mullen

lthough Queen Victoria was crowned in 1837, the style of architecture and decorative arts that bears her name actually began in the 1820s and continued in England, America, and much of Europe until 1900. Victorian style was not the invention of this iron-willed matriarch, but rather the aesthetic response of a society to industrialization.

The Industrial Revolution was a mixed blessing in Britain. Along with technological revelations, it brought crime, urban blight, and the rise of a self-indulgent *nouveau riche* class. Between the end of the eighteenth century and the middle of the nineteenth, the once profound English sense of social, civic, and artistic responsibility diminished. Wealth became in effect the motivating cultural force. As the desire for unlimited comfort spread from the wealthy to the middle class, popular aesthetics were increasingly devoid of any critical standards.

With contemporary aesthetic standards in decline, Victorian artists turned to the past for inspiration. Taking special delight in medieval ruins, they saw parallels in the Gothic art and architecture of previous centuries to their present-day Christian virtue. Yet the borrowed elements in Victorian style were completely detached from their original culture. In *Analysis of Ornament* (1856), Ralph Nicholson assailed the revivalists, stating, "A designer might...produce a perfect arrangement of forms and colours, and yet show the grossest stupidity in its application."

The early Victorians reveled in ostentation. After the Great Exhibition of 1851, the taste for ornamentation based on historical forms was passionately indulged. Victorians believed that the corpulent display of material gain gratified the eye; ornament appeased their need to have visible evidence of their social status. The exaggerated embellishment of virtually every article in the Victorian home created an atmosphere of unshakable comfort and contributed to the decidedly cluttered look of the style. While ornament might seem simply to have offered Victorians status and aesthetic pleasure, one contemporary critic argued that it served to hide the "more aberrant lusts of human nature." And, as if industrialization were the metaphor for these perverted desires, Victorians disguised the advancements of their engineers under decorative excesses that mimicked natural forms.

Victorian taste was confused by the belief that ornamentation and design were identical functions. The art critic and architect Augustus Welby Northmore Pugin criticized this idea: "How many objects of ordinary use are rendered monstrous and ridiculous simply because the artist, instead of seeking the most convenient form and then decorating it, has embodied some extravagance to conceal the real purpose for which the object has been made." Another Victorian commentator proudly replied, "Disguise is the spice of life."

Although England is recognized as having originated the Victorian style, other burgeoning commercial centers in Europe and America felt its influence, which was disseminated to all classes through the printed mass media. The surpluses created by the Industrial Revolution led to increased competition in the marketplace, as sellers sought to educate buyers to the virtues of products and services. To this end, advancements in the simultaneous printing of text and image fostered the new medium called advertising, which soon became the clarion for announcing the rewards of the Victorian life-style.

The standards governing the production of graphic arts, like those guiding the other decorative arts, were few and unequal to the strides made by technology. Victorian commercial printed matter was characterized by the era's pervasive ornamentation, often imitating contemporary architectural eccentricities; images were frequently crudely drawn and engraved; typography was decidedly poor. If a compositor lacked a lower-case *g*, for example, he would not hesitate to use an upside-down *b* in its place.

Sometimes, however, a merchant's demand for distinctive announcements did result in truly original display faces, composed of odd, and even ingenious, woodblock letters. Designers of new display faces savaged the elegant eighteenth-century Bodoni and Didot types, distort-ing and making them larger and blacker. These bastardizations, called Fat Face types, became emblems of the Victorian look. As wood engravers mastered their medium, outline, whiteline, and shadowed letterforms gained greater exposure. The Egyptian faces—squared serif letters apparently influenced by the revival of interest in that country after Napoleon's excursions—joined the Fat Faces as one of the most original typographic forms of the century. Wood display types were popularized in Britain and abroad through frequent use by commercial printers. And the distinctive Victorian style of layout—extreme variations of type size and weight crammed within a single headline—was an invention of expedience, allowing the printer to utilize every inch of precious space.

By 1845 the high-speed steam press had so increased the volume of printed matter that many townscapes were blighted by bills and posters covering every inch of available wall space. Legislation was enacted and taxes levied to counter these graphic assaults, and advertising was ultimately restricted to special areas. Yet advertisers persisted and their trade became a fact of life, eventually elevating with it the role of commercial art. By the 1860s, an influx of academically trained craftsmen and artisans had entered the commercial arts, with the result that printed matter became more visually appealing and more conceptually sophisticated—some of it even quite beautiful.

The technological advances that ushered in the Victorian style continued to alter its look throughout the century: first, as chromolithography advanced in Germany and America in the 1870s, and then, at the close of the century, as the camera gave birth to photoengraving. Little by little, designers came to rely on standardized motifs and generic ornaments sold through printing catalogues. Victorian woodcuts and engravings, and the slab-serif and Gothic types, ultimately gave way to more sinuous, organic, and curvilinear forms. Indeed, during the seventy-five years that Victorian style was dominant, it evolved from a nostalgic Gothic revival into a precursor of Modernism.

## BRITISH

Today the decorative excesses of the Victorian style seem very quaint, for, detached from the art and politics of the epoch, this printed material has a simple, nostalgic beauty. Yet the Victorians suffered from a confused belief that ornament and design were identical. Their century witnessed a decline in the stringent Renaissance standards of typography, a decline typified here by the posters and broadsides featuring Fat Face bastardizations of Bodoni and Didot types as well as Egyptian slab-serif display faces. Had the word *functionalism* been coined, Victorian designers would have rejected everything it stood for. For them, decoration was a virtue that symbolized the comfortable Victorian life-style, here exemplified by the cover of *Punch,* England's premier satiric journal, and the excessive Rococo styling on Arthur Dixon's store sign.

6. Designer unknown. Wood-engraved food packaging labels, c. 1870

7. Richard Doyle. *Punch.* Magazine cover, May 26, 1883

8. Designer unknown. Storefront sign for chemist/druggist, c. 1835. Courtesy Chris Mullen

9. Designer unknown. *Phrenology. Physiology.* Lecture poster, 1861

10. Designer unknown. *Russia, Constantinople…* Poster, c. 1852

# TWO EXTRA LECTURES

[No study can compare with that of MAN, either in magnitude or practical utility, It teaches us OURSELVES, our fellow men, our duties, and our capabilities. Phrenology puts the finger of ABSOLUTE knowledge on the whole cycle of human interest—material, social, intellectual, and moral,—every good, and its increase; every evil, and its remedy. Man's morals may be improved, his vices suppressed, his virtues developed, and Phrenology shows how. Should it not therefore, command your first attention.

**PHRENOLOGY.**     **PHYSIOLOGY.**

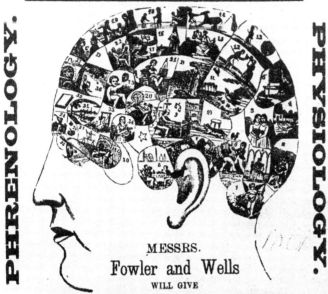

MESSRS.

## Fowler and Wells

WILL GIVE

## TWO EXTRA LECTURES,

AS FOLLOWS, IN THE

### TEMPERANCE HALL, HARTLEPOOL.

On FRIDAY Evening, July 19th, 1861,

# HOW TO TRAIN UP A CHILD.

On the Right Government, Training, and Proper Education of Children, with Advice to Young Men and Women on Self Culture and Personal Improvement. Every Parent, Teacher, and Youth should hear it.

On SATURDAY Evening, July 20th, 1861,

THE

# Perfection of Character,

Or the Moral Nature of Man, including his relations to Society and to Deity.—A future state—power to control and direct our propensities and passions, and to resist temptations—how to acquire respect, moral prudence and circumspection—the true or scientific interpretation of FAITH, HOPE, and CHARITY.

### Tickets—Front Seats, 1s.; Second do., 6d.; Back do., 3d.

Doors open at Half-past Seven, to commence at Eight. Each Lecture to close with Public Examinations.

☞ **PRIVATE EXAMINATIONS.** ☜

Professional Delineations, with Charts and full written Description of Character, and advice in regard to "WHAT TO DO," or the most appropriate occupations and pursuits in life; Faults, how to correct them; Health, how to secure and retain it; the Management of Children; Self-improvement, Marriage, &c., given during the day in private reception rooms of the Temperance Hall. Persons desiring the services of Messrs. FOWLER & WELLS, should call early, as their stay in Hartle... minates soon, and another opportunity may not occur.

9

---

Will Open on Monday Next August 24th,

IN THE

## WESLEYAN REFORM CHAPEL,

REGENT SQUARE, CHARE HEAD FIELD,

# HARTLEPOOL,

# FOR THREE NIGHTS ONLY!

Monday, Tuesday, and Wednesday, August 24th, 25th and 26th.

## Fashionable Day Performance on Wednesday

AT TWO O'CLOCK. DOORS OPEN AT HALF-PAST ONE

M. GOMPERTZ, respectfully announces to the Nobility, Clergy, Gentry, and Inhabitants of Hartlepool and its Vicinity, that he has made arrangements to Exhibit his Colossal Panorama, in the Wesleyan Reform Chapel, as above stated, there being no Room in the Town sufficiently large for the erection of this Stupendous Properties, which he has just removed from the Athenaeum, West Hartlepool, were it was last Exhibited

# M. GOMPERTZ'S

NEW AND COLOSSAL PANORAMA, ILLUSTRATING

THE WAR WITH

# RUSSIA

Painted from Drawings & Military Plans, made on the Spot, by both FRENCH & ENGLISH OFFICERS.

ACCOMPANIED BY A SPLENDID BESSON TUBA BAND.

# CONSTANTINOPLE.

# DESTRUCTION AT SINOPE

# SEBASTOPOL

## LANDING OF THE ALLIED ARMIES in the

# CRIMEA

# BATTLE OF ALMA

## Triumphant Attack of the Guards and Highlanders

UPON THE PRINCIPAL REDOUBT.

### FIELD OF THE ALMA THE EVENING AFTER THE BATTLE

CAVALRY CHARGE AT

# BALAKLAVA

### RETURN OF THE REMNANT OF LIGHT CAVALRY.

Field of Balaklava the Night after the Battle.

COMMENCEMENT OF THE BATTLE OF

# INKERMAN

### THE COMMANDERS IN CHIEF WATCHING THE PROGRESS OF THE BATTLE.

### DESPERATE STRUGGLE in the VALLEY of INKERMAN!

### FINAL REPULSE OF THE RUSSIANS

CAPTURE OF THE

# Malakhoff

# ASSAULT UPON THE REDAN.

## Pictorial Chart of the Crimea,

To conclude with M. GOMPERTZ'S DIORAMA, representing the

# CRYPT of the HOLY SEPULCHRE

17

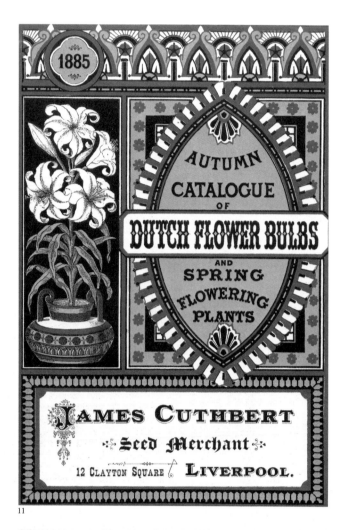

11

12

13

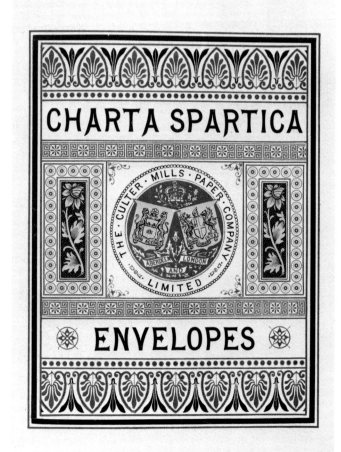

14

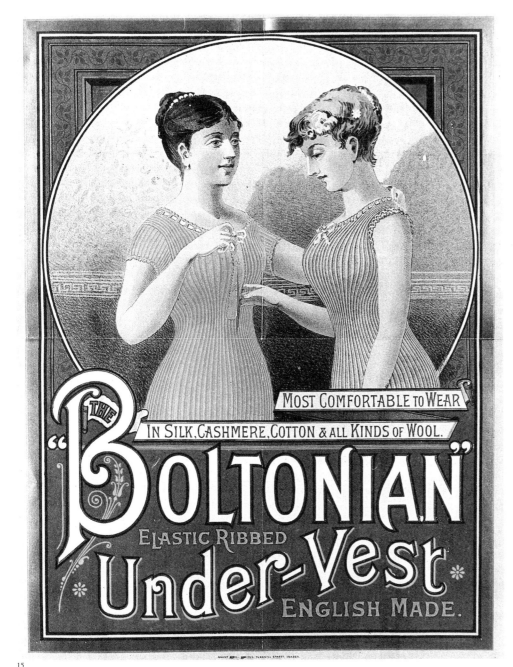

15

## BRITISH

As consumerism grew during the nineteenth century, the production of advertising announcements was left to commercial printers untutored in aesthetics. Serving their needs were an amazing variety of unique display typefaces. The printing historian Michael Twyman writes, "The jobbing and periodical printers were faced with new problems…new processes and materials…new clients…and new kinds of information to translate into print. What emerged was a new approach to design which distinguishes the 19th century printer from his 18th century counterpart, and leads to the new profession of graphic design." Owen Jones's book *The Grammar of Ornament* (1856) provided Victorian designers with examples of ancient patterns and designs used in architecture and graphics. These motifs were standardized in specimen books and sold as stock designs to the printers who serviced small businesses. The specimens also provided models from which to make customized designs like the one for the Boltonian Under-vest poster.

11. Designer unknown. *Dutch Flower Bulbs.* Type specimen from *The Printers' International Specimen Exchange,* vol. VII, London, 1885. Courtesy Chris Mullen

12. Designer unknown. *W. J. Cummins Calendar.* Type specimen from *The Printers' International Specimen Exchange,* vol. VII, London, 1885. Courtesy Chris Mullen

13. Designer unknown. *Uppingham Horticultural Society.* Type specimen from *The Printers' International Specimen Exchange,* vol. VII, London, 1885. Courtesy Chris Mullen

14. Designer unknown. *Charta Spartica Envelopes.* Type specimen from *The Printers' International Specimen Exchange,* vol. VII, London, 1885. Courtesy Chris Mullen

15. Designer unknown. *Boltonian Under-vest.* Advertisement, 1888. Courtesy Chris Mullen

16. Designer unknown. *S. G. Chalfont, Artistic Printer.* Type specimen from *The Printers' International Specimen Exchange,* vol. VII, London, 1885. Courtesy Chris Mullen

16

## AMERICAN

The dominant American graphic style of the nineteenth century drew inspiration from contemporary English and German lettering and decoration, especially as reflected in the scores of illustrated periodicals initiated around mid-century. The typography of these publications was conservative, while the editorial illustration proved to be a more important stylistic signpost. Wood engraving and lithography were the primary means of reproducing the usually over-rendered visual narratives. When *Harper's Weekly* first began publishing in 1857, its wood-engraved illustrations were limited by their mandate to represent newsworthy events as accurately as possible. Imagination came to the surface when the German-born cartoonist Thomas Nast joined the staff in 1862 and marked the periodical with his distinctive, cross-hatched editorial cartoon style. In 1871 Joseph Keppler, a Vienna-born political cartoonist trained in European lithographic techniques, founded the acerbic satirical weekly *Puck,* which not only raised the quality of American illustration but also introduced chromolithography (color printing) to cartoons. The work of Nast and Keppler also influenced the style of cartoonists working in rival (and often imitative) periodicals, such as *Judge, Jingo,* and *Truth.*

17. Rummler. *Truth.* Magazine cover, January 19, 1895

18. Designer unknown. *Harper's Magazine.* Magazine cover, December 1883

19. Grant Hamilton. *The Judge.* Magazine cover, March 22, 1884

20. Designer unknown. *Harper's Weekly.* Magazine cover, February 12, 1876

21. Designer unknown. *Jingo.* Magazine cover, October 1, 1884

22. Designer unknown. *The New York Fashion Bazar.* Magazine cover, September 1885

23. E. N. Blue. *Puck.* Magazine cover, March 23, 1887

17

18

19

20

21

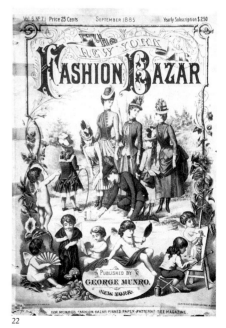

22

VOL. XXI.—No. 524.  NEW YORK, MARCH 23, 1887.  PRICE, TEN CENTS.

"What fools these Mortals be!"
MIDSUMMER-NIGHTS DREAM.

# Puck

TRADE MARK REGISTERED 1878.

KEPPLER & SCHWARZMANN, Publishers.

PUCK BUILDING, Cor. Houston & Mulberry Sts.

ENTERED AT THE POST OFFICE AT NEW YORK, AND ADMITTED FOR TRANSMISSION THROUGH THE MAILS AT SECOND CLASS RATES.

A CONTRAST.

PUCK.—I don't want to make any odious comparisons, Auctioneer Hilton; but — Mr. W. W. Corcoran is universally respected and esteemed.

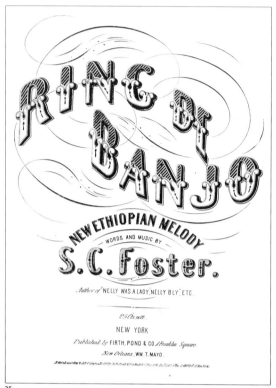

25

26

24

27

28

22

29

30

31

32

## AMERICAN

With the swing toward consumerism in America after the Civil War, the need to educate the public concerning a variety of new products caused a shift in emphasis from simple announcements to full-blown "advertisements." The same technological advances that had originally created the market surpluses and the need to compete in business also provided new economical printing methods. Chromolithography was first used for trade cards in 1840 and became a truly efficient process by the 1870s; it soon proved a formidable means of seizing viewer attention. Since advertising agents were more brokers of space than creative decision-makers, the owners of small companies themselves determined early Victorian advertising images on the basis of what they instinctively thought would be effective. The most popular themes included nationalism, patriotism, progress, and work as well as comic vignettes of all kinds. Printing firms, like Julius Bien Co., Currier and Ives, and Louis Prang and Company, eventually assumed a creative role in conceiving and producing custom and stock cuts and chromos for trade cards, song sheets, packaging, posters, and greeting cards.

24. Designer unknown. *Heinz Sweet Pickles.* Trade card, c. 1887
25. Designer unknown. *Ring de Banjo.* Sheet music cover, 1851
26. Designer unknown. *Cleveland's Baking Powder.* Trade card, c. 1886
27. Designer unknown. *Soapine.* Trade card, c. 1896
28. Designer unknown. *Arm & Hammer.* Trade card, c. 1880
29. Designer unknown. *Muzzy's Starch.* Trade card, 1882
30. Designer unknown. *Rose Leaf.* Trade card, 1865
31. Designer unknown. *Vinegar Bitters Almanac.* Book cover, 1874
32. Designer unknown. *Best in the World Superior Silk.* Trade card, c. 1880
33. Designer unknown. *Ivory Soap.* Packaging, c. 1895

33

## AMERICAN

The makers of early Victorian posters were primarily concerned with conveying verbal messages and gave scant attention to artistic design. Typography was often a conglomeration of different styles, usually with broken fonts. Broadsides would feature various discordant typefaces, often within the same word; occasional small woodcut vignettes added some interest to an otherwise dull typographical arrangement. Some of the more amusing and successful concoctions were those announcing theater and circus performances, lectures, and auctions. Another reason for the poster's lack of artfulness was that the Victorian businessman could not see his high ideal of art, modeled after Italian Renaissance paintings, as having anything to do with the ephemeral needs of practical selling. Before the end of the century, however, type designers working with foundries like the American Type Founders Co. began to teach printers how to make type more readable. And pictorial posters became fashionable when businessmen finally came to realize that pictures attract an audience more easily than words.

34. Designer unknown. *American National Caravan.* Poster, 1831. Courtesy American Antiquarian Society, Worcester, Mass.

35. Designer unknown. *Payn & McNaughton.* Poster, 1847

34

35

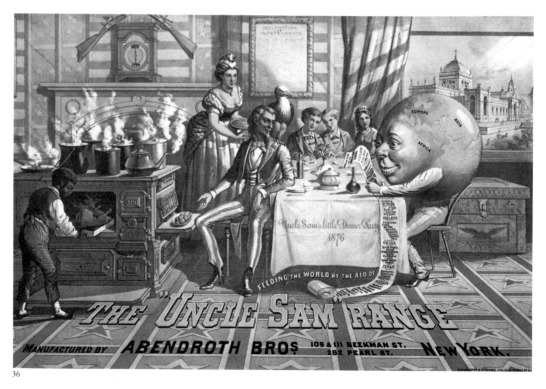

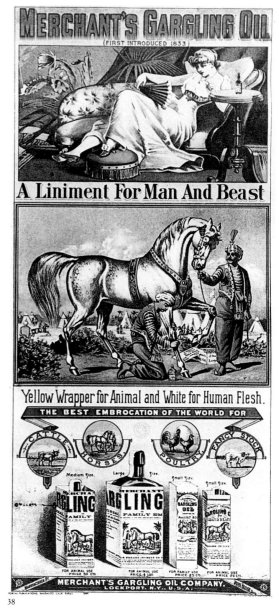

39

40

In his book *The Democratic Art,* Peter Marzio quotes a social critic of the 1870s who attacked the chromolithograph as "the quintessence of the democratization and, therefore, debasement of high culture. It represented a 'pseudo-culture,' being one of a plethora of evil media—newspapers, magazines, lyceum lectures, small colleges—that diffused through the community a kind of smattering of all sorts of knowledge, a taste for art—that is, a desire to see and own pictures." The chromo did bring cheap reproductions of great paintings into the average home, but it also provided the means for colorful imagery to enhance the most quotidian advertising and publishing. Despite their naive aesthetic prejudices, businessmen realized that color helped increase sales. For the Victorian consumer, color printing—like color television almost a century later—was a metaphor for progress and affluence.

36. Designer unknown. *Uncle Sam's Little Dinner Party.* Poster, 1876. Courtesy New-York Historical Society

37. Designer unknown. *Robert Heller, Prestidigitateur.* Poster, c. 1895

38. Designer unknown. *Merchant's Gargling Oil.* Trade card, 1894

39. Designer unknown. *Cock Robin.* Pages from children's book published by McLaughlin Brothers, 1896

40. Designer unknown. *The Hanlons, "Le Voyage en Swiss."* Poster, c. 1880. Courtesy New York Public Library, Lincoln Center

# A

## FRENCH

Like England and the United States, France benefited from the Industrial Revolution and the subsequent rise of a middle class. From the 1830s, the country also experienced a betrayal of republicanism and a return to authoritarian rule. Early French Victorian graphic style is best represented by the satirical political and social lithographs of Charles Philipon, Honoré Daumier, Grandville, Henri Meunier, and others, which were published in journals like *La Charivari* and *La Caricature* under the censorship decrees of the "citizen king," Louis Philippe. Later, during the rule of Louis Napoleon, cartoonists such as Alfred Le Petit and André Gill popularized the "big-head, little-body" caricature. In advertising, the emphasis was on the word over the image, except for the occasional comic vignette. Poor standards in typography prevailed until around 1870, when Jules Chéret singlehandedly began a poster revolution that involved the marriage of text and image and supplied the basis for French Art Nouveau.

41. Alfred Le Petit. *Les Contemporains.* Magazine cover, 1889

42. Alfred Le Petit. *Les Contemporains.* Magazine cover, 1889

43. Rouchon. *A l'Oeil.* Poster, c. 1845. Musée de la Publicité, Paris

44. Rouchon. *Punch-Grassot.* Poster, 1845. Musée de la Publicité, Paris

45. Jules Chéret. *Aux Buttes Chaumont.* Poster, 1885. Musée de la Publicité, Paris

41

42

# A L'ŒIL

## 8 Rue de Rivoli, Rue Malher, 1
### ET DU ROI DE SICILE, 1

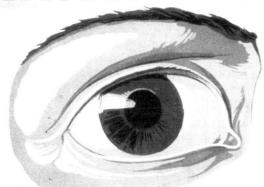

# ON DONNE À L'ŒIL

| | |
|---|---|
| 1 Belle Redingote Drap Noir, | 23. |
| 1 Pantalon Noir Belle Qualité, | 12. |
| 1 Gilet Noir, _____ id. _____ id. | 6 |
| HABILLEMENT COMPLET, | 41 fr |

# A L'ŒIL

43

# PUNCH-GRASSOT
## Recette du Bon Moine.
### ENTREPÔT GÉNÉRAL
## 13, Rue Thévenot, 15.

## DÉPOT PRINCIPAL POUR LA VENTE AU DÉTAIL
# CHEZ M. GRASSOT
## Café Minerve, Rue de Richelieu, 8
### & DANS LES PREMIÈRES MAISONS D'ÉPICERIE.

le CRUCHON, 3 f. ½ CRUCHON, 1 f. 75

44

# AUX BUTTES CHAUMONT
# Jouets
## et
# OBJETS POUR ETRENNES

### Boulevard de la Villette
### à l'Angle du Faubourg St Martin

45

HERE BEGINNETH THE TALES OF CANTER·
BURY AND FIRST THE PROLOGUE THEREOF

WHAN THAT Aprille with his shoures soote
The droghte of March hath perced to the roote,
And bathed every veyne in swich licour,
Of which vertu engendred is the flour;
Whan Zephirus eek with his swete breeth
Inspired hath in every holt and heeth

The tendre croppes, and the yonge sonne
Hath in the Ram his halfe cours yronne,
And smale foweles maken melodye,
That slepen al the nyght with open eye,
So priketh hem nature in hir corages;
Thanne longen folk to goon on pilgrimages,
And palmeres for to seken straunge strondes,
To ferne halwes, kowthe in sondry londes;
And specially, from every shires ende
Of Engelond, to Caunterbury they wende,
The hooly blisful martir for to seke,
That hem hath holpen whan that they were
seeke.

BIFIL that in that seson on a day,
In Southwerk at the Tabard as I lay,
Redy to wenden on my pilgrym-
age
To Caunterbury with ful devout
corage,
At nyght were come into that hostelrye
Wel nyne and twenty in a compaignye,
Of sondry folk, by aventure yfalle
In felaweshipe, and pilgrimes were they alle,
That toward Caunterbury wolden ryde.

46. William Morris. *The Canterbury Tales*. Page, published by Kelmscott Press, 1896

housands of visitors from England and the Continent thronged to the colossal Crystal Palace in 1851 to view the remarkable products made by the most advanced manufacturing machinery the world had ever known. Yet they found that the only truly remarkable revelation was the poor aesthetic quality of virtually all the wares on exhibit. Rather than improving industrial goods, modern machinery had virtually stamped out taste by eliminating the role of the artist in the production process.

For the English middle class, born in the wake of the Industrial Revolution, industry symbolized the final break with everything associated with the medieval social system. By the mid-nineteenth century, handicrafts and craftsmen, the last remnants of the medieval artistic tradition, were seen as beneath contempt. The essential unity and interdependence of all artistic activity was utterly rejected. An article in an issue of *The International Studio* deeply lamented this popular view, "In former days there was no demarcation between the artist and the craftsman.... In modern times we make a distinction as arbitrary as it is invidious between 'fine' arts, thereby indicating exclusively painting and sculpture on the one hand and on the other those arts which we call 'minor' or more usually 'handicrafts' or 'industries.' And if we deign to name him 'artist' at all who is neither a painter of pictures nor a modeller of statues, we apply the term to him with little more significance than we should do in the case of a cook or hair-dresser."

While most Victorians remained apathetic to this situation, social reformers—including artists, architects, and writers—did try to reestablish aesthetic standards by developing a coherent national style. The art critic Henry Cole began publishing the *Journal of Design and Manufactures* in 1847, stating in its pages that "ornament must be secondary to the thing being decorated." In *The True Principles of Pointed or Christian Architecture* (1841), Augustus Welby Northmore Pugin championed the idea of honesty in architecture and design and announced that all ornament should constitute an enrichment of the essential form. The influential artist and critic John Ruskin argued that fitness of purpose was a moral obligation, that ornamentation should be organic, and that the Gothic form was not only the best national idiom but the panacea for the modern aesthetic malaise.

Ruskin's most enthusiastic colleague was William Morris, an architect and designer whose passions fueled the Arts and Crafts Movement and whose philosophy established the ethics of modern industrial design. Morris fervently rejected those forces that would separate art from everyday life and dedicated himself to fighting ugliness in all its forms. Believing that a society unable to produce good design had at its core a faulty ethical system, Morris developed a quasi-socialist philosophy. His system decreed that craftsmen-artists-designers would themselves take direct responsibility for their creations and thus restore the pride in work that had been violated by the anonymous production line. In their handcrafted nature, Morris's earliest furniture designs for his own home constituted his first protest against the machine aesthetic.

Distressed by the absence of British leadership in applied arts, Morris founded Morris, Marshall, Faulkner and Company (also known as Morris and Company) in 1861 in order to fabricate tastefully superior handcrafted furnishings for the mass consumer. Morris further sought to recreate a medieval arts and crafts environment, patterning his utopian ideals after those of the legendary "Merrie Olde England." In Morris's plan, workshops and guilds would be training grounds for the total artist, who would work with all mediums and forms, from architecture to typography.

Certain critics considered the Arts and Crafts Movement reactionary. Morris did sometimes encourage blind admiration for the antique, and he also condoned a certain snobbish intolerance for machinery. But he had a more conciliatory side as well. Aware of the latent promise of industry, he believed that in time its miracles of ingenuity would minimize the amount of time spent in unattractive labor.

Morris was a reformer, and Arts and Crafts was decidedly a reform movement—a struggle against the encroachment of industrialism on the workingman's way of life. The design pioneer Arthur H. Mackmurdo, who in 1882 founded the Century Guild (which marked a transition from Arts and Crafts to Art Nouveau), wrote that the movement was "not an aesthetic excursion; but a mighty upheaval of man's spiritual nature." As Nickolaus Pevsner observes, "What raises Morris as a reformer of design...is...that he recognized the indissoluble unity of an age and its social system.... Morris was the true prophet of the 20th Century, the father of the modern movement. We owe it to him that an ordinary man's dwelling house has once more become a subject of the architect's thought and a chair, a wallpaper, or a vase a worthy object of the artist's imagination.... Morris the artist may in the end not have been able to reach beyond the limitation of his century; Morris the man and thinker did."

Although some Arts and Crafts objects can be assigned to an individual, most represent the collective designs of the several loosely knit yet kindred communities based on Morris's precepts in England and the United States. Arts and Crafts quickly exerted influence as a decisive philosophical shift in Victorian aesthetics. Visually, the style remained consistent with the general Victorian preference for ornament, although it did wage war against the excessive Baroque and Romantic mannerisms of the age. Yet Arts and Crafts was not monolithic, running the gamut from its most characteristic primitive Gothic to Mackmurdo's asymmetrical floral designs, the Shaker-inspired simplicity of the American designer Gustav Stickley, the elegant ornamentalism of Louis Comfort Tiffany, and the early geometric stylings of Frank Lloyd Wright.

Despite some visual evidence to the contrary, Morris encouraged the return to simple figures, colors, and ornamental backgrounds. It was his emphasis on "decorative honesty," rather than his revivalist tendencies, that proved of lasting significance. From it arose the modern concept of the "total work of art," which inspired the various Arts and Crafts designers in England and America and later the Modernists on the Continent.

31

47

48

49

50

51

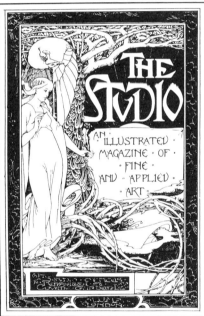

52

54

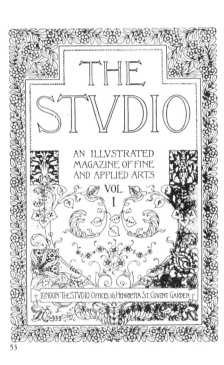

53

55

## BRITISH

In an article published in an 1899 issue of *The International Studio*, Aymer Vallance said of Selwyn Image's design of *The Century Guild Hobby Horse:* "Never before had modern printing been treated as a serious art whose province was to embrace the whole process from the selection and spacing of the type and the position of the printed matter on the page, to the embellishment of the book with appropriate initials and other decorative ornaments." Renaissance printers had, of course, been no less concerned with typographic clarity and beauty; however, when compared with most early Victorian printing, the Arts and Crafts graphic style was indeed more handsome, if not curiously original. Influenced by Gothic manuscript illumination and wall tapestries, the floral and curvilinear motifs shown here suggest a new direction in graphic presentation, one that later contributed to Art Nouveau.

47. Designer unknown. *An Exhibition of Walter Crane's Designs.* Poster, c. 1895

48. Selwyn Image. *The Century Guild Hobby Horse.* Title page, 1884

49. Wilbur Macey Stone. *Hillyer Institute.* Poster, 1895

50. Aubrey Beardsley. *Belles-Lettres.* Page, c. 1896

51. Aubrey Beardsley. *The Studio.* Magazine cover, January 15, 1894. Courtesy Chris Mullen

52–55. Designers unknown. *The Studio.* Title pages from a competition exercise, c. 1888. Courtesy Chris Mullen

56. William Morris. *The Woodpecker.* Tapestry, 1885. William Morris Gallery, Walthamstow, England

56

57

58

## BRITISH

From its inception, the handicraft revival was tinged with a Romantic antiquarianism. William Morris, who spent his whole life fighting ugliness, believed that Gothic was the best national idiom—an English art for England. *Gothic* is also the term applied to modern, sans-serif typefaces, those that reject classical Roman typography. As Morris defined it, despite its historical roots, Gothic was synonymous with change. Aubrey Beardsley's synthesis of the Gothic and the Romantic in the *Morte d'Arthur* typifies the imaginative strength of the new art. In Beardsley's work, naturalistic ornament served a formal rather than a simplistically decorative purpose. Morris further changed the basic printing practice of the late nineteenth century by returning it to the hands of artisans and craftsmen and by urging the development of a widespread English private-press movement. The pages produced by Morris's Kelmscott Press—influenced by incunabula and employing Gothic types and naturalistic motifs—were purposeful rejections of the rational and academic values of the Italian Renaissance. The lover of Renaissance typography will no doubt find the designs of Morris and his followers claustrophobic in their attempts to fill every inch of empty space with symbolic meaning, but in their time these designs opened a path to a new beauty.

57. Selwyn Image. *Jesus Hominum Salvator.* Book illustration, c. 1885

58. Edward Burne-Jones and William Morris. *Sigurd the Volsung.* Decorated page, with illustration by Burne-Jones and woodcut border by Morris, published by the Kelmscott Press, 1897

59. Aubrey Beardsley. *Morte d'Arthur.* Decorated page, 1893

60. Charles Ricketts. *Hero and Leander.* Title page, trial proof woodcut, 1894. Museum of Art, Rhode Island School of Design, Providence. Gift of Mrs. Gustave Radeke

61. Aubrey Beardsley. *Morte d'Arthur.* Page, 1893

62. Aubrey Beardsley. *Morte d'Arthur.* Frieze, 1893

63. Designer unknown. *The Book of Job.* Book cover, published by the Abbey Press, 1902

64. Gleeson White. *Sir Edward Burne-Jones, A Record and Review.* Design for book cover, from *The Studio,* 1894

65. Charles Ricketts. *The Ballad of Reading Gaol.* Artist's mark, 1898

66. Arthur H. Mackmurdo. *The Century Guild.* Artist's mark, 1884

67. C. R. Ashbee. *The Guild of Handicraft.* Artist's mark, date unknown

59

60

61

63

64

65

66

62

67

68

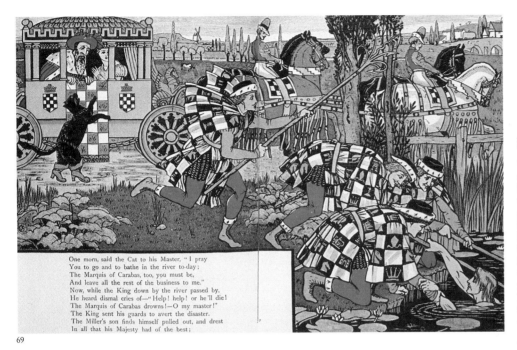

One morn, said the Cat to his Master, "I pray
You to go and to bathe in the river to-day;
The Marquis of Carabas, too, you must be,
And leave all the rest of the business to me."
Now, while the King down by the river passed by,
He heard dismal cries of—"Help! help! or he'll die!
The Marquis of Carabas drowns!—O my master!"
The King sent his guards to avert the disaster.
The Miller's son finds himself pulled out, and drest
In all that his Majesty had of the best;

69

## BRITISH

Various Arts and Crafts themes were elaborated as the style took hold in England and later on the Continent. William Morris's Gothic obsession was a major motif but only one aspect of a greater need to develop viable design standards. Owen Jones, who had designed the Egyptian, Roman, and Greek displays for the Great Exhibition of 1851, understood the need for the proper models on which to base aesthetically pleasing ornament. Jones compiled an international sampling of historical patterns and motifs in his popular *Grammar of Ornament,* which became a sourcebook for Arts and Crafts innovators. Among these was Arthur H. Mackmurdo, whose curvilinear patterns were a particularly noteworthy response to such exotic forms. Reprinted in many editions over the years, Jones's seminal work influenced designers even as late as the Art Deco era. The Arts and Crafts style also became a symbol of a certain liberalism and education, a heritage to which Walter Crane was a significant contributor. A socialist cartoonist as well as a designer of textiles, wallpaper, tiles, cards, and calendars, Crane left his most lasting mark as a children's book writer and illustrator. His series of inexpensive books were the first successful mass-market works in color for children. Crane's illustrations wed the influence of William Blake with that of Japanese woodblock prints. He was one of the first illustrators to acknowledge the relationship between illustration, typography, and page design.

68. Original Egyptian decorative designs. Page from *The Grammar of Ornament* by Owen Jones, 1856. Courtesy Chris Mullen

69. Walter Crane. *Puss in Boots.* Pages, date unknown. Courtesy Chris Mullen

70. Walter Crane. *The Alphabet of Old Friends.* Pages, date unknown. Courtesy Chris Mullen

71. Arthur H. Mackmurdo. Dining chair with fret back, 1881. William Morris Gallery, Walthamstow, England

71

70

## AMERICAN

Gustav Stickley is credited with giving the Arts and Crafts style a uniquely American flavor. Stickley is best known for his functional, straight-line furniture in the Mission or Craftsman Style. He experimented with a guild system at his furniture plant in Syracuse, New York, and for thirteen years published and designed a periodical, *The Craftsman,* dedicated to the teachings of Ruskin and Morris. In his first issue, Stickley stated his goals: to "teach that beauty does not imply elaboration or ornament; to employ only those forms and materials which make for simplicity, individuality and dignity of effect." From 1890 to 1914, a spirit of adventure seized American printers, and the Arts and Crafts book represented a brief but intense episode in printing history. The influence of incunabula and medievalism is exemplified here by the designs of Daniel Berkley Updike and Walter Crane. An "aesthetic style," based on classical Roman typography, also grew in opposition to Arts and Crafts Romanticism. In other areas, American Arts and Crafts developed its own formal vocabulary. The Keramic Studio was founded as the voice of ceramicists, and Arts and Crafts guilds and workshops arose in many parts of the country around various strong individuals, including A. E. Mathews and Elbert Hubbard. Frank Lloyd Wright was also an early proponent of Arts and Crafts ideals, but lost fervor when he realized that the cursed machine was a necessary component in the future of American design. Outlasting its European counterparts, Arts and Crafts ended in America about 1914 as an "artsy-craftsy" middle-class style.

72. Gustav Stickley. Library table. Illustration from *The Craftsman,* c. 1901

73. Designer unknown. *Keramic Studio.* Magazine cover, December 1906. Everson Museum of Art, Syracuse, N.Y.

74. Gustav Stickley. *The Craftsman.* Magazine cover, 1901

75. Daniel Berkley Updike (designer) and Robert Anning Bell (illustrator). *Altar Book.* Decorative pages, 1896. Princeton University Library

76. Walter Crane. *Arts and Crafts.* Magazine cover, April 1893. Published by the Art Worker's Guild, Philadelphia

77. Designer unknown. Original designs used for the stenciling of walls and decoration, c. 1902. From *The Craftsman*

73

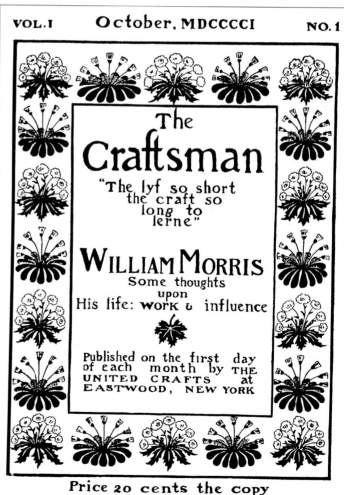

74

THE NATIVITY OF OUR LORD, OR THE BIRTHDAY OF CHRIST, COMMONLY CALLED CHRISTMAS DAY.

ALMIGHTY God, who hast given us thy only begotten Son to take our nature upon him, and as at this time to be born of a pure virgin; Grant that we being regenerate, and made thy children by adoption and grace, may daily be renewed by thy Holy Spirit; through the same our Lord Jesus Christ, who liveth and reigneth with thee and the same Spirit ever, one God, world without end.

Heb. i. 1.

GOD, who at sundry times and in divers manners spake in time past unto the fathers by the prophets, hath in these last days spoken unto us by his Son, whom he hath appointed heir of all things, by whom also he made the worlds; who being the brightness of his glory, and the express image of his person, and upholding all things by the word of his power, when he had by himself purged our sins, sat down on the right hand of the Majesty on high; being made so much better than the angels, as he hath by inheritance obtained a more excellent name than they. For unto which of the angels said he at any time, Thou art my Son, this day have I begotten thee? And again, I will be to him a Father, and he shall be to me a Son? And again, when he bringeth in the firstbegotten into the world, he saith, And let all the angels of God worship him. And of the angels he saith, Who maketh his angels spirits, and his ministers a flame of fire. But unto the Son he saith, Thy throne, O God, is for ever and ever: a sceptre of righteousness is the sceptre of thy kingdom. Thou hast loved righteousness, and hated iniquity; therefore God, even thy God, hath anointed thee with the oil of gladness above thy fellows. And, Thou, Lord, in the beginning hast laid the foundation of the earth; and the heavens are the works of thine hands: they shall

75

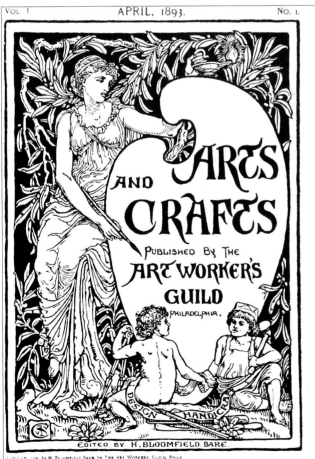

VOL I.    APRIL, 1893.    NO. 1.

ARTS AND CRAFTS

PUBLISHED BY THE ART WORKER'S GUILD

PHILADELPHIA.

EDITED BY H. BLOOMFIELD BARE.

ISSUED MONTHLY.    12 Months' Subscription, $2.00. Single copy, 20 cents.

76

77

78. Henri de Toulouse-Lautrec. *Reine de Joie.* Poster, 1892. The Museum of Modern Art, New York. Gift of Mr. and Mrs. Richard Rodgers

Ploreated madness, linear hysteria, strange decorative disease, stylistic free-for-all—such were the terms its contemporaries used to describe Art Nouveau, the first international design style. Dating from the 1880s to the outset of World War I, Art Nouveau was a rebellion against the entire Victorian sensibility, steeped as it was in the past. The exponents of the style fervently hoped to revolutionize every aspect of design in order to set a standard that would be compatible with the new age. For a relatively short period, Art Nouveau was, as one critic wrote, "one of the most imaginative innovations in the history of design."

Despite its name, Art Nouveau was born in England, the fountainhead of the European avant-garde at the time. It was a direct descendant of the Arts and Crafts Movement, specifically as practiced by Arthur H. Mackmurdo, who combined a penchant for Pre-Raphaelite Romantic symbolism with a pragmatic desire to reform design. A significant departure from the prevalent Gothicism, the cover of Mackmurdo's book *Wren's City Churches* (1883) formally employed Art Nouveau's characteristic organic, leafy motifs for the first time. Among the direct sources for the cover were Hokusai's woodblock prints and Blake's illustrations for "Songs of Innocence." Other English Art Nouveau progenitors include Aubrey Beardsley, who added a mystical quality to the new linear vocabulary, and C. F. A. Voysey, who helped bring English Art Nouveau to the Continent.

Caught between "art for art's sake" and functional aesthetics, Art Nouveau was an odd blend of art, artifice, and practicality. Like most things that insist on being totally new, it could not help reinterpreting the past: oriental art was seen afresh; Rococo art was borrowed to some degree; Celtic illuminated manuscripts were admired for their unity of design and their Romantic remoteness. The aesthetes among the Art Nouveau designers employed curvilinear and floral abstraction as a playful, yet generally functional, relief to conventional form. Yet, despite their professed revolutionary aims, they sometimes became immured in frivolous middle-class concerns. In fact, Art Nouveau designs obscured the surface of a structure just as often as the maligned Victorian ornamentation had.

Another faction of Art Nouveau practitioners, the so-called decadents, indulged wholeheartedly in the excesses of the style. In their fascination with mysticism, they developed a hierarchy of exotic goddesses and nymphets that were at once weird, fantastic, mysterious, esoteric, and decidedly kitsch.

Other Art Nouveau designers who saw the arts as servants of life sought ways to apply the lessons of modern technology to art. Interested more in the architectonic than the organic form, these rationalists generally concerned themselves with logical and geometric constructions. One of these, Lewis F. Day, stated: "Whether we like it or not, machinery, steam power and electricity…will have something to say about ornament of the future." Indeed, the more practical among these early Modernists thought that the machine could be used to disseminate beauty as well as progress or comfort throughout society. Art Nouveau did, in fact, become the first commercial art consistently used to enhance the beauty of industrial products.

With art books and magazines more available because of economical printing methods, the Art Nouveau revolution blossomed throughout the Continent. The first major stylistic upheaval in which antiquity was no longer the dominant influence, it became both a popular fashion and a bridge into the twentieth century. Savvy entrepreneurs in Europe and the United States—including Julius Meier-Graefe in Munich, Samuel Bing in Paris, Arthur L. Liberty in London, and Louis Comfort Tiffany in New York—proselytized, popularized, and, through relentless commercialism, eventually trivialized the new style.

While a common form language linked the various versions of Art Nouveau, the style developed differently in each country. In England, new simplified forms had dictated suitable decoration; in France, Le Style Moderne developed from a sense that decoration dictated form. The style came to Belgium in the early eighties, when Octave Maus established the Cercle des XX. Later Belgian developments included La Libre Esthetique, whose members espoused the whiplash linear style dominant in Brussels, and Victor Horta's "high Art Nouveau," marked by a hysterical linearism. During the mid-nineties, German Jugendstil (youth style) and, shortly afterward, the Austrian Secession were characterized by hard-edged, angular graphics, derived in part from northern printmaking techniques, and a typography decorative to the point of illegibility. The Secession was further influenced by Charles Rennie Mackintosh and the Glasgow School, whose rectilinear symmetry heralded the inevitable retreat from the purely decorative Art Nouveau style.

Although Art Nouveau was never really predominant in America, it was fashionable for a time. Tiffany's Fevrile glass, Louis Sullivan's Celtic architectural ornament, and Will Bradley's posters all drew upon Europe for inspiration. In Spain, the architect Antoni Gaudí and the exponents of Modernista saw the future graphically in terms of undulating surfaces and moving planes. In Italy, Stile Liberty never quite developed a national identity; the more original Novocento Style arose there at the turn of the century as the poet and politician Gabriele D'Annunzio called for a return to the Romantic past. In Holland, two influential Art Nouveau painters and poster artists, Jan Toorop and Johan Thorn Prikker, made sorties into the world of mystical symbolism.

By 1894, Henry Van de Velde (the Belgian architect and designer who founded the applied art school that became the Bauhaus) was the leading theorist of what he called "an art nouveau." He believed that good design was a social curative and wrote, "Ruskin and Morris chase ugliness out of man's heart, I out of his intellect." Van de Velde saw the new movement as a way for art and industry to derive a vision of the future together. Although the Art Nouveau decorative style was ultimately limited—and thus incapable of realizing such a vision—it did provide a curious stepping-stone that the Modernists would later employ to attain that future.

41

## FRENCH/BELGIAN

The stage was set for *L'Art Moderne,* the name originally given to the new style coalescing in France and Belgium during the late nineteenth century. From the 1870s almost to the end of the century, Jules Chéret had enlivened Parisian streets with hundreds of his advertising posters featuring Rococo-inspired line and a brilliant color palette. By the 1890s, other illustrators of the *bon ton,* including Henri de Toulouse-Lautrec, Théophile Alexandre Steinlen, and Pierre Bonnard, joined the ranks of innovative street artists in advertising all types of events and products with posters that wed Japanese elegance, Symbolist mystery, and the Post-Impressionist vision. From England, Arthur H. Mackmurdo's botanical cover design for *Wren's City Churches* led to the emergence of the classic Art Nouveau graphic style. By the time it was elaborated in the posters of its most significant proponents, the Swiss Eugène Grasset and the Czech Alphonse Mucha (both émigrés to Paris), Art Nouveau had become a pan-European movement.

79. Arthur H. Mackmurdo. *Wren's City Churches.* Title page, published by G. Allen, 1883. The Mitchell Wolfson Jr. Collection of Decorative and Propaganda Arts, Miami

80. Privat Livemont. *La Réforme.* Poster, 1897. Musée de la Publicité, Paris

81. Henri Meunier. *Savon Swan.* Poster, c. 1899. Musée de la Publicité, Paris

82. Pierre Bonnard. *France-Champagne.* Poster, 1891. Cleveland Museum of Art. Mr. and Mrs. Lewis B. Williams Collection, Gift of Lewis B. Williams

83. Henri de Toulouse-Lautrec. Drawing of a woman, c. 1890

84. Jules Chéret. Drawing of a woman, c. 1895

85. Théophile Alexandre Steinlen. *Gil Blas.* Magazine cover, November 1893

80

81

79

82

83

84

85

43

86

87

88

89

## FRENCH/BELGIAN

The late nineteenth-century revolution in French painting was fully appreciated by a relatively privileged few. René Martin, writing in *Le Figaro* in 1885, said that "there is far more talent shown in a poster than in many of the most discussed paintings in the salon," and by 1890 the Art Nouveau poster was the most popular form of mass art. Although the style had many guises, its most typical was the free-flowing organic form, based on floral abstraction and flat patterns, with a skipping or undulating rhythmic design. In its attempt to escape from formalism, Art Nouveau ended up with a perfect evocation of a natural form. Some thought the style would be the hope for a new tomorrow, others were sure it would result in cultural degeneracy. But, for the brief period during which it flourished, the Art Nouveau style served as a strong force in disseminating the applied arts to a mass audience.

86. Eugène Grasset. *Marque Georges Richard, Cycles & Automobiles.* Poster, 1899

87. Jean Miscelas Peske. *L'Estampe et l'Affiche.* Poster, 1898. Courtesy Posters Please, Inc., New York

88. Jean de Paléologue. *Fernand Clément & Cie.* Poster, 1894

89. Henri de Toulouse-Lautrec. *Jane Avril.* Poster, 1899

90. Henri de Toulouse-Lautrec. *Babylone d'Allemagne.* Poster, 1894. Kunstgewerbemuseum, Zurich

91. A. Turpain. *La Lumière.* Book cover, 1913. The Mitchell Wolfson Jr. Collection of Decorative and Propaganda Arts, Miami

90

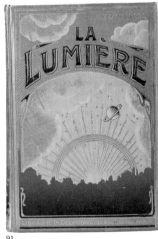

91

45

**FRENCH/BELGIAN**

The Art Nouveau aesthetic marked virtually everything from buildings to furniture to glassware. The typefaces, borders, ornaments, and dingbats that characterized Art Nouveau printing accorded with the stylistic innovations of architects and designers such as Henri Guimard and Emile Gallé. Among the artists of *la belle époque* were some of the most original type designers, Georges Auriol, Alphonse Mucha, and Eugène Grasset, who created emblematic designs for leading Parisian typefoundries, like Deberny and Company, G. Peignot and Sons, and Robert Girard & Cie. All their new typefaces were heralded by specimen booklets, which also usually contained a wide selection of imaginative and stylish vignettes (or *clichés*), used to embellish the Art Nouveau page. Such design manuals as Mucha's *Combinaisons Ornementales* and *Documents Décoratifs* served as models from which the new trends could be advanced to printers throughout France.

92. Henri Guimard. Angled cupboard. From Nozal House, c. 1904–7. Musée de la Publicité, Paris

93. Alphonse Mucha. *Combinaisons Ornementales.* Cover of type specimen book, c. 1898

94. Alphonse Mucha. *Documents Décoratifs.* Cover of type specimen book, c. 1898

95. Various designers. Ornaments and silhouettes. Specimen from Fonderies Deberny & Peignot, 1910

96. Designer unknown. Cafe sign. Bronze, 1900. The Museum of Modern Art, New York. Gift of Joseph H. Heil

97. Designer unknown. Motifs and typography, c. 1900. *Top to bottom:* Auriol Italic; Kalligraphia; Wotan; Arnold Bocklin; Aegean

92

93

94

95

96

*AABCDEFGHIJKLLM NOPQRSTTUVW XYZ*

ABCDEFGHIJKLMNOPGRSTUVWXYZ

**ABCDEFGHIJKLMNOPQRSTUVXYZ**

ABCDEFGHIJKLMNOPQRSTUVWXYZ

ABCDEFGHIJKLMNOPQRSTTUVWXYZ

97

## FRENCH/BELGIAN

Art Nouveau held such sway in the graphic arts that many contemporary artists and designers who did not otherwise consider themselves exponents of the style applied certain of its mannerisms to their work. Cartoonists in particular found that Art Nouveau traits helped them signal a contemporary look as distinguished from the more academic Beaux-Arts drawing tradition. The artists of *L'Assiette au Beurre* (The Butter Dish), which lasted from 1901 to 1912 and was one of France's most acerbic illustrated weeklies, often combined Art Nouveau exaggeration with the kind of elegant drawing of a Bonnard or Lautrec to help convey their caustic social and political messages. *L'Assiette au Beurre* in turn influenced the cartoon style of other French satiric and humor magazines, such as the nationalistic *La Baïonnette* and the lighthearted *Le Sourire*.

98. Thomaz Leal de Camara. *Visions!* Cover of *L'Assiette au Beurre,* satirizing British imperialism, 1903

99. Weiluc. *The Killers on the Roads.* Cover of *L'Assiette au Beurre,* on motorcar racing, 1902

100. Miklos Vadasz. *Princes Russes.* Cartoon from *L'Assiette au Beurre,* May 12, 1906

101. Dimitrios Galanis. *Love.* Cover of *L'Assiette au Beurre,* June 17, 1905

102. Dimitrios Galanis. Cartoon from *L'Assiette au Beurre,* commenting on French colonialism, 1902

103. Galantara. Cartoon from *L'Assiette au Beurre,* satirizing greed, 1901

104. Pierre Bonnard. *La Revue Blanche.* Poster, 1894. The Museum of Modern Art, New York

105. Marco de Gastyne. *La Baïonnette.* Magazine cover, 1917

106. Paul Iribe. *Le Sourire.* Magazine cover, 1903

98

99

100

101

102

103

104

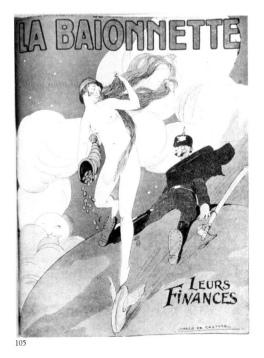

105

106

## FRENCH/BELGIAN

Jules Chéret created the most well known posters of *la belle époque*. He was awarded the nation's most prestigious award, the Légion d'Honneur, "for creating a new branch of art by applying art to commercial and industrial painting." Chéret opened the floodgates for scores of other highly skilled decorators of the urban streetscape, among them Emmanuel Orazi. However, the most emblematic Art Nouveau images are those of Alphonse Mucha, whose Byzantine style characterized by idealized portraits of women framed by cherubs, palm leaves, and mosaics helped to elevate advertising to a fine art.

107. Alphonse Mucha. *Bières de la Meuse.* Poster, 1897. Courtesy Posters Please, Inc., New York

108. Alphonse Mucha. *Waverley Cycles.* Poster, 1898. Courtesy Posters Please, Inc., New York

109. Jules Chéret. *Ed. Sagot.* Poster, 1891. Courtesy Posters Please, Inc., New York

110. Jules Chéret. *La Loïe Fuller.* Poster, 1893. Courtesy Posters Please, Inc., New York

111. Emmanuel Orazi. *Contrexéville.* Poster, 1900. Courtesy Posters Please, Inc., New York

107

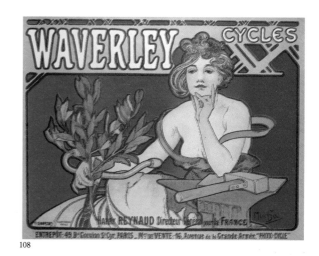

108

LIBRAIRIE
Ed. Sagot
18, Rue Guénégaud

Affiches · Estampes

109

FOLIES-BERGÈRE

La Loïe Fuller

110

CONTREXÉVILLE
SOURCE DU
PAVILLON

111

51

8. Jahrgang — Nummer 8

# Beiblatt des Simplicissimus
## Illustrierte Wochenschrift

München, den 19. Mai 1903 — Verlag von Albert Langen in München

Der „Simplicissimus" erscheint wöchentlich einmal. Bestellungen werden von allen Postämtern, Zeitungs-Expeditionen und Buchhandlungen entgegengenommen. Billige Ausgabe pro Nummer 15 Pf, ohne Frankatur, pro Quartal (13 Nummern) M. 1.80 (bei direkter Zusendung unter Kreuzband im Inland M. 2.35, im Ausland M. 2.45), pro Jahr M. 7.20 (bei direkter Zusendung im Inland M. 9.—, im Ausland M. 9.80). Die Luxus-Ausgabe, die mit besonderer Sorgfalt auf besserem Papier hergestellt wird, kostet pro Nummer 25 Pf, ohne Frankatur, pro Quartal M. 3.— (bei direkter Zusendung unter Kreuzband im Inland M. 3.75, im Rolle verpackt M. 5.—, im Ausland nur in Rolle M. 6.—) pro Jahr M. 12.— (bei direkter Zusendung im Inland M. 15.—, in Rolle verpackt M. 20.—, im Ausland nur in Rolle M. 24.—).

Zu spät (Zeichnung von J. B. Engl)

„O mei, o mei, jezt haut sich der dumm' Bua an Damm'n ob weg'n der Militari. Dös is a Unglück, jezt bist a Krüpp'l und zu nix'n mehr z' brauch'n." — „Jessas ja, an dös hon i net denkt, jezt konn i nimmer raffa."

## JUGENDSTIL

Art Nouveau arrived a little later in Germany than in England, France, and Belgium, but it nevertheless became the dominant national style between 1896 and approximately 1909. Munich was the capital of Jugendstil (youth style), being the birthplace of the Munich Secession (which represented mystical and mythological strains in the decorative arts), the headquarters of the arts journal *Pan,* which championed the new art, and home to the style's major designers and leading applied-arts schools and galleries. With the founding in 1897 of the Vereinigten Werkstätten by Peter Behrens, Hermann Obrist, Richard Riemerschmid, and others under the influence of the theorist Henry Van de Velde, Jugendstil was applied to a wide range of products, furniture, and architecture. While Jugendstil was promoted in publications such as *Kunst und Handwerk, Dekorative Kunst,* and *Deutsche Kunst und Dekoration,* it was the trendsetting cultural weekly *Jugend,* founded by Georg Hirth in 1896, that gave Jugendstil its name. Also in the same year, Albert Langen began publishing his satirical weekly *Simplicissimus,* whose Jugendstil-inspired artists profoundly influenced the expressive look and acerbic content of cartoons and caricatures elsewhere in Europe.

112. Designers unknown. *Simplicissimus.* Page of advertisements, 1909

113. Franz Von Reznicek. *Die Frau in der Karikatur.* Cover of a book by Eduard Fuchs, 1906

114. Bruno Paul. Cartoon from *Simplicissimus.* 1904

115. Bruno Paul. *Simplicissimus Ausstellung.* Poster, 1906

113

114

115

## JUGENDSTIL

Jugendstil developed into a distinctly German graphic vocabulary. Drawing on Germanic printmaking traditions and a certain Bavarian regimentation, Jugendstil was often more precise and hard-edged than its naturalist-oriented counterparts. Yet the style made allowances for its practitioners' individual approaches, as evidenced by the variety of methods, from the classical to the Romantic, seen on the illustrated covers of *Jugend.* Despite these individual mannerisms, the typical Jugendstil letter and image combination is unmistakable, whether employed as an advertisement for a restaurant, the cover of a novel, or a poster for an exhibition.

116. Arnost Hofbauer. *Topičův Salon.* Poster, 1898. Courtesy Posters Please, Inc., New York

117. Designer unknown. *Seltsame Geschichten (Curious Stories).* Book cover, 1905

118. M. Janselow. *Lustige Blätter.* Magazine cover, 1900

119. Hans Christiansen. *Jugend.* Magazine cover, 1899

120. Designer unknown. *Jugend.* Magazine cover, 1899

121. Designer unknown. *Jugend.* Magazine cover, 1900

122. Ludwig Lutz Ehrenberger. *Frz X. Thallmaier.* Poster, 1905. Courtesy Reinhold Brown Gallery, New York

116

117

118

119

120

121

122

ABCDEFGHIJKLMNOPQRSTUVWXYZ

ABCDEFGHIJKLMNOPQRSTUVWXYZ

ABCDEFGHIJKLMNOPQRSTUVWXYZ

Steckenpferd-Lilienmilch-Seife

das beste tägliche Getränk

vanHouten's Cacao

ABCDEFGHIJKLMNOPQRSTUVWXYZ

ABCDEFGHIJKLMNOPQRSTUVWXYZ

ABCDEFGHIJKLMNOPQRSTUVWXYZ

123

## JUGENDSTIL

Jugendstil designers rejected traditional methods of typography in favor of unique display typefaces that worked harmoniously with the image. Such a choice is evident in the posters by Bruno Paul and Henry Van de Velde shown here, while the work by Johan Thorn Prikker (one of Holland's significant Art Nouveau proponents) shows an all-purpose use of a traditional Gothic lettering. One-of-a-kind brushed letters were used on posters and advertisements, and a few eccentric yet emblematic faces were devised as complete alphabets. The Germans actually produced the first Art Nouveau typeface, designed by Otto Eckmann for the Klingspor Typefoundry and sold to printers throughout Europe. Many of the odder, and often illegible, faces shown here were redrawn and used as novelty types decades later.

123. Designers unknown. Jugendstil typography and advertisements. *Top to bottom:* Carmen, c. 1900; Fantasia-Grotesque, c. 1900; Sezession, c. 1902; two advertisements from *Jugend,* 1907; Eckmann-Schrift, 1896; Siegfield, c. 1900; Herold Reklameschrift, 1904

124. Bruno Paul. *Kunst im Handwerk.* Exhibition poster for Arts in Crafts in Munich, 1901. Courtesy Fairleigh Dickinson University, Madison, N.J.

125. Henry Van de Velde. *Tropon.* Poster for a food company, 1897. Courtesy Fairleigh Dickinson University, Madison, N.J.

126. Johan Thorn Prikker. *Holländische Kunstausstellung.* Exhibition poster for the Kaiser Wilhelm Museum, 1903. Courtesy Fairleigh Dickinson University, Madison, N.J.

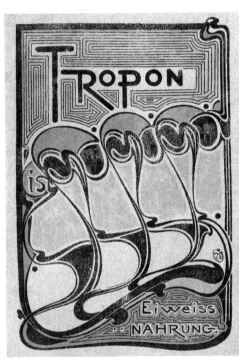

124

125

126

## GLASGOW STYLE

Inspired by traditional Celtic ornament and Aubrey Beardsley's distinctive line, the Scotsman Charles Rennie Mackintosh developed a new visual language that became known as the Glasgow Style. Because of its initial use of botanical motifs during the early 1890s, the Glasgow Style is usually linked with Art Nouveau, but it was more precisely a rejection of such motifs in favor of more functional design. As Mario Amaya writes: "Mackintosh, with bold Scots directness and a rectilinear neatness seemed to offer a solution basing many of his designs on geometry, particularly the cube." The Glasgow Four (Mackintosh, his wife, Margaret Macdonald, and J. Herbert and Frances McNair) further influenced other designers working at the time in the Scottish capital. Their work as graphic, textile, and interior designers and as architects also fascinated the Austrian Secessionists, who found it an exciting alternative to floreated abstraction.

127. Charles Rennie Mackintosh. Clock, with six columns and domino figures, 1917–19. Courtesy Chris Mullen

128. Charles Rennie Mackintosh. Highbacked ladder-back chair, 1902

129. M. G. Lightfoot. *Midsummer Night's Dream.* Book cover, date unknown. National Museums and Galleries on Merseyside, Walker Art Gallery, Liverpool

130. J. Herbert MacNair. *Liverpool Academy of Arts.* Poster, 1901. Merseyside County Art Galleries, Liverpool

131. J. Herbert McNair and Margaret and Frances Macdonald. *Glasgow Institute of the Fine Arts.* Poster, 1895. Library of Congress, Washington, D.C. Poster Collection

132. Jessie M. King. *The Arcadian.* Restaurant announcement, date unknown. Hunterian Art Gallery, University of Glasgow

133. Charles Rennie Mackintosh. *Stylized Flowers and Checkerwork.* Textile design, 1920. Hunterian Art Gallery, University of Glasgow, Mackintosh Collection

134. Charles Rennie Mackintosh. *Tulip Lattice.* Textile design, date unknown. Hunterian Art Gallery, University of Glasgow, Mackintosh Collection

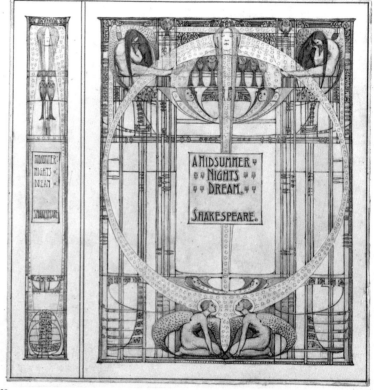

129

130

127

128

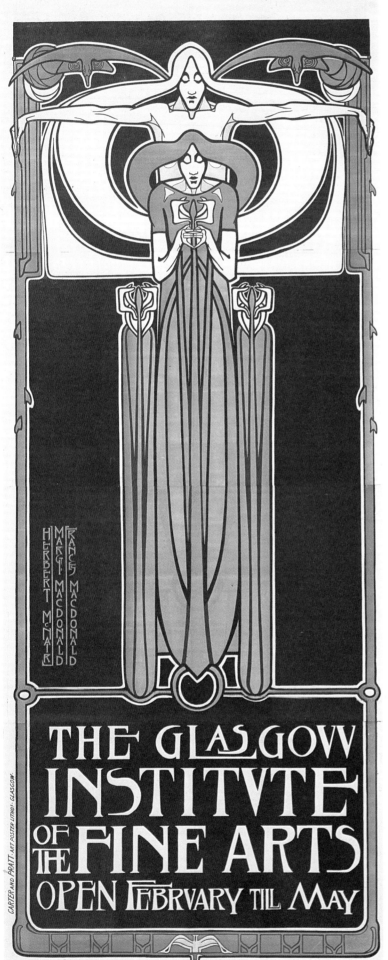

131

132

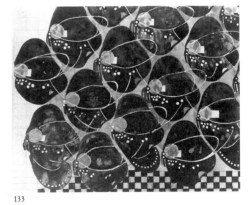

133

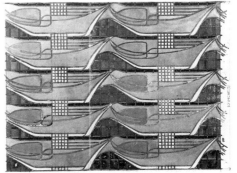

134

136

137

138

139

140

## VIENNA SECESSION

During the 1890s, the visual arts in Vienna were dominated by conservative academicians whose schools and societies refused to exhibit the new developments in European plastic and applied arts. Frustrated by unsuccessful attempts to expand the boundaries of their art and inspired by the Munich Secession's break with tradition, a group of young architects, painters, and graphic artists, including Josef Hoffmann, Joseph Olbrich, Gustav Klimt, and Koloman Moser in 1897 founded the Vereinigung Bildender Künstler Österreichs, better known as the Vienna Secession. As evidenced in their journal, *Ver Sacrum* (*Sacred Spring*), the language of Sezessionstil was akin to that of Jugendstil with added personal touches of Pre-Raphaelitism, the antique, and the classical. Yet, as the designs of many of its exhibition posters show, certain members of the Secession rejected naturalistic tendencies in favor of Otto Wagner's purist straight line and Hoffmann's simplified geometry. In this regard, their work prefigured the functionalism of future Modernists.

135. Ferdinand Andri. *Secession.* Exhibition poster, date unknown. Collection Barry Friedman Ltd., New York

136. Ferdinand Hodler. *Ver Sacrum.* Exhibition poster, 1904. Kunstgewerbemuseum, Zurich

137. Koloman Moser. *Ver Sacrum.* Magazine cover, 1899

138. Koloman Moser. *Ver Sacrum.* Page, 1899

139. Designers unknown. *Ver Sacrum.* Advertisement page, 1899

140. Koloman Moser. *Ver Sacrum.* Magazine cover, 1899

## VIENNA SECESSION

Despite their affinities with other contemporary styles, the Secessionists reaffirmed their artistic independence in their first issue of *Ver Sacrum:* "We desire an art not enslaved to foreigners. …The art from abroad should act upon us as an incentive to reflect upon ourselves; we want to recognize it, admire it, if it deserves our admiration; the only thing we don't want to do is imitate it." True to this statement, the Secessionist graphic style quickly evolved a distinctive personality, from the elegant classicism of Klimt's first exhibition poster to the group's unprecedented feats of typographic artistry.

141. Joseph Maria Olbrich. *Secession.* Catalogue cover showing the Secession Exhibition building, 1898–99. Collection Galerie Pabst, Munich

142. Alfred Roller. *Sixteenth Vienna Secession.* Exhibition poster, 1903. Kunstgewerbemuseum, Zurich

143. Koloman Moser. *Thirteenth Vienna Secession.* Exhibition poster, 1902. Graphische Sammlung Albertina, Vienna

144. Koloman Moser. *Frommes Kalendar.* Poster, 1899. Collection Barry Friedman Ltd., New York

145. Ferdinand Andri. *10th Exhibition of Vienna Secession.* Poster, c. 1901. Collection Reinhold Brown Gallery, New York

146. Gustav Klimt. *I. Kunstaustellung Secession.* Poster for the first Vienna Secession exhibition (before censorship), c. 1901. Courtesy Posters Please, Inc., New York

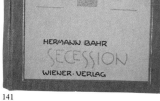

141

142

143

144

145

146

147

148

149

150

151

152

153

## AMERICAN

By 1890, a new genre of advertising known as the art poster began to flower in America. Distinct from the typographically cluttered bills of the Victorian era, these were colorful, economically rendered posters usually sponsored by a publishing house to advertise a special issue of a magazine or newspaper or a new book. The master posterist Edward Penfield wrote, "I think the American Poster has opened a new school whose aim is simplicity and good composition." While *Harper's* used Penfield exclusively, other publishers employed such artists as Will Carqueville, Frank Hazenplug, Louis Rhead, and Maxfield Parrish. The firm of Stone and Kimball, American publishers of the English arts journal the *Yellow Book,* commissioned one poster from Lautrec, but their most notable were by Hazenplug and Will Bradley. Termed the American Beardsley, Bradley also designed covers for the influential trade journal *The Inland Printer* and his own magazine, *Bradley: His Book,* dedicated to the promotion of fine typography, design, paper, and printing. By the mid-nineties, the art poster had become so popular that manufacturers were promoting contests for the most original advertisements.

147. William L. Carqueville. *Lippincott's.* Poster, January 1895. Library of Congress, Washington, D.C. Poster Collection

148. Will Bradley. *Victor Bicycles.* Poster, 1896

149. Will Bradley. *The Inland Printer.* Poster, February 1895

150. Maxfield Parrish. *Midsummer Holiday.* Magazine cover for *The Century,* 1897

151. Frank Hazenplug. *The Chap-Book.* Poster for a literary magazine, 1896. Museum für Kunst und Gewerbe, Hamburg

152. Edward Penfield. *Harper's.* Poster, 1897. The Museum of Modern Art, New York

153. Louis Rhead. *Harper's Bazar.* Cover and back cover, 1894. Library of Congress, Washington, D.C. Poster Collection

154. Arthur Dow. *Modern Art.* Poster for a book published by Louis Prang, 1895. Library of Congress, Washington, D.C. Poster Collection

154

156

157

## AMERICAN

By the turn of the century, Charles Dana Gibson could command $100,000 for one hundred black-and-white line drawings featuring his Gibson Girl. This graphic invention became a fashion rage and a boon to magazine circulation. Many other specialized illustrators and cartoonists shared Gibson's limelight—such was the commercial power of graphic art before radio or film. *Life* was called "the gentle satirist," criticizing yet also promoting the Gilded Age life-style through its smart writing, humorous graphic commentary, and delightful illustration. The Art Nouveau-inspired graphic styles of Clarence Coles Phillips and John Cecil Clay epitomized both the sophisticated bias of the magazine and the elegant graphic look of the day.

155. Charles Dana Gibson. Gibson girls. Sketches, c. 1902

156. John Cecil Clay. *Butterflies.* Magazine cover for *Life,* August 4, 1904

157. Coles Phillips. *Life.* Magazine cover, June 10, 1909

158. Coles Phillips. *Life.* Magazine cover, February 20, 1908

159. Coles Phillips. *Life.* Magazine cover, January 14, 1909

160. Coles Phillips. *Life.* Magazine cover, December 2, 1909

161. John Cecil Clay. *Harvesting.* Magazine cover for *Life,* October 5, 1905

162. Coles Phillips. *Light Consumes Coal, Save Light, Save Coal.* Poster, c. 1915–16. The Mitchell Wolfson Jr. Collection of Decorative and Propaganda Arts, Miami

158

159

155

160

161

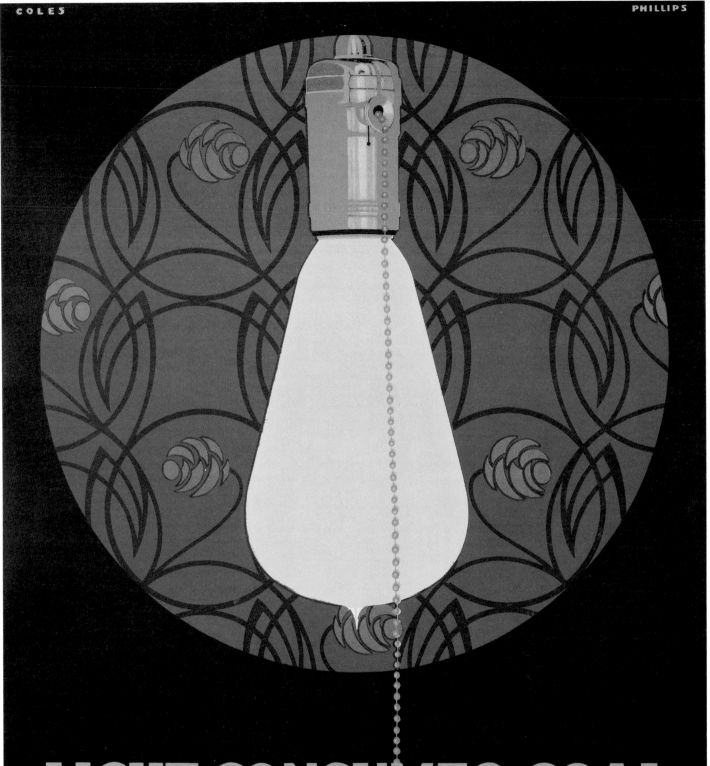

164

165

166

167

## AMERICAN

Unlike European Art Nouveau designers, American graphic artists did not employ the style to change the spiritual, cultural, or political world. For them, the style was consistent with both the commercial and technological requisites of the age. *The Burr McIntosh Monthly* (the first American magazine to list an art director on its masthead) as well as the monthly *Harper's Bazar* employed anonymous cover artists who simply followed the dominant graphic trends. The General Electric trademark conforms to the prevailing modes of lettering yet has surprisingly and effectively passed the test of time, being just shy of one hundred years old and virtually in its original form. The advertising artist for the cereal cleverly designed the frame to look like an Art Nouveau motif, while the popular cartoonist Hy Mayer's personal style instinctively fits the period in which he worked. Only the monthly, *The Masses,* a Greenwich Village–based Socialist magazine, displays any of the ideological fervor of the European movements. But even this cover, inspired by Art Nouveau (or perhaps by *Simplicissimus),* is atypical since the magazine usually took a quasi-realistic, crayon-cartoon approach.

163. Will Hope. *The Masses.* Magazine cover, June 1916

164. Hy Mayer. *Rice & Hutchins Shoes.* Advertisement, 1900

165. *Shredded Wheat.* Advertisement in *Life* magazine, July 1905

166. Designer unknown. *The Burr McIntosh Monthly.* Magazine cover, March 1905

167. Designer unknown. *Harper's Bazar.* Magazine cover, August 1902

168. A. L. Rich. *GE.* Corporate trademark for General Electric, c. 1890 (A registered trademark of General Electric Company)

168

## ITALIAN

Italy was not a major contributor to the legacy of Art Nouveau and, in fact, it was the 1904 exhibition in Turin that made the world aware that the style was on the wane. Much of Italian Art Nouveau was derived from other nations' artistic developments, like Pre-Raphaelitism and Symbolism; Art Nouveau in Italy was even called Stile Liberty, with reference to the London emporium. Yet Italy's contributions should not be entirely excluded. Italian Art Nouveau was partly a geographical phenomenon: the closer a region was to Austria, the greater the Viennese influence and the more playful its symbolic motifs. The Romantic poet and politician Gabriele D'Annunzio evolved a form of literary Art Nouveau, which he later developed into the reactionary Novocento Style, a celebration of Roman virtues and modernistic design. The major practitioners of Italian Art Nouveau are no less imaginative. Giovanni Mataloni and Marcello Dudovich created eye-catching advertising with their personal yet contemporary styles. Leonetto Cappiello, who earned his fame in Italy and France, produced hundreds of exuberant lithographic posters and blended both Art Nouveau and Art Deco in his style.

169. Giovanni Mataloni. *Incandescenza Lampada con Reticella a Petrolio.* Poster for oil lamps with incandescent mantles, 1896. The Mitchell Wolfson Jr. Collection of Decorative and Propaganda Arts, Miami

170. Leonetto Cappiello. *Livorno, Stagione Balneare.* Poster for a summer resort, 1901. The Mitchell Wolfson Jr. Collection of Decorative and Propaganda Arts, Miami

171. Marcello Dudovich. *Rassegna·Tecnica dell'Esposizione Internazionale de Milano 1906.* Poster, 1906. The Mitchell Wolfson Jr. Collection of Decorative and Propaganda Arts, Miami

172. Marcello Dudovich. *Fisso l'Idea.* Poster, 1911. The Mitchell Wolfson Jr. Collection of Decorative and Propaganda Arts, Miami

169

170

171

172

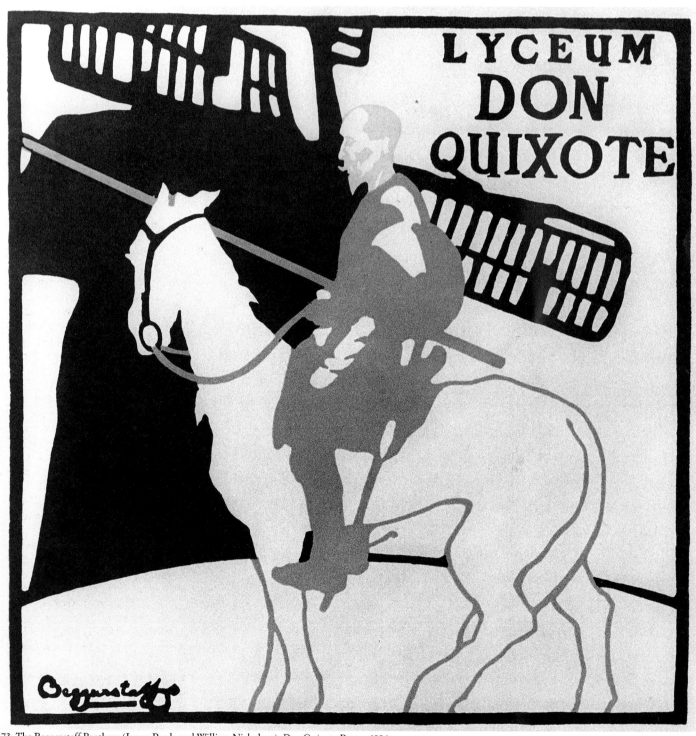

173. The Beggarstaff Brothers (James Pryde and William Nicholson). *Don Quixote.* Poster, 1896

**B**y the close of the nineteenth century, industry had become an accepted fact of life. Even billowing smokestacks, once the harbingers of industrial evil, had become symbols of progress in advertising imagery. Yet, despite the increasing need for distinctive advertising, the antagonism between art and industry continued. As a rule, manufacturers and retailers were not interested in achieving superior design and printing for their advertising, being more concerned with selling their products in the most convenient and often the most garish manner. Businessmen dictated their preferences to visually unimaginative advertising agents; the agents would then job out commissions to printers, who in turn produced standardized layouts.

Graphic design did flourish in a few contexts, however. Certainly in France from the mid-1870s to 1890s, posters promoting cabarets, theater, circuses, music halls, and other cultural events dominated the streets and were immensely important decorations to the urban environment. In addition, some commercial packaging and advertising benefited from the skills of famous French artist-designers.

On the other hand, German designers did not generally collaborate with industry, as pointed out in 1910 by Dr. Hans Sachs, editor of *Das Plakat,* the respected international poster journal: "Here the old prejudices of the bourgeois against art and artists still reign. For the bourgeois manufacturer would no more think of having his products promoted by a 'flighty' artist…than an artist of this time would degrade his brush for such profane ends." At the close of the Victorian era, the aesthetic movements influenced by William Morris's prejudices against industry still dominated English design.

This state of affairs eventually changed, though in different ways in each of the industrialized nations. In Germany, advertisements remained drearily historical, despite exposure to French genius during the first major poster exhibit in 1894 in Hamburg. Yet at exactly the same time the commercial arts were beginning to flower in England through a unique approach to poster design. James Pryde and William

Nicholson, painters and brothers-in-law calling themselves the Beggarstaffs, opened a studio dedicated to revitalizing the art of the business-advertising poster. Their unadorned, Japanese-inspired designs made from simple pieces of cut colored paper communicated product information in the most economical yet powerful fashion. In an effort to interest manufacturers in their approach, the Beggarstaffs made dummy posters for generic products, such as "no-name soap" or "no-name coffee," which they offered for sale at trade expositions. Although they sold relatively few designs before returning to painting, they had considerable influence on what would become known as the "object" poster in Europe and America.

After 1900 the great artificial flower of Art Nouveau began to wither. Charles Rennie Mackintosh had already revived the square and Otto Wagner the straight line—both paving the way for more functional design. On May 19, 1903, the architect Josef Hoffmann, the banker Fritz Wärndorfer, and the designer Koloman Moser registered the name Die Wiener Werkstätte (The Vienna Workshops) for their new organization. Hoping to improve the aesthetics of all sorts of durable goods, from picture postcards to rugs and tea services, the Werkstätte built its ethic upon Wagner's idea of *gesamtkunstwerk* (the complete work of art). It developed into a series of workshops presided over by twelve "generalists," whose designs covered the entire field of applied art and were executed by more than thirty-six master craftsmen. Although it continued until 1932, well into the Modernist era, the Werkstätte was essentially a handicrafts guild. Its costly products were sold to a bourgeois clientele and, therefore, were only peripheral in bridging the gap between art and industry.

The bridge was completed in Berlin in 1907, when the architect Hermann Muthesius and his colleague, Harry Graf Kessler, founded the Deutscher Werkbund. This confederation of ideologically diverse architects and industrial and graphic designers—one critic termed it "an association of the most intimate enemies"—came together in order to find the best way to represent its work to

industry at home and abroad. Though modeled on Morris, the Werkbund was more than another version of Arts and Crafts: it realized that the most effective way to overcome the evils of industrialism was to cooperate with industry rather than to return to handicrafts. As one member described it, the Werkbund's purpose was "to overcome the alienation that had arisen between those who invent and those who carry out." Within these broad purposes, some sought to promote a particularly German quality in their work, while others hoped to solve the problems of contemporary social renewal.

Peter Behrens, architect, teacher, graphic designer, and one-time exponent of Art Nouveau, was among the most versatile of the Werkbund members. In 1907 Behrens was summoned to Berlin by Emil Rathenau, the enlightened president of Allgemeine Elektrizitäts-Gesellschaft (AEG), and presented with the task of formulating a uniform design style for AEG, not only for its graphics but for its buildings, interiors, and products as well. Behrens became the first corporate design director and succeeded in bringing the concept of *gesamtkunstwerk* into the machine age. The former Art Nouveau theorist Henry Van de Velde was equally significant to the Werkbund, in that his work also underwent a transition from symbolism to rationalism.

In the first years of contact between design and industry, the poster was the testing ground that demonstrated that collaboration was both possible and profitable. In 1896, Munich saw the birth of the Jugendstil poster, but after the turn of the century, Berlin, the center of commerce, became the home for the exciting movement known as Berliner Plakat or Plakatstil. It was the perspicacious printing agent Ernst Growald who was instrumental in persuading artists and merchants to work together. Of all the talented Berlin posterists, Lucian Bernhard was the first, in 1906, to veer away from decorative tendencies by focusing on one product image and bold yet minimal lettering. This approach, called the *sachplakat* or object poster, had a marked influence on international graphic style for decades to follow. 73

MARCO-POLO-TEE

174

Hermann Scherrer.
Breechesmaker
Sporting=Tailor
München
Neuhauserstr.32

LVDWIG HOHLWEIN

175

Complete Sporting News

The New York Times.

176

177

178

## PLAKATSTIL

A loyal servant of business before the turn of the century, the poster reached its creative and communicative peak between 1900 and 1930. Thanks to communications directors like Peter Behrens at AEG, designer and industry became happily ensconced in a mutually beneficial relationship. Artists, printers, and publishers united to raise the poster to a high industrial art. To further this end, Dr. Hans Sachs founded the Friends of the Poster Society and its monthly organ, *Das Plakat,* which showcased the work of significant up-and-coming German posterists. Although other influential journals and annuals were published in Germany, Europe, and the United States, *Das Plakat,* with its finely printed covers, tip-ins, and fold-outs, gave its readers the most striking display of contemporary work. The Munich artist Ludwig Hohlwein, whose work evinced a lively yet tasteful use of type and image, was among the most important proponents of Plakatstil (poster style) worldwide.

174. Ludwig Hohlwein. *Marco Polo Tee.* Poster, 1910. Collection Reinhold Brown Gallery, New York

175. Ludwig Hohlwein. *Hermann Scherrer.* Poster, 1907. Collection Reinhold Brown Gallery, New York

176. J. D. Smith. *The Complete Sporting News, The New York Times.* Car card, 1925. Courtesy Fairleigh Dickinson University, Madison, N.J.

177. Walter Kampmann. *Das Plakat.* Magazine cover, 1921

178. Walter Schnackenberg. *Das Plakat.* Magazine cover, 1921

179. Pirchan. *Mitteilungen des Vereins Deutscher Reklamefachleute.* Poster, 1913. Courtesy Fairleigh Dickinson University, Madison, N.J.

180. Peter Behrens. *AEG (Allgemeine Elektrizitäts-Gesellschaft).* Trademark, 1908

180

179

## PLAKATSTIL

Even in Berlin, where it was called the Berliner
Plakat, Plakatstil was a universal style without
direct links to any specific school or movement.
In fact, the only requisite for a successful poster
is that it attract attention immediately, given that
it must compete for the viewer's eye with many
other things on the street. The hallmarks of this
poster style were bold lettering, a simple central
image, and distinctive, eye-catching colors—in
short, an accessible message made aesthetically
pleasing. The examples here show a variety of
approaches to achieve one common result.

181. Burkhard Mangold. *Winter in Davos.*
Poster, 1914. Courtesy Posters Please, Inc.,
New York

182. F. G. Cooper. *Keep Cool Electrically.*
Poster, 1925

183. C. B. Falls. *Bert Williams.* Poster, date
unknown. Library of Congress, Washington,
D.C. Poster Collection

184. Willrab. *Problem.* Poster for cigarette
company, c. 1918

185. Robert Hardmeier. *Waschanstalt Zürich
AG.* Poster for a laundry firm, 1905. Kunstgewerbemuseum, Zurich

186. Louis Oppenheim. Self-promotional
advertisement from *Das Plakat,* 1919

181

182

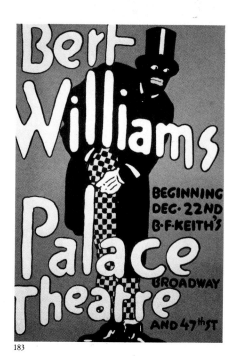

183

184

185

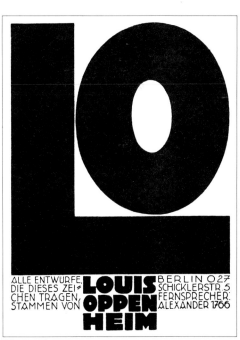

186

188

189

## PLAKATSTIL

From an early age, Lucian Bernhard was a master of the *sachplakat* (object poster). In 1906, at sixteen, he created his famous poster for Priester Matches, which shows two simple red matches with yellow tips against a dark brown background and the word *Preister* in blue block letters dropped out of the background. This masterpiece of economy became the archetype for much subsequent advertising, such as Hans Rudi Erdt's poster for Opel automobiles. Before he left Berlin for New York in the 1920s, Bernhard had produced hundreds of similarly composed posters for major corporations, including those for Stiller Shoes and Adler Typewriter, as well as many logos and typefaces. Plakatstil held such sway that poster printers convinced advertisers to reduce their images to the size of postage stamps, which were then placed on envelopes and other items of mass distribution. With poster columns and hoardings on every street and advertising stamps on virtually anything portable, customers could not help but receive the advertisers' product messages.

187. Various designers. Advertising stamps, 1905–11.

188. Lucian Bernhard. *Stiller Shoes.* Poster, 1908. Courtesy Reinhold Brown Gallery, New York

189. Lucian Bernhard. *Adler Typewriter.* Poster, 1908. Courtesy Reinhold Brown Gallery, New York

190. Hans Rudi Erdt. *Opel.* Poster, 1911. Courtesy Reinhold Brown Gallery, New York

190

## WIENER WERKSTÄTTE

Josef Hoffmann and Koloman Moser earned enough recognition as Secessionists to propagate their ideas to a new generation of artists, but they lacked control over the means of their production. The founding of the Wiener Werkstätte in 1903 was, like Morris's Arts and Crafts movement, a means for these artists to wrest command of creation and distribution. Hoffmann described their goals as "to establish intimate contact between public, designer and craftsman, and to produce good, simple domestic requisites." The graphic arts bound the group together. Hoffmann's architecture had graphic rather than plastic values, and his love of simplicity and whiteness contributed to the evolution of Modernism. Many of the patterns created by the Werkstätte's graphic artists and reproduced in the magazine *Die Flache (The Surface)* were applied to textiles and other crafts. In 1907 the group initiated a collection of affordable postcards for sale through retail outlets. Werkstätte design is based on the use of the square and balances negative and positive space so that the pictorial weights of background and foreground are equalized. Original Gothic typefaces, geometric borders, and lettering that emulated handwriting characterized all their printed matter: geometry became more important than symbolism. Yet a love of filiform trifles persisted in Hoffmann's decorations for the Fledermaus nightclub and in the posters used to advertise its events.

191. Josef Hoffmann. Hoffmann chair, 1904
192. Moritz Jung. Postcard, 1908
193. Max Bernirschke. Decorative ornament, from *Die Flache,* 1903
194. Designer unknown. *Cabaret Fledermaus.* Poster, date unknown. Courtesy Galerie Pabst, Munich
195. Josef Bruckmuller. *Die Flache I.* Magazine cover, 1903
196. Moritz Jung. *Kinderspielwaren.* Specimen sheet from *Die Flache,* 1903
197. Moritz Jung. *Kinderspielwaren.* Specimen sheet from *Die Flache,* 1903
198. Oskar Kokoschka. *Kunstschau.* Exhibition poster, 1908. Collection Galerie Pabst, Munich

191

192

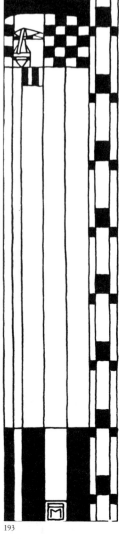

193

194

195

196

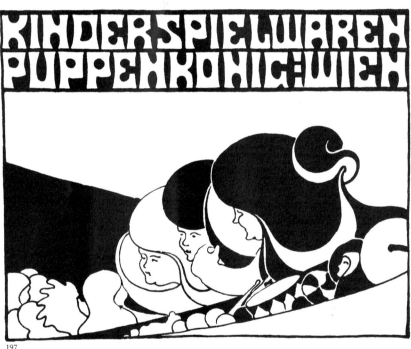

197

198

199. Otto Dix. *Der Krieg.* Book cover, c. 1918. Courtesy Ex Libris, New York

n the late nineteenth century, a new internationalism based on the belief that man had the ability to solve social problems through rational effort linked philosophers, scientists, and artists throughout Europe. Although Expressionism was born in Kaiser Wilhelm's Imperial Germany in 1905, there was nothing particularly German or imperial about it. While indebted to the Nordic tradition, its unorthodox visual language was more accurately a synthesis of pan-European trends: Jugendstil's black-and-white linear patterning, Impressionism's new scientific theories of vision, Fauvism's violent color palette, Van Gogh's and Gauguin's emotionality, Russian mysticism and spiritualism, and developments in Western science at the beginning of the new century. A personal calligraphy, based on an inner search for symbolism, replaced tired artistic conventions and soon emerged as a potent graphic art in Germany and abroad.

German Expressionism did not begin as an applied arts movement, nor was it allied with the industrial culture developing in Germany—although Expressionist architecture, film, theater, book illustration, and advertising design did eventually emerge. It began as a group of idealistic young men and women, previously excluded from the German arts establishment, became caught up in an international youth movement. The first group of Expressionists, called Die Brücke (The Bridge), formed in 1905; its members had studied architecture together at the Kunstgewerbeschule (arts and crafts school) in Dresden. Its most notable participants—including Erich Heckel, Ernst Ludwig Kirchner, Max Pechstein, Karl Schmidt-Rottluff, and Emil Nolde—embraced the idea that individualism was essential to artistic renewal. But being accustomed to the spiritual togetherness common in German universities at the time, they united into a brotherhood for strength against a hostile world.

Brücke artists believed painting had a greater value than architecture in the hierarchy of social usefulness. These "figurative" Expressionists turned away from objective reality so that their art might yield an inner, imaginative expression rather than an impression. Rejecting complete abstraction, they were rooted in the past by their emphasis on the human figure and their reliance on a humanistic Romanticism. Yet, at the same time, originality was a compulsion for them. Within the different traits of each individual's art, they generally favored Gothic expression and ignored the tenets of classical beauty, for to them pure expression had little to do with beauty. With hurricane-like speed, their periodicals, like the Berlin-based *Der Sturm* (The Storm), promulgated Expressionist ideas among the international arts community.

The second major Expressionist group, Der Blaue Reiter (The Blue Rider), was founded in 1912. Its leading proponents, the Russian Wassily Kandinsky and the Munich-born Franz Marc, cultivated the abstract as a universal source of symbols. These "abstract" Expressionists broke with optical reality in order to find a psychological basis for aesthetic pleasure. Their 1912 periodical, *Der Blaue Reiter Almanach,* championed the birth of a new spiritual epoch after the inevitable decline of nineteenth-century materialism.

Expressionism soon developed into a distinctive, primitive visual language. Its stark woodcuts and lithographs using very few but violent colors were characterized, according to the historian Helmut Rademacher, by "deformations, heightened intensity of expression and the treatment of reactions to psychic acts by an ecstatic pathos...." Influenced by the dominant style of caricature in acerbic satire magazines like *Simplicissimus* and *Jugend,* Expressionists distorted and elongated human figures and landscapes to create a mood of excitement within outlined and shaded forms. When employed as book or periodical illustrations, their images were rarely literal representations of texts but, rather, subjective evocations of an essence.

Before World War I, the urge for social change was expressed in largely metaphysical terms; political or cultural criticism was merely implied. During the war, some artists took prowar, nationalist positions, while others promulgated pacifist and cautionary messages. After Germany's defeat, with the abdication of the kaiser and the outset of the 1918 German revolution, many Expressionists became activists, allying themselves with left-wing parties to produce agitational posters, publications, and graphics. The Expressionist style defended the revolution, made calls to work and against strikebreaking, and even combated Bolshevism. In 1918, Dr. Adolph Behne, founder of the Arbeitsrat fur Kunst (Labor Office for Art), wrote about this new propagandistic trend: "They do not advertise for a firm but for an idea. They do not address themselves to a special public but to every sort of public....That is why they need to use new forms...." A month after the November revolution, the November-gruppe—including, among others, Pechstein, Oskar Kokoschka, Erich Mendelsohn, Otto Dix, and George Grosz—issued a battle call: "The future of art and the gravity of recent days compell us revolutionaries of the spirit (Cubists, Expressionists and Futurists) to union...." Although similar groups sprang up throughout Germany, feuds among pacifist, socialist, communist, and liberal factions made unity difficult.

The end of Expressionism came between 1920 and 1922. In the wake of the doomed Weimar Republic, the flame of political passion was extinguished. For artists, the incompatibility of their wishes and the political reality caused disenchantment with activism. It was also inevitable that the excitement of the novel and the unprecedented, which had given rise to German Expressionism, should lose its attraction once all facets of the style had been developed. A whole graphic repertoire of Expressionist forms, types, and color applications, created in the heat of feeling, was left to those who irresponsibly applied it to products as a stylistic veneer. An almost endless flood of artificial Expressionism debilitated the movement. With the coming to power of Adolf Hitler in 1933, Expressionist artists were denounced as degenerate, as "artistic pollution," and their legacy expunged from memory. Yet, even after World War II, Expressionist philosophy and graphic style continued to dramatically influence the practice of art and design.

200

201

202

203

204

205

## GERMAN

The decorative trivialities of the Munich Seccession provoked the Expressionist revolt. An inner search for personal symbolism—for a personal calligraphy—took the place of artistic conformity. The Expressionists believed that their art could be a force in the improvement of the human race. Having exposed the brutality of war, they went on to portray the harshness of German society in the postwar era. Examples here show the primitive woodcut style that distinguished the postwar Expressionists and became emblematic of the style as it took its place among other early Modernist movements.

200. Ernst Ludwig Kirchner. *Almanach auf des Jahr 1920.* Cover of almanac published by Fritz Gurlitt Verlag, 1920

201. Conrad Felixmüller. *Rettet Euch Menschen.* Woodcut, 1917

202. Conrad Felixmüller. *Der Kampf mit dem Engel (The Struggle with the Angel).* Title page, 1917

203. Ernst Ludwig Kirchner. *Umbra Vitae (Shadows of Life).* Page with woodcut illustrations from a book of poems by Georg Heym, 1924

204. Ernst Ludwig Kirchner. *Künstlergruppe Brücke.* Head piece, 1913

205. Emil Nolde. *Der Anbruch (A New Beginning).* Cover with woodcut illustration from a publication edited by Otto Schneider and J. B. Neumann in Berlin, January 1919

206. Hans Hoerl. *Die Aktion (The Action).* Cover of political publication, 1924

207. Franz Marc. *Der Sturm (The Storm).* Magazine cover, 1912

208. Conrad Felixmüller. *Der Weg (The Way).* Cover, with woodcut illustration, from a monthly periodical for Expressionist literature, art, and music, edited by Walter Blume, May/June 1919

206

207

208

## GERMAN

Expressionism's final years, from 1918 to 1922, were a period of great excitement, fostered by the belief that artists could actually contribute to the shaping of a new society. Artists issued political manifestos and proclamations; journals were published with inspirational titles like *The Beginning, The New Germany,* and *Mankind;* and posters called for international reconciliation. Art made valuable contributions to the political spirit, and politics were at the core of all Expressionist endeavor, including cinema and theater. Ultimately falling prey to its own excesses, Expressionism was rejected by its own proponents. The Nazis vilified the Expressionists in their notorious *Degenerate Art* exhibit, thereby insuring that the style will forever be a symbol of protest and revolt.

209. Otto Freundlich. *Entartet "Kunst" Ausstellungsführer.* Cover of *Degenerate Art* exhibition catalogue, 1938

210. Oskar Kokoschka. *Nieder mit dem Bolschwismus (Down with Bolshevism).* Poster, 1919. The Museum of Modern Art, New York

211. Heinz Fuchs. *Arbeiter Hunger (Worker Hunger).* Poster, 1918–19. Courtesy Ex Libris, New York

212. Max Pechstein. *An die Laterne (To the Lamppost).* Poster, 1919. Staatliche Museen Preussischer Kulturbesitz, West Berlin, Kunstbibliothek mit Museum für Architektur, Modebild und Grafik-Design

213. Hans Poelzig. *Der Golem (The Golem).* Poster for the film based on the novel by Gustav Meyrink, 1920. The Museum of Modern Art, New York

214. Paul Leni. *Expressionismus und Film (Expressionism and Film).* Book cover, 1926. Courtesy Ex Libris, New York

215. Max Pechstein. *An Alle Künstler! (To All Artists!).* Poster, 1919

209

210

211

212

213

214

215

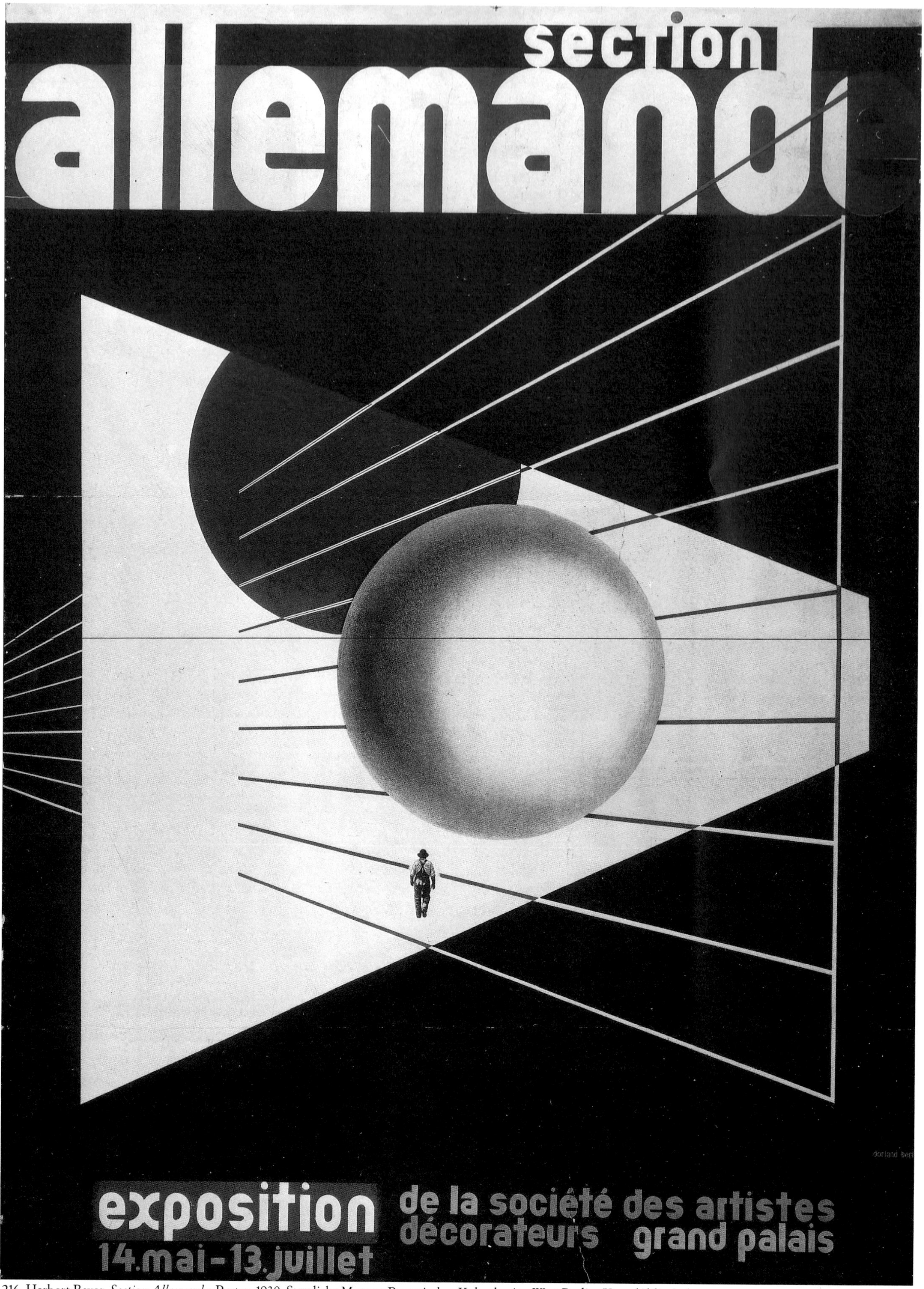

216. Herbert Bayer. *Section Allemande.* Poster, 1930. Staatliche Museen Preussischer Kulturbesitz, West Berlin, Kunstbibliothek

As pervasive as their influence is today, Modernist art and design were, from the outset, never completely accepted by the majority. The early Modernists encountered opposition from those believing their philosophies subversive, elitist, or both. What we call the Modernist era—roughly between 1908 (from the beginnings of Cubism) to 1933 (when Hitler came to power)—was a time of profound political, social, and cultural turmoil throughout the world. Various art forms, from architecture to film to typography, posed challenges to social systems made obsolete by rapidly changing machine age technologies. The different Modernist groups comprised activists who sought both to free art from its bourgeois ornamental superstructure and to influence the politics of contemporary life. Although the Futurist label was applied to only the Italians and the Russians, at the heart of the entire Modernist spirit was a forward-looking—and decidedly utopian —ethic. The most emblematic typeface of the age was even christened Futura.

The machine was the most cogent symbol of the Modernists' glorified, often sentimentalized, future; as Fernand Léger said, "The machine has altered the habitual look of things." To smash the old visual language and create a new one were the professed aims of the Modernist artist—aims expressed through abstract painting and sculpture, functional architecture, austere furnishings, and asymmetrical typography. The media were formidable tools: Modernism was propagated by highly publicized demonstrations and exhibitions as well as through numerous manifestos reprinted in avant-garde periodicals, almanacs, and newspapers, all having relatively wide distributions. The Modernist movement was not a monolith but rather a confluence of disparate groups and individuals who intersected at times to share ideas. While they all concurred with the desire to smash academic aestheticism, they rarely could reach consensus on the means to do so.

Cubism was the seminal experiment on which the form languages of the other movements were built. It marked the final break with reliance upon nature for subject matter and the complete rejection of decorative tendencies. As such, Cubism was despised by the bourgeoisie, yet eventually its surface mannerisms were borrowed by the day's leading fashion stylists. The Cubist practice of integrating random, collaged letterforms into paintings significantly influenced the free-form typography of subsequent movements.

Futurism, originally formulated by the Italian poet F. T. Marinetti in 1908, was the first to raise the Modernist banner on an international platform. This noisy proclamation of the Italian avant-garde curiously wed its theories of dynamic Modernism to militant patriotism. Being at once revolutionary and traditional, Futurism revealed the inconsistencies of living equally for the present and the future. Suprematism, developed by the Russian writer and painter Kasimir Malevich in 1913, synthesized Cubism and Futurism into an early geometric abstraction and added a metaphysical component. Suprematism found an opponent in Vladimir Tatlin's Constructivism, which sought to encompass all human spiritual, cognitive, and material activity. Originating in 1916 in Zurich and later continuing in Berlin, Dada was decidedly antiart and politically active. The Dutch De Stijl group, founded in 1917 by Theo van Doesburg, Piet Mondrian, and others, detached itself from Expressionist excesses in favor of a universal harmony devoid of emotional overtones

Although the plastic arts figured prominently in these movements, the applied arts were the ones to reach the broadest constituency. The first Modernist battles, like the progressive ones at the turn of the century, were waged against the industrialists, who controlled public taste and used it for their own functions and interests. A proper relationship between art and industry, Modernists believed, would dispel the hegemony of the industrialist. Through arts and crafts workshops in design schools such as the Bauhaus at Weimar and the Vkhutemas in Moscow, students were encouraged to produce utilitarian materials fit for everyday use. Reduced to their functional essence, these new products had no precedents in the decorative arts of the past. In theory at least, the masses, not the bourgeoisie, became the primary consumer.

The Modernist style was perhaps most immediately recognizable in a multitude of graphic communications: posters, brochures, books, handbills, and letterheads. The first substantial change occurred in typography. The classical symmetrical arrangements first erupted into Cubist, Futurist, and Dadaist typographic collage images, then evolved into the more disciplined, yet decidedly revolutionary, asymmetrical New Typography. Originating in Soviet Russia and Germany, the New Typography was quickly adopted in other centers of avant-garde activity, including Holland, Hungary, Czechoslovakia, and Poland, and was finally codified into a total revision of the rules of traditional commercial layout. Its principles were promulgated worldwide in philosophical essays and technical manuals by El Lissitzky, László Moholy-Nagy, Paul Renner, and its most devout (and rigid) adherent, Jan Tschichold. To these designers the rules of the old typography, practiced since the age of Gutenberg, violated the criterion of fitness for purpose in design.

The Polish advertising designer and painter Henryk Berlewi, who formed the Group of Abstract Constructive Art, wrote that advertising design "must rest on the same principles as prevail in modern industrial production." Logically, therefore, photography replaced realistic, decorative, or otherwise sentimentalized illustration. Photomontage, a completely mechanistic means of illustration, became an effective propaganda weapon and the most popular tool of the new graphic design. When used together, asymmetrical typography, geometric layout, and photographic illustration defined the radical new form language of Modernist design. Yet, as initial resistance to this powerful aesthetic turned into acceptance by commercial type foundries, printing firms, and advertising agencies, the honest Modernist characteristics were appropriated into Moderne, a bastardization of both the functional and the decorative approach.

## FUTURISM

The task of redefining the spiritual and material world at the outset of the new century fell to those artistic pioneers who commanded the shock troops of Modernism. The first upheaval was led by the Italian writer, poet, and critic F. T. Marinetti, who in 1909 published the first Futurist manifesto as a call for artists to battle: "There can be no nostalgia! No pessimism! There's no turning back!" Marinetti espoused a permanent artistic and political revolution. Possessed by false patriotism, he believed that war would be a cleansing process. He rejected the bourgeois material values of the ruling class in favor of the emerging Fascism of Benito Mussolini. Marinetti and the poets, painters, and sculptors who embraced Futurism's "new religion of speed" mythologized the machine—first the automobile and later the airplane—as a totem of the modern spirit. The metal book shown here is a symbol of Futurism's affinity for the machine age. In Futurist graphics, this affinity was translated into a kinetic style marked by free-verse poetics and onomatopoeic noise; Cubist collages were an important influence typographically. For Marinetti, such works described in visual terms "the whirling world of steel, pride, fever and speed."

217. Filippo T. Marinetti. *Les Mots en Liberté Futuristes.* Book cover, 1919. Courtesy Ex Libris, New York

218. Filippo T. Marinetti. *Montagne + Vallate + Strade × Joffre (Mountains + Valleys + Streets × Joffre).* Book cover, Futurist manifesto, 1915. Courtesy Ex Libris, New York

219. Gino Severini. *Serpentine Dance.* Page from *Lacerba,* July 1, 1914. The Beinecke Rare Book and Manuscript Library, Yale University, New Haven, Conn.

220. Tullio D'Albisola. *Parole in Liberta Futuriste.* Metal cover for a book by Filippo T. Marinetti, 1932. Courtesy Ex Libris, New York

221. Filippo T. Marinetti. *Zang Tumb Tumb.* Book cover, 1912. Courtesy Ex Libris, New York

222. Filippo T. Marinetti. *Dizionario Aereo.* Book cover, date unknown. Courtesy Ex Libris, New York

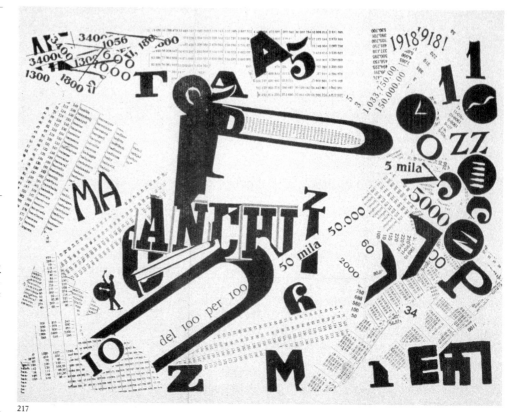

217

218

219

TULLIO D'ALBISOLA

MARINETTI
DELL'ACCADEMIA D'ITALIA
PAROLE in LIBERTÀ
FUTURISTE
TATTILI—TERMICHE OLFATTIVE

LITO-LATTA
SAVONA
EDIZIONI FUTURISTE DI POESIA
PIAZZA ADRIANA 30 ROMA

F. T. MARINETTI FUTURISTA
ZANG
TUMB TUMB
ADRIANOPOLI OTTOBRE 1912
TUUUMB in LIBERTÀ
PAROLE TUuuuM TUuuuM TUuuuM
EDIZIONI FUTURISTE
DI " POESIA "
Corso Venezia, 61 - MILANO
1914

F. MARINETTI — F. AZARI
PRIMO
DIZIONARIO AEREO
ITALIANO
EDITORE MORREALE
MILANO

223

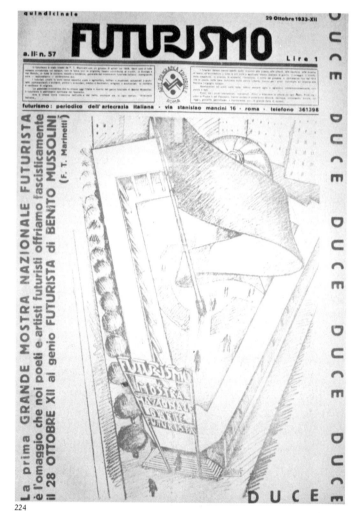

224

225

226

## FUTURISM

Futurist graphic style derived from the theory that the energy of the universe must be shown in painting and graphics as dynamic sensation and, further, that motion and light destroy the materiality of solid bodies, continually transforming reality. These theories required a new approach to pictorial creation, which the painter Umberto Boccioni identified in his *Manifesto of Futurist Painting* as a means to construct "dynamic sensation," "lines of force," and "the battle of planes." The newspaper, magazine, and book covers shown here demonstrate how these principles were applied to the graphic arts and also suggest how the early Futurist experimentation with free verse led to handmade book-objects and picture-poems. The Futurist revolution then went on to tackle the cinema, fashion, household objects, and even the mails with the intention of renewing all aspects of human life.

223. Designer unknown. *Futurismo.* Page from Futurist publication, 1932. Courtesy Ex Libris, New York

224. Designer unknown. *Futurismo.* Front page, October 1933. Courtesy Ex Libris, New York

225. Ivo Pannaggi. *Raun.* Book cover, 1932

226. V. Paladini. *Dino Terra, L'Amico dell'Angelo.* Photomontage, 1927. Courtesy Ex Libris, New York

227. Enrico Prampolini. *Broom.* Cover of an international magazine of the arts, c. 1921. Courtesy Ex Libris, New York

228. Designer unknown. *Stile Futurista.* Book cover, December 1934. Courtesy Ex Libris, New York

229. Enrico Prampolini. *Vulcani.* Book cover, date unknown. Courtesy Ex Libris, New York

227

228

229

## FUTURISM

Fortunato Depero was indefatigable in his propagation of Futurist principles. He promoted the art of the Futurist book, founded and directed the machine-art magazine *Dinamo,* produced Futurist radio programs, designed costumes and furniture, opened the Casa d'Arte Futurista in Italy and New York, and invented an "onomalanguage," a free-word, free-sounding expressive verbal rigmarole. Representing the so-called second stage of Futurism (from 1919 to about 1930), Depero was the individual most responsible for putting the often inaccessible Futurist theory into practice, particularly in the service of business. His synthesis of dynamic and expressionistic graphic forms was undeniably original. Believing that product advertising was the proper means by which to stimulate a dialogue with the public, he took on assignments for Campari, Magnesia San Pellegrino, and Venus Pencils as well as for numerous magazines and books. The historian Giorgio Ruggeri writes: "In Depero one rediscovers applied art...a heritage of so many new directions in art."

230. Fortunato Depero. Theater costumes for mechanical men, c. 1927

231. Fortunato Depero. *Depero Futurista.* Bolted book cover for an exhibition catalogue, 1927

232. Fortunato Depero. *Dinamo.* Advertisement for a magazine, 1933. Museo Depero, Rovereto, Italy

233. Fortunato Depero. *Magnesia S. Pellegrino.* Poster, 1931. Museo Depero, Rovereto, Italy

234. Fortunato Depero. *Campari.* Advertisement, c. 1931

235. Fortunato Depero. *Bitter Cordial Campari.* Advertisement, c. 1923

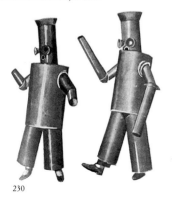

230

231

232

233

bozzetto di padiglione      per la ditta **DAVIDE CAMPARI & C.**

234

235

236

237

Soaring to Success !

# DAILY HERALD

— the Early Bird.

238

## VORTICISM

Vorticism, named by Ezra Pound in 1914 (from the vortex, the center of all energy), was one of Britain's most vehement avant-garde movements. Although linked by common artistic and philosophical threads to Marinetti's Futurism, Vorticism, as proposed by its leading spokesmen, Pound and Wyndham Lewis, differed from Futurism in some respects. It enthusiastically embraced Futurism as a revolutionary frame of mind while seeking to dissociate itself from Futurism as a visual style peculiar to a group of Italian artists, whose manifestos and spokesmen had made it the best publicized art movement on the Continent. Yet, the differences in form and practice between the two were actually often negligible. Lewis edited and designed the Vorticist's leading periodical, *Blast,* which, in keeping with the avant-garde spirit, was intended to shock—not only by its name but by its cover, size, and Gothic typography. It was printed in violent pink or puce, "the color of an acute sick-headache," said a critic. At best, its style conveyed a dogged aggressiveness as its writers tackled the issues of the day, hoping to destroy everything old and decadent in its path. *Coterie* was a less inflammatory Vorticist literary journal. E. McKnight Kauffer, an American expatriate who became a leading Modernist designer in Britain, created his first and most famous poster apparently under the influence of Lewis.

236. Wyndham Lewis. *Blast.* Cover for a Vorticist magazine, July 1915. Courtesy Ex Libris, New York

237. William Roberts. *Coterie.* Cover for a literary periodical, 1919. Courtesy Chris Mullen

238. E. McKnight Kauffer. *Flight of Birds.* Poster for the *Daily Herald,* 1919. Victoria and Albert Museum, The National Museum of Art and Design, London

## CONSTRUCTIVISM

Before Constructivism, there were several Russian prerevolutionary artistic experiments, including Cubo-Futurism, Rayonnism, and the mystical, nonobjective Suprematism of Kasimir Malevich. Developed by Vladimir Tatlin, Constructivism became an early Soviet youth movement, an artistic outlook that aimed to encompass the whole spiritual, cognitive, and material activity of man. By declaring themselves for the revolution, Constructivists expected to be able to introduce their own programs for the future. Lazar El Lissitzky sought to create a modern art that would take the viewer out of the traditional passive role and make him an active spectator. In fact, throughout the course of Russian art history (particularly with Russian Orthodox religious iconography), there runs a strong belief that art must have some redeeming social purpose, a purpose to be achieved by eliciting certain physical responses. Lissitzky's civil-war-era poster *Beat the Whites with the Red Wedge* not only tried to convince viewers of the legitimacy of the Bolshevik cause; it wanted them to vigorously strive for revolution. Under the influence of Suprematism, Lissitzky wrote that the square was "the source of all creative expression." His children's book *Of Two Squares* was a fable about the cooperation of a black and red square in dispersing chaos and establishing a new order.

239. El Lissitzky. *Of Two Squares.* Cover *(top left)* and pages from a children's book about the Russian Revolution and the triumph of Bolshevism, Dutch De Stijl Edition, 1922

240. El Lissitzky. *Beat the Whites with the Red Wedge.* Poster, 1920. Courtesy Szymon Bojko

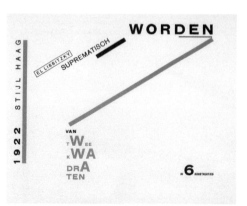

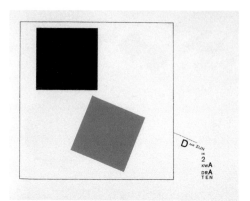

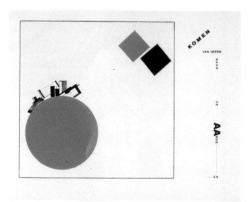

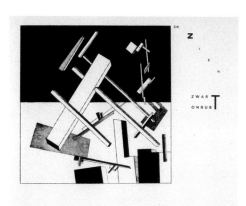

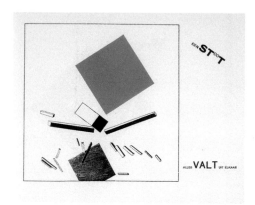

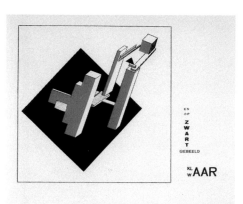

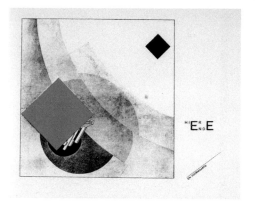

239

## CONSTRUCTIVISM

The Constructivists practiced their own brand of collectivism in which the individual and his work were subordinate to the group. More important than either their artistic innovation or political commitment was their fusion of the two into a single art reflecting their revolutionary times. In the minds of many, it was Constructivist typography that was most identified with the art of revolution. Yet the basic style (the result of individual work by, among others, Lissitzky, Alexander Rodchenko, Alexei Gan, Solomon Telingater, Gustav Klutsis, and Varvara Stepanova) developed in response to technological limitations and material shortages as well as from an understanding of Modernist theories. Lissitzky formulated his typographical design for Mayakovsky's book of polemical poems, *For the Voice,* on the idea of the "kinetics of succeeding pages," somewhat akin to the movement of film. Rodchenko believed that graphic design must be a coded sign, unambiguous, objectified, free from ornament. Gan and Telingater made typographical pictures that followed the demands of the texts being illustrated. Lettering was expected to function on both a substantive and an emotional level.

241. Gustav Klutsis. Photomontage for a special tribute to Lenin, 1924. Courtesy Szymon Bojko

242. El Lissitzky. *For the Voice.* Pages from a book of poems by Vladimir Mayakovsky, 1923. Courtesy Ex Libris, New York

243. Solomon Telingater. *The Word Belongs to Kirsanov.* Pages, 1930

244. El Lissitzky. *Broom.* Magazine cover, 1922. Courtesy Ex Libris, New York

245. Vladimir Mayakovsky and Alexander Rodchenko. *Give Pencils Which Are Good.* Poster for the Moscow Polygraphical Division, date unknown. Courtesy Ex Libris, New York

246. Alexander Rodchenko. *GUM (Government Universal Store).* Advertisement for watches, text by Vladimir Mayakovsky, 1923

241

242

243

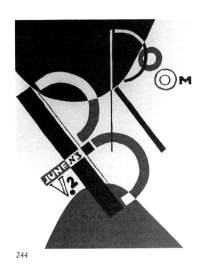

244

245

## CONSTRUCTIVISM

By 1921, the New Economic Policy was in place and the Soviet Union was on the path to economic normalcy and political stability, or so everyone hoped. About this time, Rodchenko, Tatlin, Stepanova, and other members of the INKHUK (Moscow's Institute for Artistic Culture) abandoned painting and sculpture for domestic design. What they called Productivism was their attempt to manufacture materials for everyday use—textiles, dishware, clothing, furniture, and so on—in a direct and efficient manner. Rodchenko, Stepanova, and others made advertising for commercial enterprises, like the GUM department store, as well as for theatrical and cultural events. Together with Mayakovsky, Rodchenko also formed an advertising partnership that created propaganda for nationalized commerce, education, and services. Calling themselves "advertising constructors," Mayakovsky wrote the poems and slogans and Rodchenko designed images that caught the eye with their strong geometry, bright color, and bold lettering.

247. Alexander Rodchenko. *Rezinotrest.* Poster for a rubber conglomerate, 1923. Courtesy Szymon Bojko

248. Alexander Rodchenko. *Three Mountains Beer.* Poster, 1923. Courtesy Ex Libris, New York

249. Alexander Rodchenko. *Baby Dummies.* Poster for the Rubber Trust promoting baby pacifiers, 1923. Courtesy Ex Libris, New York

250. Alexander Rodchenko. *Rezinotrest.* Poster promoting the production of galoshes for export, 1923. Courtesy Ex Libris, New York

251. Alexander Rodchenko. Poster urging Soviet citizens to become stockholders, 1923. Courtesy Ex Libris, New York

252. Varvara Stepanova. *Death of Tarelkin.* Theater poster, 1922. Courtesy Szymon Bojko

253. Alexander Rodchenko. Poster advertising Leningrad Publishing House, 1925. Courtesy Ex Libris, New York

247

248

249

250

251

252

253

254

255

256

257

258

259

260

## CONSTRUCTIVISM

Anatoly Lunacharsky wrote, "If the revolution can give art its soul, then art can endow the revolution with speech." And despite Lenin's lack of confidence in the avant-garde, it was certainly the intention of many of its designers to create a proletarian art. Yet after Lenin's death in 1924 tolerance among Soviet leaders for the avant-garde began to wane. Despite some exuberant typographic work by the leading designers, many of the Soviet periodicals of the early 1920s were printed on gray paper with lackluster type. Collage and photomontage were the only graphic techniques that both the progressives and conservatives accepted as effective communications. Montage (from the French word *monter,* meaning to mount) developed simultaneously in the late teens in Germany and Russia. Photomontage, the making of a new image from two or more photographs, was, as Hannah Hoch wrote, "a tool to integrate objects in the world of machines and industry into the world of art." Montage as a film technique was also powerfully used in the Soviet cinema. The book jackets shown here suggest a trend in late Constructivist design away from "phonetic" typography to primarily "optical" expression.

254. Designer unknown. *From Easel to Machine.* Cover for a Constructivist manifesto, 1922. Courtesy Ex Libris, New York

255. El Lissitzky. *Rabbi.* Cover for the text of a play, 1922. Courtesy Ex Libris, New York

256. G. Bershadeskii. *The Flying Proletariat.* Cover for a book of poems, 1925. Courtesy Ex Libris, New York

257. Solomon Telingater. *At the Top of My Voice.* Photomontage book cover, 1931. Courtesy Ex Libris, New York

258. El Lissitzky. *Brigade of Artists.* Book cover, date unknown. Courtesy Ex Libris, New York

259. Designer unknown. *BOCC.* Book cover, date unknown. Courtesy Ex Libris, New York

260. Alexander Rodchenko and Vladimir Mayakovsky. *The Youth of Mayakovsky.* Book cover, 1931. Courtesy Ex Libris, New York

261. Officers of the Red army

261

## CONSTRUCTIVISM

Soviet cinema was a truly revolutionary communications medium, as was the printed material used to promote it. Soviet film posters, which began to appear in quantity during the mid-twenties, were only somewhat influenced by typical Constructivist graphic design. The leading posterists, such as the Stenberg brothers and Semion Semionov, developed a distinctive style employing sans-serif type as a pictorial element and a combination of photomontage with a painted image. The Stenberg brothers worked within a highly sophisticated sense of two-dimensional space. Their images were on different planes that turn and slide one on top of another; space is suggested more by one's sense of vertigo than by traditional perspective. Of most interest was the Stenbergs' translation of the exclusively black and white films into vibrant, colorful posters. The color palette of all the posterists was quite unique amid the symbolic red and black colors of Constructivism. Yet the high quality of film posters, like that of the films themselves, lasted for only a brief time. By the early 1930s, the Stalinist ritual of harsh cultural criticism began to take its toll.

262. V. N. Lenin, c. 1919

263. Designer unknown. *My Destiny.* Movie poster, 1929. Courtesy Ex Libris, New York

264. Nikolai Prusakov and Grigory Borisov. *I Hurry to See the Khaz-Push.* Poster for an Armenian film, 1927. Courtesy Ex Libris, New York

265. Designer unknown. *Flying Luck.* Movie poster, c. 1928. Courtesy Ex Libris, New York

266. Designer unknown. *Symphony of the Donbas.* Movie poster, 1931. Courtesy Ex Libris, New York

267. Georgy and Vladimir Stenberg. *Charles Ray in the Movie* Punch. Poster, c. 1928. Courtesy Ex Libris, New York

268. Semion Semionov. *The Turkish Railway.* Movie poster, 1929. Courtesy Ex Libris, New York

269. Designer unknown. *The Knot.* Movie poster, c. 1927. Collection Reinhold Brown Gallery, New York

262

263

264

265

266

267

268

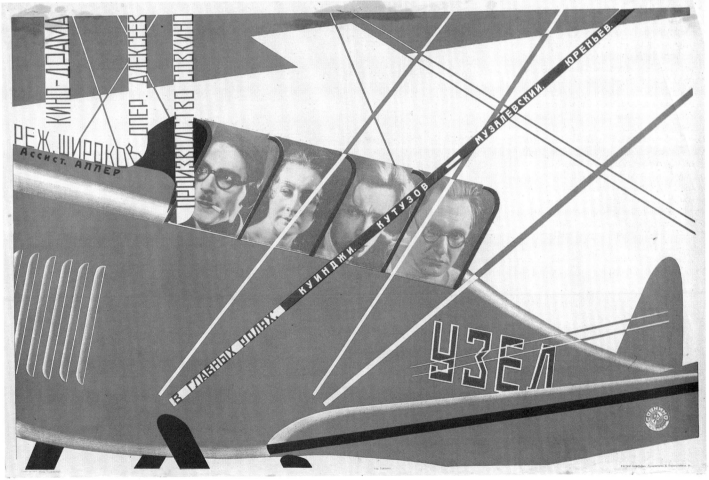

269

270

## CONSTRUCTIVISM

Constructivism's theory and style were exported
to Europe through manifestos, periodicals, and
the personal efforts of its leading proponents.
Lissitzky, for example, spent a good deal of time
with Kurt Schwitters in Hanover, working on the
Dada periodical, *Merz,* and with Ilya Ehrenburg
in Berlin, publishing the Constructivist journal,
*Objet.* In 1922 the Polish painter and designer
Henryk Berlewi was inspired to create his
abstract Mechano-Faktura (mechanical art) constructions after hearing Lissitzky lecture in War-
saw. Two years later, he co-founded Reklama-
Mechano, an advertising agency whose work
came to best represent Polish Constructivism.
The Czech poet and artist Karel Teige adapted the
Constructivist language to the needs of his
nation's avant-garde. In Belgium, Fred Deltro
produced a series of caricatures of the ruling class
that were based on Constructivist-inspired geometry. The cover for the Dutch professional advertising magazine, *De Reklame,* shows how a typical
Lissitzky-like design can be used simply as a
decorative motif.

270. Designer unknown. *De Reclame.* Cover of
a Dutch advertising magazine, 1926. Courtesy
Fairleigh Dickinson University, Madison, N.J.

271. Juryi Roshkov. Photomontage for a
Vladimir Mayakovsky poem, 1925. Courtesy
Szymon Bojko

272. Henryk Berlewi. *Composition in Red and
Black (Mechano-Faktura Compositions).* Print,
1922. Courtesy Ex Libris, New York

273. Karel Teige. *Ma Buch (My Book).* Book
cover, 1922. Courtesy Ex Libris, New York

274. Fred Deltro. *Jeu de Massacre.* One of
twelve pochoirs for a book by Henri Barbusse
(Bruxelles Editions Socialistes), 1920. Courtesy
Fairleigh Dickinson University, Madison, N.J.

271

272

273

274

## DE STIJL

De Stijl (The Style) was defined by the architect H. P. Berlage as "unity in plurality." Taking its name from a magazine edited from 1917 to 1931 by the Dutch painter, designer, and writer Theo van Doesburg, it was not a group in the usual sense. Most of those connected with De Stijl were associated only briefly and some of the most important never met at all. De Stijl concerned itself with developing a utopian style and spirit; it was not merely about the stylization of things. Anything emotional was taboo. All De Stijl design was based on the rectangle and the use of black, white, gray, and the primary colors, as evidenced in the graphic work of van Doesburg and Vilmos Huszar during World War I. After the war, many of the De Stijl artists went their separate ways, and van Doesburg replaced them with kindred artists from abroad, like El Lissitzky. The format and layout of his magazine also became purer and reductive, more in line with the internationalism of the New Typography.

275. Gerrit Rietveld. *Red/Blue Chair,* 1918

276. Vilmos Huszar. *De Stijl.* Magazine cover, 1917. Courtesy Ex Libris, New York

277. Vilmos Huszar. *Miss Blanche Egyptian Cigarettes.* Poster, 1926

278. Vilmos Huszar, *De Stijl.* Magazine cover, 1917. Courtesy Ex Libris, New York

279. Theo van Doesburg. *Alphabet,* 1919

280. László Moholy-Nagy and Theo van Doesburg. *Grundbegriffe der Neuen Gestaltenden Kunst.* Cover of a Bauhaus book, 1925. Courtesy Ex Libris, New York

281. Piet Zwart. Logos for IOCO, 1922–23

282. Vilmos Huszar. *Ex Libris Voor Lena de Roos.* Bookplate, 1922–24

275

276

277

278

279

THEO van DOESBURG BAUHAUS

GRUNDBEGRIFFE DER NEUEN GESTALTENDEN KUNST

BÜCHER 6

280

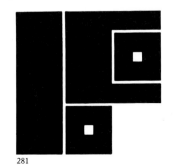

281

282

IDEE UND AUFBAU DES STAATLICHEN BAUHAUSES WEIMAR VON WALTER GROPIUS

BAUHAUSVERLAG G.M.B.H. MÜNCHEN

283

284

ALLES Lebendige OFFENBART SICH dem MENSCHEN durch das Mittel DER BEWEGUNG

ALLES Lebendige OFFENBART SICH IN FORMEN

SO IST ALLE FORM BEWEGUNG

UND ALLE BEWEGUNG OFFENBAR IN FORM

DIE FORMEN SIND GE=FÄSSE DER BEWEGUNG UND BEWEGUNGEN DAS WESEN DER FORM.

286

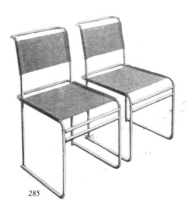

285

STAATLICHES BAUHAUS IN WEIMAR 1919-1923

287

## BAUHAUS

By 1914 a reform movement had begun in Germany to change the method and quality of art education by combining the fine and applied arts into a single curriculum. The early Modernist Henry Van de Velde was placed in charge of the Weimar Kunstgewerbeschule, and Peter Behrens ran the Düsseldorf School of Arts and Crafts. In 1919 the architect Walter Gropius was appointed director of an institution that merged the Weimar Academy of Fine Art and the Weimar Kunstgewerbeschule. His first action was to reconstitute the school, to be called Das Staatliche Bauhaus, on the model of William Morris's Arts and Crafts workshops. Gropius was proudly anti-academic: his teachers were called *masters* and his students *apprentices* and *journeymen* to signify that the school was working in the real world. Workshops, not studios, provided the basis for Bauhaus teaching, in which craftsmen and fine artists would introduce students to the mysteries of creativity and help them achieve a formal language of their own. A preliminary course called *Vorkurs,* developed by Johannes Itten, was an introduction to all forms of art, as well as a testing ground for students. For its first four years, no official Bauhaus graphic style was evident. Shown here are various Bauhaus projects influenced by Expressionism, Dada, Constructivism, and De Stijl.

283. László Moholy-Nagy. *Idee und Aufbau des Staatlichen Bauhauses Weimar.* Book cover, c. 1923. Courtesy Ex Libris, New York

284. Oskar Schlemmer. Bauhaus logo, 1922. Courtesy Ex Libris, New York

285. Marcel Breuer. Steel chairs, 1926. Courtesy Ex Libris, New York

286. Johannes Itten. *Utopia.* Page from Bauhaus typographical book, 1921. Courtesy Ex Libris, New York

287. Herbert Bayer. *Staatliches Bauhaus in Weimar, 1919–1923.* Cover for the first Bauhaus exhibition catalogue, 1923. Courtesy Ex Libris, New York

288. Joost Schmidt. *Bauhaus.* Poster, 1923. Courtesy Ex Libris, New York

289. Margit Terry-Adler. *Utopia, Documente der Wirklichkeit I/II.* Book cover, 1921. Courtesy Ex Libris, New York

290. Joost Schmidt. *Weimar Bauhaus.* Book cover, 1924. Courtesy Ex Libris, New York

291. Walter Gropius (architect). Bauhaus School, Dessau

288

289

290

291

## BAUHAUS

From the outset, Gropius believed that the
Bauhaus should avoid imposing any particular
style and that students should have the opportunity to develop their individuality. In distanc-
ing itself from the De Stijl ethic of a strictly
defined geometric, impersonal style, the Bauhaus
drifted toward a quasi-Expressionist style. When
Theo van Doesburg came to teach at the Bauhaus, he encouraged Gropius to move in the
direction of a more avant-garde Constructivism.
The arrival of the Hungarian painter and
designer László Moholy-Nagy furthered the
interest in typography, printing, and photography and strengthened the Constructivist faction at the school. Although criticized for his
methods, Moholy-Nagy prevailed in developing
an asymmetrical typography that was both clear
and convincing. When the Bauhaus was forced
to move to Dessau, Gropius modified the curriculum and established a typography workshop,
first under Herbert Bayer and then under Joost
Schmidt (who changed the course title to *Commercial Art*). Among Bayer's many design contributions was his Universal Alphabet, which
rejected all capital letters. By the late twenties,
the Bauhaus style was the quintessence of functional graphic design.

292. Herbert Bayer. Sketch for an advertising
sign, 1924. Courtesy Ex Libris, New York

293. Herbert Bayer. *Bauhaus-Ausstellung.*
Postcard, 1923. Courtesy Ex Libris, New York

294. Ludwig Hirschfeld-Mack. *Farben Licht-
spiele.* Advertisement, c. 1925. Courtesy Ex
Libris, New York.

295. Herbert Bayer. *Einladung...zum Bart-
Nasen-Herzensfest.* Party invitation, 1928. Courtesy Ex Libris, New York

296. Herbert Bayer. *Kandinsky's 60th.* Birthday poster, 1926. Kunstgewerbemuseum, Zurich

297. Joost Schmidt. *Yko.* Advertisement, 1924.
Courtesy Ex Libris, New York

298. Herbert Bayer. Universal alphabet, 1925.
Courtesy Ex Libris, New York

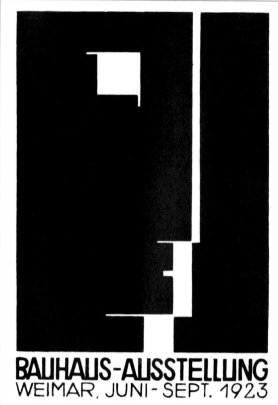

293

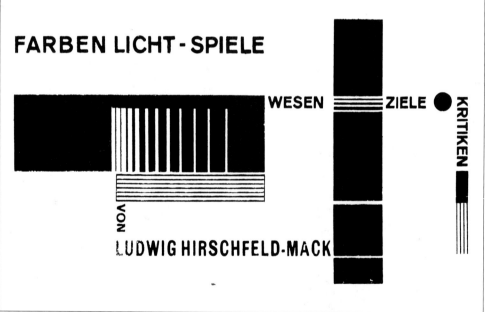

294

292

295

296

297

298

299

300

301

302

303

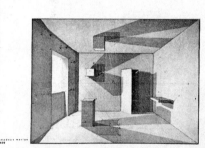

304

305

306

## BAUHAUS

Soon after the Bauhaus moved to Dessau, it became well known to the general public and, thus, associated with a style—anything geometric, functional, or modern. Gropius himself never ceased to deny the existence of a Bauhaus style. Oskar Schlemmer said of this perceived style that it "became a rejection of yesterday's styles, a determination to be 'up-to-the-minute' at all costs—this style can be found everywhere but at the Bauhaus." Actually, the design of Bauhaus materials was consistently determined by functional requisites, not by the obsession with style. The essential features of all Bauhaus publications were order, asymmetry, and a basic rectangular grid structure. Decoration was limited to the use of heavy rules, circles, and rectangles of type metal. Photography and montage replaced realistic drawing as illustration. The sans-serif typeface was regarded as essential, and in 1925 Bayer's proposal to drop capital letters from all printed matter was accepted. Rather than conforming to a style, Bauhaus objects may be more properly described as having fitness of purpose.

299. László Moholy-Nagy. *Gropius Bauhaus Bauten, Dessau (Bauhaus Book 12)*. Book jacket, 1930. Courtesy Ex Libris, New York

300. Joost Schmidt. *Offset 7*. Book jacket, 1926. Courtesy Ex Libris, New York

301. László Moholy-Nagy. *Malerei, Fotografie, Film (Painting, Photography, Film)*. Book jacket, 1925. Courtesy Ex Libris, New York

302. Herbert Bayer. *Kandinsky: Punkt und Linie zu Fläche (Kandinsky: Point and Line on Plane)*. Book jacket, 1926

303. Herbert Bayer. *Bauhaus*. Magazine cover, 1928. Courtesy Ex Libris, New York

304. Joost Schmidt and Xanti Schawinsky. *Bauhaus*. Magazine cover, January 1929. Courtesy Ex Libris, New York

305. Herbert Bayer. *Bauhaus, Dessau*. Book cover, 1927. Courtesy Ex Libris, New York

306. László Moholy-Nagy. *Von Material zu Architektur (Bauhaus Book 14)*. Book cover, 1929. Courtesy Ex Libris, New York

## NEW TYPOGRAPHY

The New Typography is most simply defined as a rejection of the classical rules of typographic symmetry. In a 1927 essay, El Lissitzky traces its development back to Marinetti's *parole in liberta,* Wyndham Lewis's layout for *Blast,* and the Dadaist photomontager John Heartfield's layout for the magazine *Neue Jugend.* El Lissitzky's typography was the first formal application of the new approach, and his sans-serif letterforms, limited range of primary colors, and geometricized forms were to become lasting clichés in advertising typography. Lissitzky was one of the first to absorb the lessons of modern art movements and apply them usefully to communications, and Moholy-Nagy, in turn, adapted Lissitzky's basic premises to his Bauhaus course. In 1924 Max Burchartz opened his advertising agency, Werbau, to work in the new style for industrial clients. In 1925 a young professor of typography from Leipzig, Jan Tschichold, who had no direct connection with the Bauhaus, collected and analyzed the significant examples of modern work in a special issue of *Typographische Mitteilungen* titled "Elementare Typographie." Three years later, Tschichold formulated and codified the fundamental principles of asymmetry in *Die Neue Typographie (The New Typography),* with which he sought to change the basic practices of the German printing industry. While asymmetric design afforded more variety and could be more readily accommodated to the new layout techniques, the type historian Herbert Spencer argues that "Tschichold's attempt to strictly codify modern typography...was neither necessary nor relevant." And thus, by its very nature, it contradicted the free spirit of modern typography.

307. Jan Tschichold. *Graphische Werbekunst.* Exhibition poster, 1926. Courtesy Ex Libris, New York

308. Anton Stankowski. *Hill auch in Witten!* Advertisement, 1925

309. Jan Tschichold. *Die Hose.* Movie poster, 1927. Courtesy Ex Libris, New York

310. Jan Tschichold. *Typographische Mitteilungen.* Magazine cover, 1925. Courtesy Ex Libris, New York

311. Max Burchartz. *Schubertfeier der Staedtischen Buehnen, Essen (Schubert Festival).* Poster, 1928. The Museum of Modern Art, New York. Gift of Philip Johnson

312. Jan Tschichold. *Laster der Menschheit (Lusts of Mankind).* Movie poster, 1926. Kunstgewerbemuseum, Zurich

313. Jan Tschichold. *Casanova.* Movie poster, 1927. Kunstgewerbemuseum, Zurich

314. Joost Schmidt. *Uber Type Foundry.* Page from type catalogue, 1932. Courtesy Ex Libris, New York

307

309

308

311

312

313

314

### NEW TYPOGRAPHY

A fresh, new typography was badly needed that
would not depend on ready-made layouts and
would express the spirit, life, and visual sensibility of its day. And it was achieved in Czechoslovakia from the late twenties to early thirties. In
his years as design director for the Prague publishing house Druzstevni Prace, Ladislav Sutnar
practiced his own version of the New Typography
in a memorable series of book jackets for works
by Upton Sinclair and George Bernard Shaw. His
jacket for *Nejmenši Dům (Minimum Housing)* is a
masterpiece of simplicity and visual clarity. Sutnar
found photography the perfect medium for
reproducing reality and giving the reader a terse,
pointed message. His poster for an exhibition of
modern trade in the city of Brno employs a
dramatic collage of architectural and industrial
products in an animated counterpoint to the
economical typography. And Karel Teige's title
page for Konstantin Biebl's poem recalls the
typecase designs in Lissitzky's *For the Voice.*

315. Ladislav Sutnar. *Československo Brno 1929.*
Poster, 1929. Courtesy Ex Libris, New York

316. Karel Teige. *S Lodí Jež Dováží a Čaj a Kávu
(With the Ship Comes Tea and Coffee).* Title pages
from book of poetry by Konstantin Biebl, 1928.
Courtesy Ex Libris, New York

317. Zdeněk Rossmann (author and designer).
*Písmo a Fotografie v Reklamé (Lettering and Pho-
tography in Advertising).* Book jacket, 1938. Courtesy Ex Libris, New York

318. Ladislav Sutnar. *Nejmenši Dům (Minimum
Housing).* Book jacket, c. 1930–31. Courtesy Ex
Libris, New York

319. Ladislav Sutnar. *Poutlásky.* Book jacket for
Upton Sinclair novel, c. 1930. Courtesy Ex Libris,
New York

320. Ladislav Sutnar. *Drobnosti.* Book jacket
for George Bernard Shaw work, c. 1930. Courtesy
Ex Libris, New York

321. Ladislav Sutnar. *Obraceni Kapitana Brass-
bounda (Captain Brassbound's Conversion).* Book
jacket for George Bernard Shaw play, c. 1930.
Courtesy Ex Libris, New York

Zdeněk Rossmann

# písmo a fotografie

## v reklamě

Index

322

323

324

325

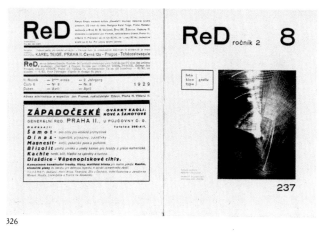

326

237

327

## NEW TYPOGRAPHY

The New Typography was inspired to some degree by a general degradation of typography, but it was also a response to new printing technologies that allowed designers to break free from the confines of the traditional typecase and curiously anticipated the later freedoms of phototypography. Tschichold's rigid rules were perhaps intended more for the untutored job printer, who required guidelines, than for those skilled and imaginative designers who already possessed communications skills. Shown here are examples of the New Typography that, though decidedly influenced by the spirit of Constructivism and De Stijl, nevertheless break the rules of earlier Modernist typography. The Czechoslovakian designer and art director Ladislav Sutnar demonstrates in the magazine covers for *O Bydlení (About Living)* and *Žijeme (For Life)* how a type and photo combination can signal a commitment to modern life. Karel Teige's cover and contents spread for *Red* suggest his affinity with the Bauhaus. And Yugoslav designer Ljubomir Micić plays with Constructivist forms on the covers of the arts journal *Zenit*.

322. Ladislav Sutnar. *O Bydlení (About Living)*. Cover of an avant-garde interiors magazine, photomontage with typography, 1932. Courtesy Ex Libris, New York

323. Ladislav Sutnar. *Žijeme (For Life)*. Cover for an "Illustrated Magazine of Modern Times," 1931. Courtesy Ex Libris, New York

324. Ladislav Sutnar. *Žijeme (For Life)*. Magazine cover, 1931. Courtesy Ex Libris, New York

325. Karel Teige. *Red*. Magazine cover for a "Monthly of Modern Culture," 1929

326. Karel Teige. *Red*. Magazine pages, 1929. Courtesy Ex Libris, New York

327. Ljubomir Micić. *Zenit*. Cover of a magazine devoted to contemporaneous European art movements, 1924. Courtesy Ex Libris, New York

328. Ljubomir Micić. *Zenit*. Magazine cover, 1924. Courtesy Ex Libris, New York

328

329

330

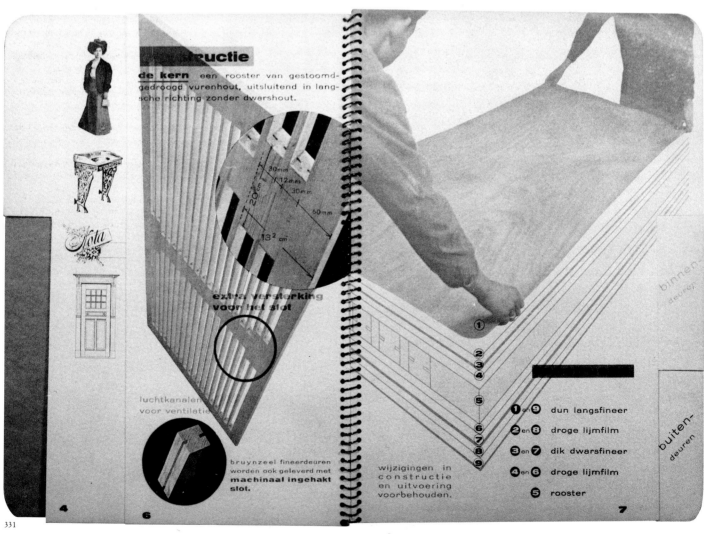

331

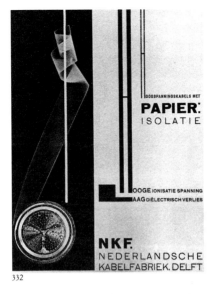

332

333

## NEW TYPOGRAPHY

Purified De Stijl typographics, emphasis on horizontal and vertical lines, use of the rectangle, and primary colors arranged in masses characterize the work of Piet Zwart and Paul Schuitema, the leading Dutch proponents of the New Typography. Zwart was one of the first in Holland to add photography to typographic elements, thus dramatically clarifying complicated messages. Schuitema followed suit and, by superimposing photographs in primary colors under typographic designs, was able to simulate cinematic motion. Both men applied their dynamic functionalism to business catalogues and advertisements for products and services as various as electrical wire, cables, cheese, broadcasting and paper companies, and the Dutch postal service (PTT), enlivening with typographic excitement some otherwise banal printed matter.

329. Paul Schuitema. *Rindless Cheese.* Advertisement for P. Van Berkel Ltd., date unknown. Courtesy Ex Libris, New York

330. Piet Zwart. *Hommage à une Jeune Fille.* A free-form typographic composition devised by the placement of elements from a typecase, 1925. Courtesy Ex Libris, New York

331. Piet Zwart. *Bruynzeel Architectural Products.* Catalogue spread, 1935. Courtesy Ex Libris, New York

332. Piet Zwart. *Papier.* Advertisement for Dutch cable manufacturing company, 1925

333. Piet Zwart. *Breakdown.* Advertisement for NCW cable, c. 1925

334. Piet Zwart. *PCH.* Brochure for Broadcasting Station Scheveningen announcing ship-to-shore communication, 1928. Courtesy Ex Libris, New York

334

125

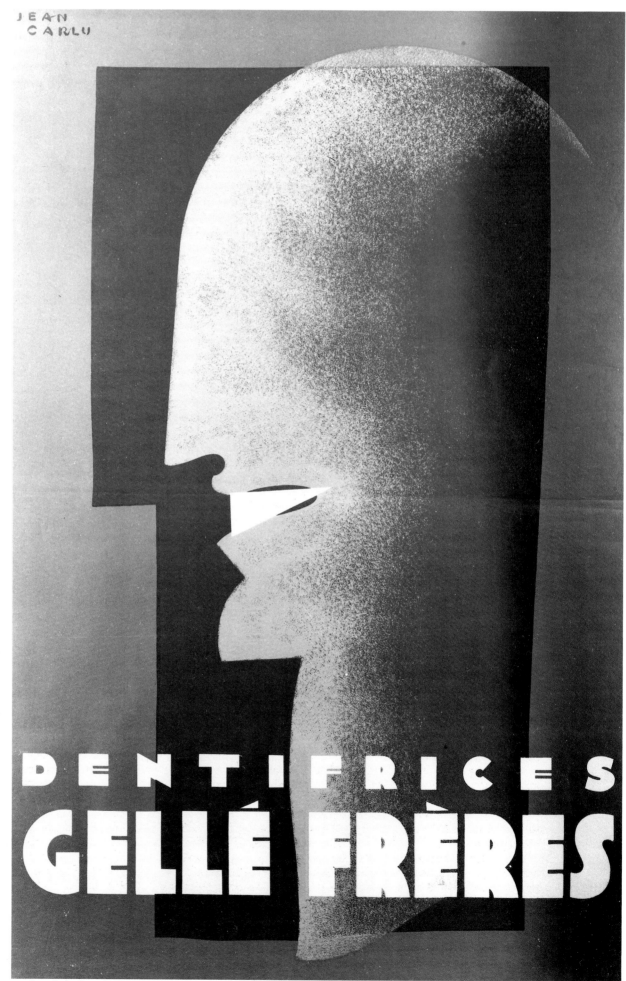

335. Jean Carlu. *Dentifrices Gellé Frères*. Poster for toothpaste, 1927. Musée de la Publicité, Paris

While Modernist designers struggled after World War I to transform society with their utopian ideals of function and fitness, Moderne or Modernistic design—a fashionable amalgam of the new reductive forms and the old decorative tendencies—was taking the consumer world by storm. In contrast to the perceived solemnities of the Modernist Bauhaus, these often frivolous and shocking manifestations of the Jazz Age were forged into a broad international style called Art Deco, later termed "the last of the total styles" by the historian Bevis Hillier.

Under different names in various countries, Art Deco universally affected architecture, furniture, clothing, and graphic arts between the world wars. As Art Nouveau began to wane, designers affiliated with the Société des Artistes Décorateurs realized that the middle class required another unthreatening style as an alternative to the increasingly abstract (and, for many, inaccessible) Modernism. Despite the prevailing Modernist philosophy, the compulsion of the European public for ornament persisted.

Art Deco was thus not retrogressive but responsive to contemporary wants. While, for instance, the couturier Paul Poiret despised Cubism, he found that certain of its elegant visual traits could be incorporated into a new decorative and luxurious style. The style also acknowledged and responded to the demands of industrial culture, including the availability of new materials such as plastics, ferroconcrete, and vita-glass. Geometric rather than asymmetric, rectilinear rather than linear, Art Deco was inspired by Art Nouveau, the Ballets Russes, North American and Aztec Indian art, and even by certain aspects of the Bauhaus. And, with the discovery in 1922 of Tutankhamen's tomb near Luxor, Art Deco ornament became a unique confluence of Egyptian ziggurats, sunbursts, and lightning bolts with a bit of the zigzag line of the Charleston added for good measure. With its Modernist characteristics, curious historical references, and controlled anarchy, it came to symbolize both efficient modern living and the elegant life-style. Art Deco reemphasized the end of traditional design, but unlike classical Modernism, it was founded on a mania for the new.

When the Exposition Internationale des Arts Décoratifs et Industriels Modernes opened in 1925, it covered two banks of the Seine and stood as a monument to both the excesses and the dichotomies of Art Deco. Most of the French exhibits, like E. J. Ruhlmann's furniture pavilion, were oppressively ornate when compared to the few decidedly Modernist structures, such as Konstantin Melnikov's angular glass Soviet pavilion and Le Corbusier's L'Esprit Nouveau. Exhibits from the Netherlands, Britain, and Austria evinced similar decorative obsessions. By the close of the exhibition, Art Deco's influence, like its ubiquitous sunray motif, fanned around the world.

Graphic design was practiced with the same frenzy as the other decorative arts. Art Deco's progressive yet unchallenging motifs provided not only an acceptable metaphor for the glory of machine-age culture but an effective code for consumerism as well. Advertising typography and layout acted as the primary communicators of the Art Deco graphic style. The official lettering on most signs and buildings at the 1925 exposition, Peignot, became one of the typographic emblems of the age. In addition, the elegant specimen sheets of Moderne display faces produced by type foundries served as paeans to the style. The French master advertising posterists, like A. M. Cassandre, Paul Colin, Jean Carlu, Charles Loupot, and Leonetto Cappiello, skillfully disseminated the Art Deco language to the public. In England, the American E. McKnight Kauffer imbued his advertisements and book jackets with Cubist and Futurist characteristics.

In 1929, the Parisian designer A. Tollmer published his book *Mise en Page,* which codified the Art Deco approach to layout. Subsequently translated into English, it became more universally used by advertising designers and printers than Jan Tschichold's *New Typography,* published the year before. Although the illustrations in *Mise en Page* are more anarchic and carnival-like than those in Tschichold's book, Tollmer's premise actually derives from the same Modernist typographic experiments. "Henceforth the art of layout is free of its bonds…," he wrote. "It must carry conviction of its own accord. The public must receive from it what in amorous terminology one might call 'the fatal dart.' In order…to obtain a freer variety of possible combinations, it became necessary to abandon the horizontal and vertical scheme…to develop an alternative…of obliques and curves. At this point we come to the modern technique, and more particularly to the technique of modern advertising."

As a pure style without ideology, Art Deco could be applied to any subject or theme. Its distinctive graphic look was identifiable regardless of national origin. And it was also nonpartisan: the Italian and German fascists applied it to their propaganda, as did the French communists, Spanish leftists, and British socialists. Its heroic and futuristic visual language was equally appropriate in the service of electrical appliances or despotic regimes.

International design magazines and annuals saturated the world market with Art Deco—in packaging, book and magazine design, and advertising. American advertisers balked at first at Art Deco's Modernist aspects but eventually responded to its combination of a rarefied esthetic quality with an up-to-date tempo. According to the historian Roland Marchand, during the 1926 New York Art Directors' annual exhibition, "Modern art forms were the predominant trend….The public seemed to want atmosphere, particularly in fantastic and eccentric forms."

Not all American design was based on such fantasies, however. The 1930s was the age of the industrial designer, who derived new Moderne forms from the science of aerodynamics. Late Deco's raybands and motion lines were not mere ornaments but symbols of Streamline technology. The Streamline era was inaugurated, celebrated, and ended at the 1939–40 New York World's Fair. The world was on the brink of war. Art Deco's international dominance soon petered out in the face of wartime austerity. The 1960s, another period of expanded consumerism, was to witness a nostalgic revival of the style.

## FRENCH

As early as 1911, the stage had been set in Europe for a new decorative style. The Martine School of Decorative Art had been founded by Paul Poiret, and the Société des Artistes-Décorateurs were pursuing plans for an exhibition that would unite artist, manufacturer, and craftsman at a major decorative art exposition to be held in 1915. Owing to the war, however, the landmark Paris Exposition Internationale des Arts Décoratifs et Industriels Modernes did not take place until 1925. When it finally opened, the Expo was accused of demonstrating the vacuity of decoration for the sake of decoration, despite the presence of Le Corbusier's and Melinkov's Modernist pavilions. It was a triumph of Moderne over Modern, of design linked to art, not to the machine. The magazine-cover images shown here combined the decorative frenzy with Neo-classical and Cubist elements (and a touch of Modigliani). These ingredients made for a new stylized gesture, the hallmark of the Art Deco style.

336. Charles Loupot. *Exposition Internationale des Arts Décoratifs et Industriels Modernes.* Poster, 1925. The Mitchell Wolfson Jr. Collection of Decorative and Propaganda Arts, Miami

337. Designer unknown. *La Revue Ford.* Magazine cover, 1927

338. Georges Lapape. *Vogue.* Magazine cover, October 15, 1924. Courtesy *Vogue,* The Condé Nast Publications Inc.

339. Bolin. *Vogue.* Magazine cover, November 1, 1926. Courtesy *Vogue,* The Condé Nast Publications Inc.

340. Eduardo Benito. *Vogue.* Magazine cover, May 1, 1926. Courtesy *Vogue,* The Condé Nast Publications Inc.

341. Eduardo Benito. *Vogue.* Magazine cover, October 15, 1927. Courtesy *Vogue,* The Condé Nast Publications Inc.

337

336

338

339

340

341

342

343

130

344

345

## FRENCH

Despite Modernism's efforts to simplify design, the urge to decorate and be decorated was not dead, never having been totally renounced by the middle class, whose creature comforts demanded ornament of some kind. Art Deco was a symbolically appropriate style for this purpose, since it made overt references to luxury and extravagance. The influential French fashion designers catered to such demands not only in their clothing design but also in their packaging. The perfumer Coty, for example, commissioned the craftsman René Lalique to produce ornate labels for his bottles. Parisian department stores like Les Grands Magasins, Galeries Lafayette, and Au Bon Marché gave special attention to those products in all departments—from cosmetics to liquors to tobaccos—that evoked the *au courant* spirit.

342. Designer unknown. Fan advertising champagne, date unknown. Courtesy John and Margaret Martinez

343. Designer unknown. *Cocktail Grand Luxe.* Advertisement card, 1932

344. Designer unknown. *Campeones.* Cigarette package, c. 1928. Courtesy Rikuyo-sha Publishing, Inc., Tokyo

345. Designer unknown. *Rhum.* Package design, c. 1928. Courtesy Rikuyo-sha Publishing, Inc., Tokyo

346. Designer unknown. Face powder box, c. 1930. Courtesy Rikuyo-sha Publishing, Inc., Tokyo

347. Designer unknown. Face powder box, c. 1930. Courtesy Rikuyo-sha Publishing, Inc., Tokyo

346

347

### FRENCH

Modern and Moderne eventually came to co-exist as stylistic alternatives. In the 1930s, however, the austerity of Modernism interested only an intellectual minority, and the preference for things "modernistic" was considerably more far-reaching. Art Deco was, in fact, one of the first mass-produced styles to find acceptance with most consumers. Moderne styling became a popular graphic idiom. Following the fashion illustration of the day, posterists created works that gave the era its own unique graphic language, one that was decorative and anti-Impressionistic. Typefoundries promoted novelty display typefaces through richly illustrated specimen sheets and periodicals. The most influential of these was Deberny & Peignot's *Divertissements Typographiques,* which spotlighted the two most emblematic types of the epoch, Peignot and Bifur, both designed by A. M. Cassandre.

348. A. M. Cassandre. *Deberny & Peignot.* Advertisement on a delivery truck, 1925

349. Designer unknown. Toy truck, with advertisement for St. Raphaël wine, date unknown

350. René Vincent. *Les Automobiles Georges Irat.* Poster, 1923. Courtesy Posters Please, Inc., New York

351. Paolo Garretto. *Amilcar.* Poster, 1929. Courtesy Posters Please, Inc., New York

352. Designer unknown. *Arts & Decoration.* Advertisement pages from a periodical, 1928

353. Leonetto Cappiello. *Lampe Osmine.* Poster, 1920. Mitchell Wolfson Jr. Collection of Decorative and Propaganda Arts, Miami

354. Designer unknown. *Flit Soldier.* Three-dimensional advertisement, c. 1930

348

350

349

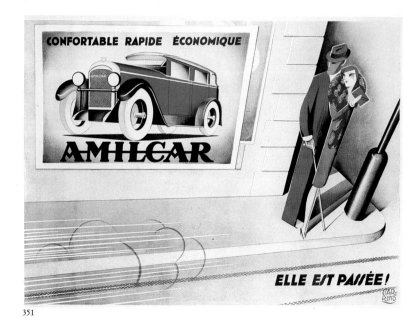
351

352

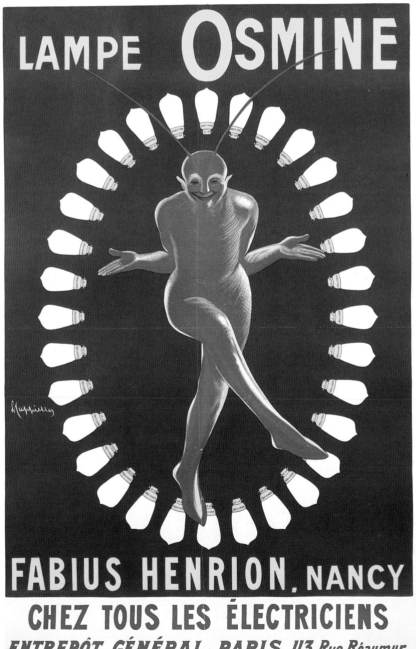

353

354

133

355

356

357

## FRENCH

Paris was the wellspring of the contemporary poster during the nineteenth century and also its capital between the wars. Not tied to any one movement, the leading French graphic designers drew inspiration from various sources. Georges Barbier owed his style both to oriental art and to the scenic design of Diaghilev's Ballets Russes, the spectacle that revolutionized the European dance world. Influenced by Leonetto Cappiello's virtuosity, the Frenchmen A. M. Cassandre (Adolphe Jean-Marie Mouron) and Jean Carlu and the Swiss Charles Loupout and Paul Colin became the most significant posterists associated with the Art Deco era. They embraced Cubist and Constructivist trends yet transcended their clichés, thereby revolutionizing the poster and dominating French advertising.

355. A. M. Cassandre. *L'Intransigeant.* Poster for the newspaper, 1925. Courtesy Reinhold Brown Gallery, New York

356. Jean Carlu. *Disques Odéon.* Poster for records, 1929. Gewerbemuseum, Basel, Museum für Gestaltung

357. A. M. Cassandre. *Grand Sport.* Poster, 1925. Courtesy Reinhold Brown Gallery, New York

358. A. M. Cassandre. *Wagon-Bar.* Railway poster, 1932. Courtesy Reinhold Brown Gallery, New York

359. Georges Barbier. *Paulette Duval/Vaceslav Svoboda.* Poster, 1920. Courtesy Posters Please, Inc., New York

360. Designer unknown. *Encyclopédie des Arts Décoratifs et Industriels Modernes.* Twelve-volume set of encyclopedias on Paris Art Deco, 1925. The Mitchell Wolfson Jr. Collection of Decorative and Propaganda Arts, Miami

360

358

359

## GERMAN

In no other country was the struggle for style more important than in Germany. That that nation gave the highest value to style as a mode of expression was evidenced, for example, by its development of Expressionism and its assimilation of Bauhaus modes as a national style. Commercial designers between the wars thus had a rich Modernist tradition from which to develop a distinctly German strain of Art Deco. Karl Schulpig, one of the top trademark designers, successfully combined Bauhausian geometry and Expressionistic iconography in much of his work. Schulz-Neudamm's poster for Fritz Lang's film *Metropolis* was an appropriately decorative rendering of a Futurist theme. Rectilinear form prevailed in most German illustration.

361. Karl Schulpig. Self-promotional advertisement, 1925

362. Schulz-Neudamm. *Metropolis.* Film poster, 1926. The Museum of Modern Art, New York. Gift of Universum-Film Aktiengesellschaft

363. Herzig. *Tanztee und Tonfilm.* Cover of a song book, 1928

364. Designer unknown. *Georg Gerson.* Promotional advertisement for printing and advertising firm, 1923

361

362

363

364

INTERNATIONALE MONATSHEFTE FÜR BAUKUNST · RAUMKUNST · WERKKUNST

DIE PYRAMIDE

SIEBEN STÄBE · VERLAGS-UND DRUCKEREI · GESELLSCHAFT M·B·H · BERLIN-ZEHLENDORF

FERNSPR = ZEHLENDORF

NR.3007 · POSTSCHECK ·

KONTO = BERLIN 33607

BANK · KONTO = DARMSTÄDTER

U. NATIONALBANK · FILIALE

BERLIN-LICHTERFELDE · W.

365

AUTORISIERTE OPEL-VERTRETUNG
GENERAL-VERTRETUNG ERNST MAG
FÜR BERLIN UND PROVINZ BRANDENBURG

LUDWIG FLATAU

AUTOMOBILE · MOTORRÄDER · WASSERFAHRZEUGE
REPARATURWERKSTATT · ZUBEHÖR ·
ERSATZTEILLAGER · TANKSTELLE

FERNSPR · WESTEND 2253
BERLIN-
CHARLOTTENBURG 5
KAISERDAMM 105

366

KONRAD BEICHT
ARCHITEKT B·D·A

HOCHBAU UND INNENAUSSTATTUNG
BANK = DRESDNER BANK, FILIALE LIEGNITZ
POSTSCHECK-KONTO = BRESLAU NR.35073
BÜRO UND WOHNUNG = FERNSPRECHER 3225
ATELIER = FERNSPRECHER 3225

367

BUCHDRUCKEREI DER

UNION DEUTSCHE VERLAGSGESELLSCHAFT STUTTGART

368

## GERMAN

The German professional design and advertising magazines, notably *Die Reklame* and *Gebrauchsgraphik,* promoted various, and sometimes seemingly contradictory, definitions of modernity. Hence, they presented Bauhausian graphic motifs as appropriate for all kinds of advertising and editorial layout; to the purists, such a linking of the Bauhaus with Art Deco was sacrilegious. But for those who believed that the Bauhaus method was the future of commercial design, the widespread acceptance by non-Bauhaus designers and printers of its Modernist motifs should have been cause for celebration.

365. Paul Pfund. *Die Pyramide.* Letterhead design for a monthly art magazine, c. 1929

366. Paul Pfund. *Ludwig Flatau.* Letterhead design for an auto dealer, c. 1929

367. Paul Pfund. *Konrod Beicht, Architekt.* Letterhead design for an architect, 1929

368. Designer unknown. *Buchdruckerei der Union Deutsche Verlagsgesellschaft, Stuttgart.* Advertisement for a printing firm from *Das Plakat,* 1919

369. Leonard. *Gebrauchsgraphik.* Magazine cover, 1930

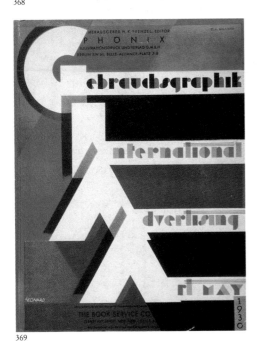

369

## SWISS

A haven for those fleeing the war, neutral Switzerland continued to develop its exemplary advertising style (Werbestil), giving special emphasis to the poster. Swiss artists had been exposed earlier to the movements and styles flowering elsewhere in Europe, yet it was not until the late twenties, as poster historian Alain Weill writes, "that the Swiss poster developed in decisive fashion, to create a typically Swiss style. This style is doubtless the assimilation of two opposing influences: France on one side, Germany on the other." Among those who visited Paris was Herbert Matter, who studied with Fernand Légér and Amédée Ozenfant and worked briefly for Deberny & Peignot. Matter's *PKZ* poster epitomizes the pictorial simplicity of this era. Other Swiss posterists studied in Berlin under the German master O. H. W. Hadank; among those who studied in Munich was Otto Bamberger, who originated the "object poster" in Switzerland.

370. Designer unknown. *Cigarettes Sato.* Poster, 1933. Kunstgewerbemuseum, Zurich

371. Reno. *Serodent, La Santé des Dents.* Poster, 1932. Kunstgewerbemuseum, Zurich

372. Herbert Matter. *PKZ.* Poster, 1928. Österreichisches Museum für Angewandte Kunst, Die Neue Sammlung, Vienna

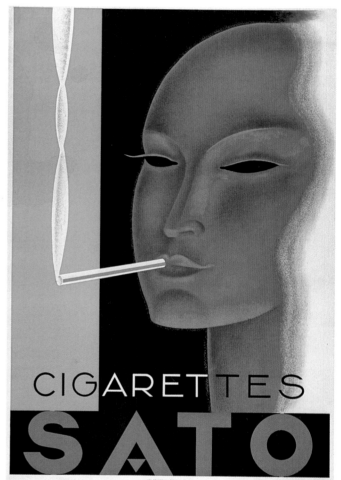

370

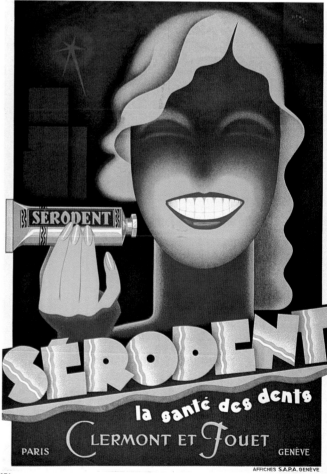

371

.WOLFSBERG ZÜRICH

MOTOR
COMPTOIR
ZÜRICH 1932
AUTOHALLE 4.–7.
LETZIGRABEN MÄRZ

374

375

## SWISS

The Deco era was known for its sleek, fast automobiles. Along with planes and ships, they were the most potent and prized symbols of modernity. The Swiss, especially, conducted a love affair with the car, and many of their finest and most characteristically Art Deco posters were devoted to motorcar races and exhibitions.

373. Otto Baumberger. *Motor Comptoir Zürich.* Poster, 1932. Kunstgewerbemuseum, Zurich

374. Designer unknown. *Genève.* Poster, 1936. Kunstgewerbemuseum, Zurich

375. Kaspar Ernst Graf. *Grand Prix Suisse, Automobile, Berne.* Poster, 1934. Kunstgewerbemuseum, Zurich

376. Noel Fontanet. *Automobil-Ausstellung.* Exhibition poster, 1930. Kunstgewerbemuseum, Zurich

376

143

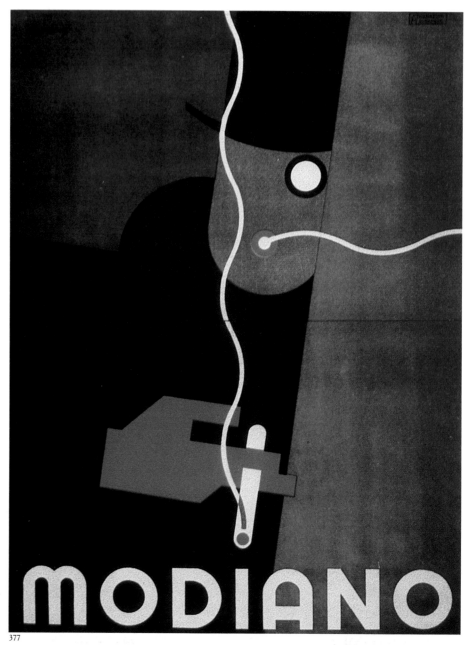

377

378

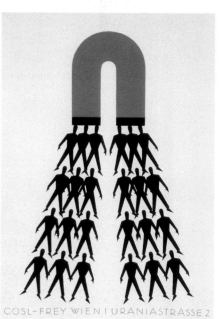

379

380

381

## EASTERN EUROPEAN

Other forms of Art Deco emerged in the various European capitals. Deco was the dominant visual code between the wars, and it was impossible to pick up a graphic design magazine or annual during this time and not find at least one of its characteristic traits—undulating geometric patterns, airbrushed raybands, decorative sunbursts, and so on. In a special 1930 issue of the German printers' journal *Archiv* dedicated to Hungarian Modernism, there appears Robert Bereny's poster showing a haughty gent smoking Modiano cigarettes, a masterpiece of witty Deco styling. About his work Bereny said, "The poster should be painterly, for the simple reason that, psychologically speaking, the human being regards everything that is painted as painterly." Advertisements here by the Austrian poster masters Julius Klinger, the partners Cosl and Frey, and Emil Preetorius typify the German reductivist Deco style. And the poster for LOPP by an unknown Polish designer underscores the universality of Art Deco.

377. Robert Bereny. *Modiano.* Poster for cigarettes and cigarette paper, 1928

378. Julius Klinger. *Wasserkraft-Elektrizitäts.* Poster for an Austrian hydroelectric utility, 1922

379. Cosl-Frey. Self-promotional poster for design studio, c. 1930. Courtesy Fairleigh Dickinson University, Madison, N.J.

380. Julius Klinger. *Spessl.* Poster, 1923. Courtesy Fairleigh Dickinson University, Madison, N.J.

381. Emil Preetorius. *Kathreiner Weine.* Austrian poster, date unknown. Courtesy Fairleigh Dickinson University, Madison, N.J.

382. Designer unknown. *LOPP.* Polish poster for an aviation company, date unknown. Courtesy Fairleigh Dickinson University, Madison, N.J.

382

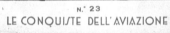

384

385

383

386

387

## ITALIAN

The Italian pavilion at the 1925 Paris exposition was decked out in antique Roman appointments consistent with D'Annunzio's rhetoric about the glorious Italian past. Only a single room displayed innovative design: Marinetti's exhibit of three Futurists, Balla, Boccioni, and Depero, who had not succumbed to the Novocento reaction. Italian decorative art between the wars was an odd coupling of both Modernist and classical conceits. Italian art, unlike its counterpart in Germany, thrived under Fascism. Yet Futurism, despite Mussolini's sanction, lost much of its vitality when used as the regime's propaganda tool. A Futurist-inspired, decorative style of illustration, layout, and typography eventually dominated Italian commercial design before the war.

383. Designer unknown. *Fiera di Fiume.* Postcard, 1929. The Mitchell Wolfson Jr. Collection of Decorative and Propaganda Arts, Miami

384. Designer unknown. *Le Conquiste dell' Aviazione.* Pamphlet cover, 1928

385. Designer unknown. *Italian Fascist Youth Battalion Handbook.* Cover, 1929

386. Giovanni Riccobaldi. *Via Mostra Mercato dell'Artigianato, Firenze.* Postcard, 1936. The Mitchell Wolfson Jr. Collection of Decorative and Propaganda Arts, Miami

387. Designer unknown. *Gioventi Fascista.* Magazine cover, 1933

388. Designer unknown. *Roma Chicago New York Roma.* Poster, 1933. The Mitchell Wolfson Jr. Collection of Decorative and Propaganda Arts, Miami

388

### ITALIAN

Mussolini liked to call Italian artists, architects, and industrialists his "producers." They were indeed arms of the party, for their products were consistently used to represent the new order. However, not all graphic design of the period showed the *fasci* or Mussolini as central motifs. From before World War I, Italian industry and business had successfully employed the talents of graphic designers like Federico Seneca, whose distinctive posters for Buitoni products, Perugina chocolates, and Modiano cigarettes made him one of the most sought-after posterists of the era. Venna's cover for *Gran Bazar* demonstrates a typical use of the Deco-style cartoon in advertising and editorial illustration.

389. Federico Seneca. *Buitoni.* Poster, 1927. Courtesy Steven Guarnaccia

390. Lucio Venna. *Carnevale (Gran Bazar).* Magazine cover, 1930

391. Antonio Seguini. *Modiano: I Campionato Interprovinciale Radiomotociclistico per Giovani Fascisti.* Poster, 1933. Fotografie Industriali e Pubblicitarie Documentari Cinematografici, Civici Musei Udine

392. Designer unknown. *Calendario.* Title page from a commemorative calendar of Fascist military campaigns, 1934

389

390

391

MVSN

CREDERE

COMBATTERE

OBBEDIRE

CALENDARIO XI
A CVRA DELL' VFFICIO
STORICO ED A BENEFI-
CIO DELL' OPERA DI PRE-
VIDENZA DELLA MILIZIA

XII

LC

392

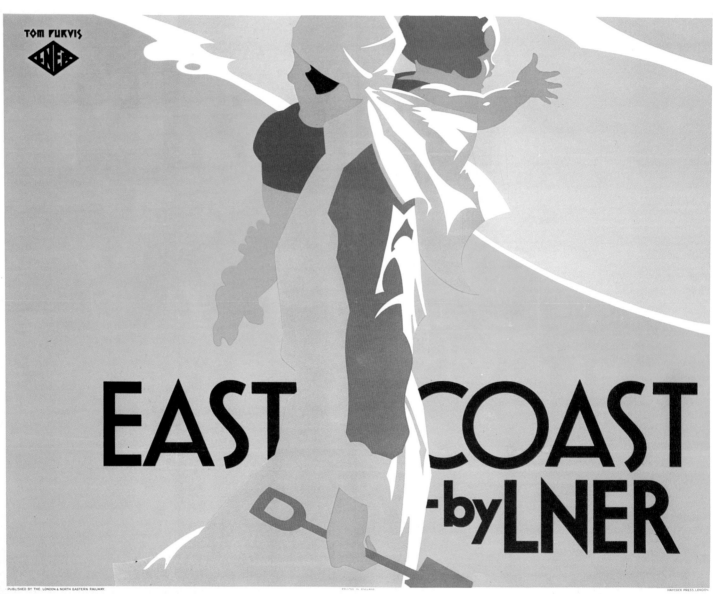

393

394

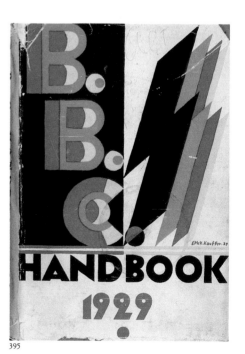

395

## ENGLISH

About 1919, English design, which had been deeply committed to decorativism for almost a century, emerged from the Victorian era to embrace a functionalism consistent with the needs of contemporary industry. Particularly in the fields of architecture and industrial design, Britain soon became a model of modern industrial production. By the 1925 exposition, decorative design, influenced by Modernist art and practiced by Duncan Grant and Vanessa Bell, came in for a reappraisal. E. McKnight Kauffer imbued his graphic designs (as well as his murals, textiles, and carpets) with forms similar to those of Le Corbusier and Léger. In 1930, Aldous Huxley, who often wrote on matters of typography and design, stated in *The Studio*: "The contemporary style has evolved out of the harsh artistic puritanism of a Cubism which, in its first violent reaction against prettiness, would suffer nothing but straight lines and angles, into something more ripe and humane, for which there is yet no convenient name." The book jackets and posters here reveal many of the formal concerns with color, geometry, and pattern that constituted the English Art Deco vocabulary.

393. Tom Purvis. *East Coast by Liner.* Poster, 1935. Courtesy Chris Mullen

394. Halliwell. *Speed Your Message.* Poster, 1931. The Mitchell Wolfson Jr. Collection of Decorative and Propaganda Arts, Miami

395. E. McKnight Kauffer. *BBC Handbook.* Book jacket, 1929. Courtesy Chris Mullen

396. Wallace and Tiernan. *The Year Book of the London School of Printing and Kindred Trades.* Book cover, 1929. The Mitchell Wolfson Jr. Collection of Decorative and Propaganda Arts, Miami

397. E. McKnight Kauffer. *You Can Be Sure of Shell.* Poster, 1934. Courtesy Chris Mullen

**THE YEAR BOOK**

OF THE LONDON SCHOOL OF PRINTING AND

KINDRED TRADES · 61 STAMFORD STREET · LONDON · S·E·1

NINTH SESSION, 1929-1930

396

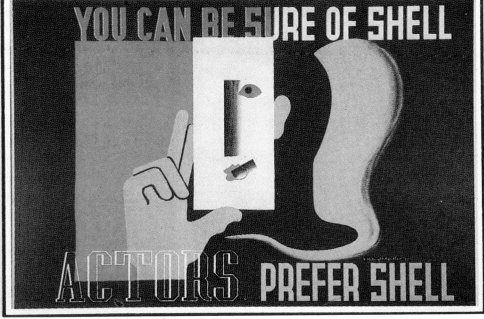

397

### ENGLISH

With the founding in 1919 of the British Institute of Industrial Arts and the Design and Industrial Association, British art and industry conclusively joined forces. Graphic designers actively participated in this relationship, contributing to significant advertising campaigns for manufacturers and services, including the London Underground, the four national railway corporations, and Shell–Mex and B.P. oil companies. The designer most responsible for advancing the British graphic style of the Deco era was Frank Pick. In directing the advertising for the London subways, Pick understood the need for a cohesive design system. In addition to architectural systematization, he had the subway map redesigned and commissioned a unique alphabet from Edward Johnson, who designed an early sans-serif alphabet that was soon adopted in different forms by Modernists throughout the world. Pick also commissioned Kauffer's Cubist-inspired posters of the early twenties, which made people appreciate modern art almost despite themselves. The Shell Company, whose advertising was directed by Jack Baddington, treated the public to an ever-changing display of posters on the sides of its delivery trucks.

398. A. Rogers. *Speed.* Poster, 1930. London Transport Museum

399. Ashley Eldrid Havinden. *Den Neuen Plymouth.* Poster (German version of English original), 1929. Courtesy Posters Please, Inc., New York

400. Dora Batty. *R.A.F. Display—Colindale Station.* Poster, 1932. London Transport Museum

401. Designer unknown. *Curtiss Flying Service.* Poster, c. 1929. Courtesy Santoro Collection, London

398

399

400

401

402

403

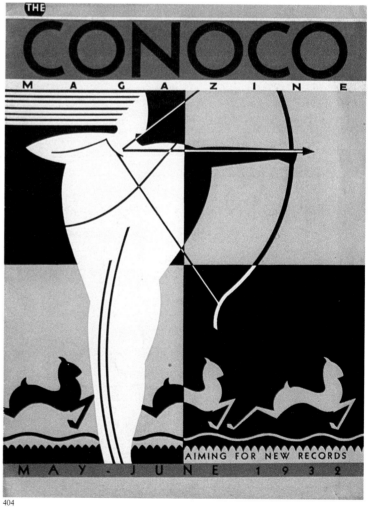

404

405

## AMERICAN

Writing in 1933, the American interior designer Donald Deskey defined the style that had taken his country by storm: "From the chaotic situation arising out of an era of prosperity without precedent for decoration, produced by Expo '25 …a style emerged…or, better still…a common denominator—the modernist style. I believe this term is a pure Americanism. It originated from the hysteria created by Expo and serves to denote the kind of work produced in the period 1925–29 which has no connection with anything produced previously.…The clichés of the past were exchanged for an ill-digested present-day formula. Self-styled designers blindly applied ornament to the surface of form—in itself badly planned. Their ornamental syntax consisted almost entirely of…the zigzag, the triangle, fawn-like curves.…In the meantime the really modern style was defined in other than modernist terms and was only concerned with outside appearances and the surface of things." For Deskey and others, Art Deco was the style of the age but also its scourge.

402. Designer unknown. *High Voltage Railway Electrification.* Sculptural inlaid panel designed for the Westinghouse Pavilion, Chicago World's Fair, 1933. The Mitchell Wolfson Jr. Collection of Decorative and Propaganda Arts, Miami

403. Designer unknown. *General Electric— Mazda Lamps.* Advertising display for lightbulbs, 1925. The Mitchell Wolfson Jr. Collection of Decorative and Propaganda Arts, Miami

404. Designer unknown. *Conoco Magazine.* Cover, May/June 1932

405. Frank Lloyd Wright. Adhesive seal, small paper bag, and trade card for V. C. Morris Store, 1942. The Mitchell Wolfson Jr. Collection of Decorative and Propaganda Arts, Miami

406. Charles Chappel. *Contact.* Advertisement from specimen book, 1930

407. Designer unknown. *Contact.* Advertisement from specimen book, 1930

406

407

## AMERICAN

Also known as Jazz Modern, the Zig Zag Style, Depression Moderne, and Manhattan Modern, American Art Deco was fed by revivals of North American Indian, Aztec, and Egyptian art. Deco artists sought to create a style that combined simplicity with dynamism. Even during the worst period of economic depression, the style was associated with glamor, luxury, and extravagance. Motifs such as greyhounds, pyramids, obelisks, lightning bolts, and sunrays put the stamp of modernity on everything from oceanliners to jewelry boxes. As Jeffrey Meikle writes, Deco motifs also suggest the "staccato rhythm of the assembly line." Graphic stylists like Merle Armitage and Fortunato Amato created print environments that could induce the consumer to buy a product—whether magazine, book, or toaster—because it was modern.

408. Fortunato Amato. *Stage.* Magazine cover, September 1937

409. Merle Armitage. *George Gershwin.* Title pages of book, 1938

410. Clarence Hornung. Logo for A. I. Friedman, c. 1938

411. Julius J. Stern. *Stella.* Trademark, 1937

412. Designer unknown. *Reveille.* Trademark, 1936

413. Designer unknown. *Barkon Lighting.* Trademark, 1937

414. Designer unknown. *RCA.* Trademark for Radio Corporation of America, 1928

415. Designer unknown. Decorative display types, from *Commercial Art Advertising Layout,* c. 1928

416. Designer unknown. Advertisements for *Town & Country,* employing contemporary geometric ornament, c. 1928

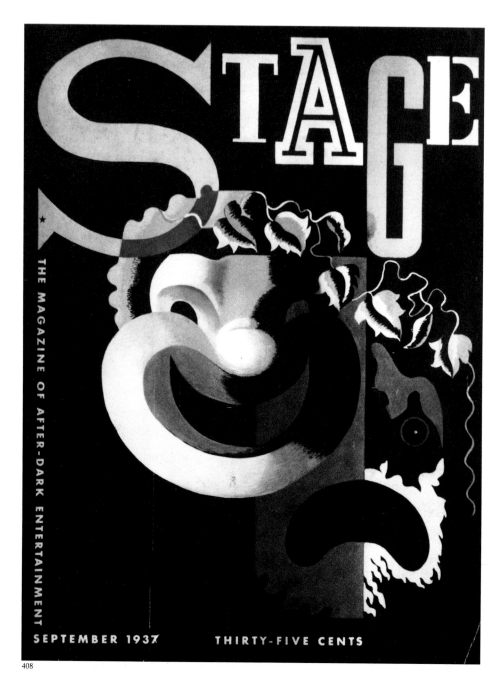

408

409

410

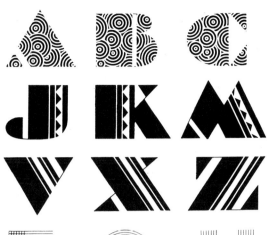

415

411

412

413

414

## The Younger Set
...is sophisticated
...speedy
...expensive

JUST when it is being quiet and good through having inveigled Papa into buying a bauble of pearls and diamonds, TOWN & COUNTRY appears to remind it that it must dash over to Antibes...that it can't get through the season without some new riding togs...that its style will be perpetually cramped sans one of those new little roadsters ■ The Younger Set wants to know and wants to buy...It won't put up with dull suggestions...TOWN & COUNTRY gossips easily and brilliantly about sports...clothes...the theatre...about all the people whom the Younger Set will break its young neck to know...Supported by its brilliant advertising pages Miss Graduate and Mr. Freshman are the most formidable buying force in the country

SINCE 1925 TOWN & COUNTRY has published in excess of a million lines of advertising ANNUALLY... over 1600 pages

416

## The man about town
won't be told what to like

He knows that already... But he depends on TOWN & COUNTRY to tell him where to get it...He may be in doubt about a plage, a piece of furniture, or a new celebrity...TOWN & COUNTRY settles the matter for him...He accepts its opinion on arts and necessities as he accepts his man's on cuff-links and Chablis

TOWN & COUNTRY reflects the good taste he is accustomed to...in cars...houses... horses...yachts...He is a many-sided person...difficult to please...TOWN & COUNTRY saves him the bore of selection by elimination...He takes its judgment on faith because its pages are closed to the doubtful and mediocre...

SINCE 1925 TOWN & COUNTRY has published in excess of a million lines of advertising ANNUALLY...over 1600 pages ◀

HARPER'S BAZAAR

MARCH 1st 1938

AN

AMERICAN FASHIONS

A.M. CASSANDRE

15 FR. IN PARIS        50 CENTS        2/6 IN LONDON

418

419

420

421

## AMERICAN

John Dos Passos characterized the American decorative style as "the shop-window world of Fifth Avenue." City of the Empire State and Chrysler buildings, New York was the Deco capital of America. And the covers of the magazines published in New York were like its shop-windows, complete with fanciful, dreamlike, and symbolic decorative illustration. New York was also the mecca for modernistic European artists. The posterist A. M. Cassandre came from Paris to design covers for *Harper's Bazaar,* as did Paolo Garretto, who worked regularly for *Fortune, The New Yorker,* and *Vanity Fair,* and M. F. Agah, who landed the prestigious art directorship at *Vanity Fair.*

417. A. M. Cassandre. *Harper's Bazaar.* Magazine cover, March 1, 1938

418. John Held, Jr. *Life.* Magazine cover, June 24, 1926

419. Paolo Garretto. *Fortune.* Magazine cover, February 1932

420. Designer unknown. *Film Fun.* Magazine cover, 1925

421. M. F. Agah. *Vanity Fair.* Magazine cover, December 1929

422. Georges Schreiber. *Manhattan Melody.* Vase, 1951. The Mitchell Wolfson Jr. Collection of Decorative and Propaganda Arts, Miami

422

159

## STREAMLINE

Streamlining was more than a distinctly American modern style, it was the metaphor of a new epoch. The marriage of art, industry, and science, it was passionately practiced by a new profession of industrial designers, who applied themselves to the aerodynamic redesign of all sorts of machinery, from airplanes to pencil sharpeners. Though its look related to Art Deco, its trappings were not just surface trivialities; while symbolizing an age of speed, it also proclaimed great optimism. Americans learned about modern design through the ephemera of streamlined commercial culture, specifically its advertising. One of the leading proponents of Streamlining, Walter Dorwin Teague, said the graphic style embraced "Beaux Arts principles, moderne qualities, billboard art, and industrial styling." The billboard designs here demonstrate the streamlining of graphic art.

423. H. M. A. Strauss. Schematic for patent registration for electric food mixer, 1938. Courtesy Eric Baker

424. J. C. Leyendecker. *Jantzen Swimsuits*. Billboard advertisement, date unknown. Courtesy Fairleigh Dickinson University, Madison, N.J.

425. Designer unknown. *Lipton's Tea*. Billboard advertisement, date unknown. Courtesy Fairleigh Dickinson University, Madison, N.J.

426. Designer unknown. *Lafayette Radio*. Billboard advertisement, 1936. Courtesy Fairleigh Dickinson University, Madison, N.J.

427. Otis Shepard. *Wrigley's Spearmint Gum*. Billboard advertisement, 1936. Courtesy Fairleigh Dickinson University, Madison, N.J.

428. Alexey Brodovitch. *Schaum Beer*. Proposal for a billboard, 1933

429. Otis Shepard. *Platz Dark Beer*. Proposal for a billboard, 1935

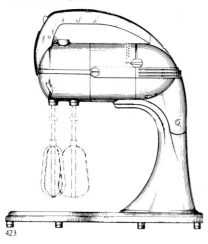

423

424

425

426

427

428

429

BEALL

RURAL ELECTRIFICATION ADMINISTRATION

U. S. DEPARTMENT OF AGRICULTURE

431

432

433

## STREAMLINE

During the late thirties, with America still feeling the tragic effects of the Depression, the government's Works Progress Administration commissioned graphic designers to produce posters and other informational graphics for the public good. Artists and small studios around the country created (many anonymously) hundreds of WPA posters encouraging literacy, personal hygiene, and good habits in the workplace. Many of these posters were stylistically influenced by the European Modernists (particularly those artists forced by the Fascists to emigrate to the United States) and by the machine aesthetic, popularized in exhibitions like the one at New York's Museum of Modern Art. Lester Beall created a series of posters for the Rural Electrification Administration intended as reminders that the Department of Agriculture is always working for the citizenry. His use of photography and strong, symbolic color is reminiscent of work done at the Bauhaus. In 1941, Jean Carlu was commissioned by Charles Coiner, Vice President of N. W. Ayer, to render a defense poster, with memorable results.

430. Lester Beall. *Rural Electrification Administration.* Poster, 1937. Library of Congress, Washington, D.C. Poster Collection

431. Designer unknown. *Keep Your Teeth Clean.* WPA poster, 1936. Library of Congress, Washington, D.C. Poster Collection

432. Robert Muchley. *Work with Care.* WPA poster, 1936. Library of Congress, Washington, D.C. Poster Collection

433. Jean Carlu. *America's Answer! Production.* Poster, 1941. Library of Congress, Washington, D.C. Poster Collection

434. Josef Albers. *Machine Art.* Exhibition poster for the Museum of Modern Art, 1927. Courtesy Ex Libris, New York

434

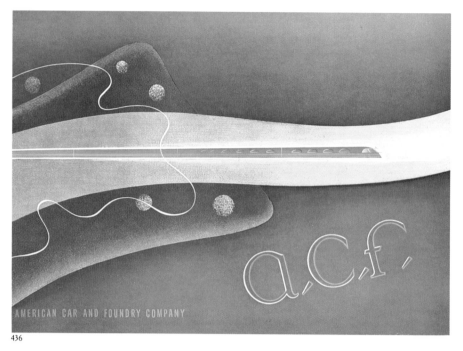

436

## STREAMLINE

"A Century of Progress," the 1933 Chicago
World's Fair, was the first American exposition
extensively devised by industrial designers. It
announced the new machine age in all its futuristic majesty. Yet it was the 1939–1940 New York
World's Fair, "The World of Tomorrow," that
epitomized the designer's utopia. Walter Dorwin
Teague, Norman Bel Geddes, Henry Dreyfuss,
and Raymond Loewy (all graphic designers at
one time) designed the major pavilions that testi-
fied to the more efficient, prosperous, and beautiful America of the future. The Trylon and
Perisphere, devised by architects Wallace K.
Harrison and J. André Fouilhoux, was the cen-
terpiece of the fair and symbol of this future.
Nembhard N. Culin's poster advertising the fair
is typical of the Streamline graphic style. The
future was a common leitmotif for many
illustrators and designers working at the time, as
evidenced by the catalogue and magazine covers
shown here.

435. Jim Nash. *Mobilgas.* Trademark, 1933
436. Leo Rackow. *A.C.F. (American Car and
Foundry Company).* Catalogue cover, 1938. The
Mitchell Wolfson Jr. Collection of Decorative
and Propaganda Arts, Miami
437. Designer unknown. *Popular Science.*
Magazine cover, 1938
438. Hugh Ferriss. *Creative Art.* Magazine
cover, August 1931
439. Charles Egri. *PM.* Magazine cover, Feb-
ruary/March 1939
440. Designer unknown. *Science and Mechan-
ics.* Magazine cover, September 1932
441. Nembhard N. Culin. *The New York
World's Fair in 1939.* Poster, 1939. The Mitchell
Wolfson Jr. Collection of Decorative and Propaganda Arts, Miami
442. Designer unknown. Trylon and Perisphere salt-and-pepper shakers, 1939

435

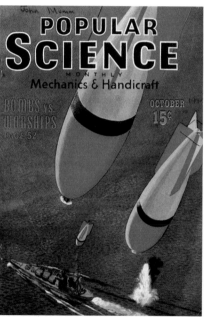

437

438

439

440

441

442

443

444

## DUTCH

It is difficult to pinpoint a specifically Dutch Art Deco style. P. A. H. Hofman's poster for the Utrecht Industries Fair conforms most clearly to the Deco formula. The other examples do not fall neatly into one category, but since they are decidedly influenced by Modern precedents, might be considered Art Deco. The magazine *Wendingen (Upheaval)*, edited by H. Th. Wijdeveld after World War I, was a champion of eclectic modernity when compared with the asceticism of a De Stijl journal. The magazine cover by Samuel Schwartz shows a Surrealist current popular in Dutch advertising posters at the time. The cover for the annual promotional piece for G. H. Bührmann's papermill, *Papiermolen*, was apparently designed to represent the dominant trend.

443. Samuel L. Schwartz. *Wendingen*. Cover of a magazine of early twentieth-century design and architecture, c. 1931. Courtesy Fairleigh Dickinson University, Madison, N.J.

444. Designer unknown. *Papiermolen*. Cover for a paper promotion, 1933

445. P. A. H. Hofman. *Industries Fair, Utrecht, Holland*. Poster, 1930. The Mitchell Wolfson Jr. Collection of Decorative and Propaganda Arts, Miami

445

446. Kurt Schwitters and Theo van Doesburg. *Kleine Dada Soirée.* Poster for Dada event, 1922. Courtesy Reinhold Brown Gallery, New York

"Dada means nothing," declared the Romanian-born poet Tristan Tzara, yet the term was to become highly charged. Dadaists rejected all forms of bourgeois art, including those, like Expressionism, once deemed revolutionary but later neutered, they felt, by middle-class acceptance. Dada was invented by a German refugee, the philosopher-poet Hugo Ball, and his companion, Emmy Hennings, in 1916 in neutral Zurich at the height of World War I. The two were joined, in Zurich and in New York, by other émigré artists who had found safe haven from the horrors of a war they blamed on the decadence of Western civilization. Dadaists scorned the idea that art was the highest form of human expression and sought to destroy the traditional barriers within artistic endeavor: the poet became a typographer, the painter a poet. While they rejected all theory and most types of organization, Dadaists developed a unique syntax and vocabulary in poetry, theater, and graphic design.

Between 1916 and 1918, the Zurich Dadaists were involved at the Cabaret Voltaire with a series of outrageous antiart happenings, reported on by Ball, Richard Huelsenbeck, Jean Arp, and Sophie Täuber-Arp in the Dada review named after the cafe. As organized by Tzara, the Dada evenings were influenced by the outlandish showmanship of the Italian Futurists. Concurrently in New York, Dada leaders Marcel Duchamp and Francis Picabia concerned themselves with revealing, and hastening, the aesthetic decomposition of Western art. (Duchamp's scandalous "ready-mades" had foreshadowed his later Dadaist concoctions.) Dada also developed a stronghold in Paris, where it evolved during the mid-twenties into Surrealism, described by the art historian Lucy Lippard as "housebroken Dada."

Immediately after the war, many of the exiles, the majority of whom were German, returned to Berlin to carry on a decidedly politicized Dada. Expressionism, which had begun by bringing Germans so many welcome truths, had become something of an official national style; aimed at inwardness, abstraction,

the renunciation of all objectivity, it was the natural enemy of Dada. In Berlin, Huelsenbeck joined forces with the painter Raoul Hausmann, the satirist George Grosz, and the brothers Wieland Herzfelde and John Heartfield, to turn Dada into a sharper weapon of attack against both the old and new ruling orders. During his first lecture on Dada in 1918, Huelsenbeck stated the Dada position: "For the first time Dadaism poses no longer in an aesthetic manner before life. It lacerates all the great words: ethic, culture, 'interiorisation,' which are only covers for weak muscles." In a polemic titled *Art Is in Danger,* Grosz stated, "If we artists were the expression of anything at all, then we were the expression of the ferment of dissatisfaction and unrest." His group soon shed the last remnants of Dada's pretense to art in favor of agitation in the service of the Spartacist, and later the communist, cause.

In its revulsion from the duplicitous Social Democratic Party then ruling the ill-fated Weimar Republic, Dada declared a satiric shadow government. Its members adopted official-sounding titles like *Oberdada, Welt-Dada, Dadaosopher,* and *Propagandada* and published parodistic manifestoes and pamphlets like *What Is Dadaism and What Does It Want in Germany?* (1919). Yet, despite its rhetoric, one could argue that Dada's real loyalty was not to politics but rather to Dada itself—a decidedly logical concept in the Dada scheme of things.

A distinct Dadaist graphic style evolved from combining the random methods of Cubist *collés* and Futurist *parole a liberta* with the efficiency and economy of mechanical-reproduction techniques. Widely scattered and mixed typography characterized the numerous Berlin Dada periodicals, while the Zurich magazines or Picabia's *391* had more crammed, jumbled pages. Dada's anarchic layouts capitalized on the contrast between a page of type and a single word stamped across it like a slogan or on words boldly isolated as in cheap posters and advertisements—all as far removed as possible from elegance and good taste.

Simultaneously employed in Berlin and Moscow, the most lasting Dada innova-

tion was photomontage. Heartfield (the art director and co-founder with Grosz and Herzfelde of the publishing house the Malik Verlag) pioneered this mechanical art and was its most exemplary practitioner, but Hausmann also took credit for its discovery. "On the wall of almost every house was a colored lithograph depicting the image of a grenadier...," Hausmann wrote about his revelation. "To make this military memento more personal a photographic portrait of a soldier had been used in place of the head. This was a stroke of lightning, one could...make paintings entirely composed of cut out photographs....I began to realize this new vision by using photographs from magazines...[and] decided to call these works photomontages. This term translated our aversion to playing artists, and considering ourselves as engineers...from that came our preference for overalls." Less aesthetically concerned than other Dadaists, Heartfield made montage political postcards that said in image what was prohibited in words by government censors.

Germany had two other, comparatively apolitical Dada groups. In Cologne, Max Ernst, Theodor Baargeld, and Jean Arp fomented trouble in the unorthodox reviews *Der Ventilator* and *Die Schammade.* In Hanover, Kurt Schwitters conducted a one-man movement, parallel and sometimes merging with Dada, called Merz. A poet, painter, typographer, and advertising-design consultant, Schwitters published his stylistically influential review, *Merz,* from 1923 to 1932. Its design, drawing inspiration from El Lissitzky's Constructivism and Van Doesburg's De Stijl, was more geometric than that of the Berlin journals.

Dada's extreme ribaldry and irreverence seduced disaffected artists for only a brief time. After 1922, with Germany in social, political, and economic chaos, many of Dada's proponents moved either inward toward Surrealism or outward toward Constructivism and the New Objectivity. Although they drifted away from the Dada style, Grosz and Heartfield continued to produce trenchant political commentary until the Nazis put an end to their efforts and they left Germany.

447

448

449

450

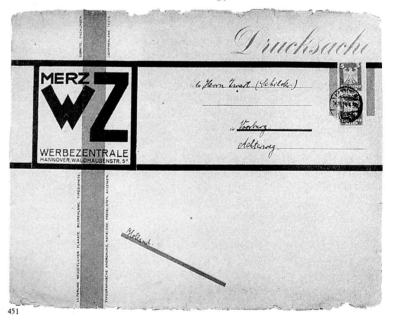

451

Although certain stylistic traits immediately identify a Dada painting or graphic work, the styles of the individual artists were more various, being influenced by Expressionism, machine imagery, and geometric abstraction. Dada, moreover, owes its typographic concoctions to Marinetti's *parole in liberta,* and indeed much of its theatrics were borrowed from the Futurists. Shown here is a sampling from the stacks of Dada literature issued from the Dada capitals: Zurich, Berlin, Cologne, Hanover, Paris, and New York. While the first two issues of the Zurich periodical *Dada* are conventional in appearance, by *Dada 3* Tristan Tzara, the editor, has introduced the organized chaos that typifies Dada's graphic expression. The cover of *Der Dada,* designed with dismembered type taken from newspapers and official organs, suggests contempt for officialdom. *Mecano,* edited by Theo van Doesburg and published in 1922, was something of a supplement to *De Stijl.* Adopting Dada graphic characteristics, it counted among its missions poking fun at the solemnities of the Bauhaus. *Merz* began publishing irregularly in 1923 as the organ of Kurt Schwitters's one-man movement and, unlike other Dada periodicals, was eventually designed according to the principles of the New Typography. Schwitters devoted complete issues to advertising and typography. The *Dada Siegt!* poster announcing a 1920 Cologne exhibit is typical of Dada's deliberate rejection of the traditional rules of typography.

447. Designer unknown. *Dada.* Pages from magazine edited by Tristan Tzara, c. 1917–21. Courtesy Ex Libris, New York

448. Marcel Janco. *Dada 3.* Magazine cover, with woodcut illustration, 1918. Courtesy Ex Libris, New York

449. Raoul Hausmann. *Der Dada.* Cover for the German Dadaist publication, 1919. Courtesy Ex Libris, New York

450. Theo van Doesburg. *Mecano.* Cover of Dutch Dada magazine publishing experimental poetry and typography, c. 1922. Courtesy Ex Libris, New York

451. Kurt Schwitters. Letterhead for *Merz,* c. 1923. Courtesy Ex Libris, New York

452. Max Ernst/Johannes Baargeld. *Dada Siegt!* Poster, 1920. Courtesy Reinhold Brown Gallery, New York

453. Kurt Schwitters. *Merz 4.* Magazine cover, 1923. Courtesy Ex Libris, New York

454. Kurt Schwitters. *Merz.* Magazine pages, 1923. Courtesy Ex Libris, New York

DADA siegt!
WIEDERERÖFFNUNG
der polizeilich geschlossenen Ausstellung
Schildergasse 37.
DADA IST FÜR RUHE UND ORDEN!
DADA ruht nie. —— DADA vermehrt sich.
Hoch die Präsidenten
der internationalen Bewegung DADA und ihre untergeordneten Organe.
(präsidial beamten vereinigt euch!)

Weshalb bin ich nicht
dieser mutige Vogel?

Eilfrachtbrief

Druckerei HERTZ, Köln, Mühlenbach 38

452

453

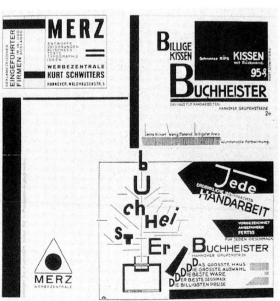

454

455

456

457

458

459

Many Dada happenings took place in nightclubs and cabarets like Zurich's Cabaret Voltaire and Berlin's Club Dada. The nightclub Schall und Rauch became a meeting place for the Berlin Dadaists; George Grosz designed many of its theatrical sets and, with other members, including Hannah Hoch, created covers for its house organ and program. Owing to the fierce factional struggles in the German government, Berlin Dadaists were more politically involved than those in other cities. John Heartfield's avowedly left-wing *Die Neue Jugend,* an outlet for early Dada manifestos, was disguised as a prospectus for a Grosz portfolio to avoid the strict censorship of newspapers. Heartfield perfected the technique of photomontage as a polemical tool. Kurt Schwitters, who was less interested in politics, became a design consultant and was able to fine-tune his typography through *Merz.* In three issues devoted to the "fairy tale," he developed *Die Scheuche (The Scarecrow),* illustrated with type forms, which owes much to Lissitzky's *Of Two Squares.*

455. P. Erkens. *Schall und Rauch.* Cover illustration for a cabaret program/magazine, November 1920

456. Hannah Hoch. *Schall und Rauch.* Cover illustration for a cabaret program/magazine, April 1920

457. John Heartfield. *Im Zeichen der Rationalisierung.* Photomontage, political poster, 1927

458. John Heartfield. *Neue Jugend.* Front page of a left-wing monthly publication, published by Der Malik Verlag, June 1917

459. George Grosz. *Schall und Rauch.* Cover illustration for a cabaret program/magazine, March 1920

460. Kathe Steinitz, Kurt Schwitters, and Theo van Doesburg. *Die Scheuche (The Scarecrow).* Cover for children's book, 1925. Courtesy Ex Libris, New York

461. Kathe Steinitz, Kurt Schwitters, and Theo van Doesburg. *Die Scheuche (The Scarecrow).* Pages from a children's book, 1925. Courtesy Ex Libris, New York

460

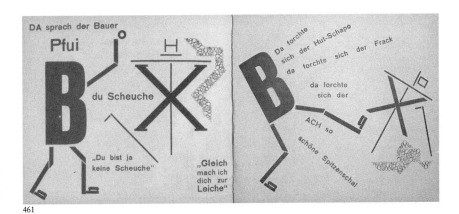

461

In 1917, George Grosz, John Heartfield, and Weiland Herzfelde founded the Malik Verlag in order to publish Communist periodicals, manifestos, and portfolios as well as low-priced novels of social interest. Following *Die Neue Jugend,* the trio collaborated on a series of small journals, which regularly changed names due to government banning orders. In the Dada tradition, the first one, *Jedermann Sein Eigner Fussball (Every Man His Own Football,* one issue only), includes Heartfield's first attempt at satirical montage, showing a fan with the heads of government superimposed and asking the question, "Who is the most beautiful?" *Die Pliete (Bankrupt)* is less Dada-oriented in its emphasis on continued social struggle and violent political revolution; one of its covers features a conventional cartoon showing Noske, the chief of Weimar security forces, after he violently suppressed a workers' protest demonstration. The trio used their journals to attack the concept of an art that had no relevance whatsoever to the working class. Malik continued to publish books after the demise of Dada in the early twenties, with Heartfield as its art director devoted to perfecting the montage technique for jacket designs. He also became a frequent contributer to the *Arbeiter Illustrierten Zeitung (AIZ),* the Communist workers' newspaper, for which he did his most powerful anti-Fascist montage/cartoons.

462. John Heartfield. *Jedermann Sein Eigner Fussball (Every Man His Own Football).* Publication cover, February 1919. Fairleigh Dickinson University, Madison, N.J.

463. John Heartfield. *AIZ (Workers' Illustrated Times).* Photomontage cover, c. 1930

464. George Grosz and John Heartfield. *Die Pliete (Bankrupt).* Illustrated magazine/newspaper cover, 1919

465. John Heartfield. *Drei Welten: Gesammelte Erzählungen.* Jacket for book by Isaac Babel, 1931. Courtesy Fairleigh Dickinson University, Madison, N.J.

466. John Heartfield. *Deutschland, Deutschland Über Alles (Germany, Germany, Above All Others).* Jacket for book by Kurt Tucholsky, 1929. Courtesy Fairleigh Dickinson University, Madison, N.J.

467. John Heartfield. *Das Geld Schreibt.* Jacket for book by Upton Sinclair, 1930. Courtesy Fairleigh Dickinson University, Madison, N.J.

468. John Heartfield. *Petroleum.* Jacket for book by Upton Sinclair, 1927. Courtesy Fairleigh Dickinson University, Madison, N.J.

462

463

464

465

466

467

468

469. Klimaschin. *USSR Agricultural Exhibition, 1939.* Poster, 1939. The Mitchell Wolfson Jr. Collection of Decorative and Propaganda Arts, Miami

lthough avant-garde Soviet artists were enthusiastic in propagating the revolution, Lenin had little confidence that their abstract visual language could communicate effectively with a predominantly illiterate population. He also suspected that the young, trailblazing Constructivists and Productivists had a hidden aesthetic agenda that superseded the needs of the infant government. Lenin had his own agenda: he wanted to shock the Russian people out of their backwardness. Fervently believing that their new art would accomplish this goal, the revolutionary artists argued that advanced artistic ideas reflected advanced political ideas. From 1918 to 1922, under the auspices of Anatoly Lunacharsky, modern Soviet graphic design applied its daring experiments in the service of social change. But as the revolution became set on an increasingly conservative course, those leaders who disapproved of progressive art forced its practitioners to abandon their methods in favor of less radical approaches. By the time Stalin came to power, many of those who still refused to sacrifice their ideals were either pressured into exile or met worse fates at home.

Nevertheless, Stalin appreciated the power of the image in a country where such a large percentage of the population was illiterate. He understood that folk art was a ready-made communications tool, although he rejected its traditional, often religious subject matter. Posters became a direct medium for educating the peasant in almost every aspect of daily life—from the efficacy of bathing, to instructions on how to drive a tractor, to warnings against laziness, intoxication, and waste. A somewhat jaundiced article in a 1931 issue of *Fortune* refers to the posters' "bold splashes of color [that] appeal to a people who see only drabness in their daily life. [The posters'] naivete commends them more strongly to men and women who, like children and savages, love to look at similar pictures."

In 1932 the Communist Party abolished the remaining cultural organizations in which Modernists were members and instead set up monolithic unions of Soviet writers, architects, composers, and artists who conformed to official art forms. In 1934 a new doctrine called Socialist Realism, devised by Stalin and Maxim Gorky, was presented at the first Soviet Writers' Congress. Socialist Realism rejected formalism, along with the plastic arts and design, deeming them "the bourgeois influences on art." Idealized scenes of leaders and workers replaced more abstract images, while staid typographic treatments forced out the dynamic, asymmetrical layouts of the New Typography. Though figurative painting was most preferred, photography and montage were acceptable and continued to be practiced by artists like Alexander Rodchenko.

The repressive Soviet regime was not the only one to feel enmity against the European avant-garde and its perceived elitism. Since the end of World War I, Modernist artists and designers in Germany had supported left-wing political organizations against the oligarchy, the old-guard militarists, and Adolf Hitler's National Socialist party. In 1929 the Nazi ideologist Alfred Rosenberg founded the Militant League for German Culture to combat avant-garde influences. Upon coming to power in 1933, Hitler exacted his revenge by expunging all actual and symbolic traces of his artist-enemies. He even outlawed modern sans-serif typefaces in favor of the medieval German Fraktur (eventually, realizing Fraktur's problems of legibility, he declared that Fraktur should be outlawed as a Jewish invention). In 1937, at the opening of his infamous *Degenerate Art* exhibition at the newly built House of German Art, Hitler railed that "works of art that cannot be understood but need a swollen set of instructions to prove their right to exist and find their way to neurotics who are receptive to such stupid...nonsense will no longer openly reach the German nation....With the opening of this exhibition has come the end of artistic lunacy and with it the artistic pollution of our people."

Hitler and Joseph Goebbels, the cunning Nazi Minister of Propaganda, replaced Modernist art with classically heroic, Romantic depictions of the Aryan Superman or with equally overbearing images in a more realistic style (which were not too formally different from those of Soviet Socialist Realism). The propaganda poster actually played a greater role in the Nazis' rise to power than is generally realized: when the radio was shut off, the cinema dark, and the political meetings over, the poster still stood on every street corner. One master of the agitational political poster, the artist Mjölnir, was given the Teutonic honorific of Reich Plenipotentiary for Artistic Formulation. Even Ludwig Hohlwein, one of the virtuosos of the objective style in poster design, became a treasured propagandist for his keen ability to portray Aryan beauty.

Much of the early Italian fascist printed propaganda used Futurist and Art Deco styles to advertise Mussolini's cult of personality; on the other hand, most comparable German ephemera were unadorned, stark, and monumental, more consistent with other Nazi visual motifs. Hitler had formed the opinion that the masses were malleable, either already corrupt or corruptible. There was no place in his propaganda for a qualifying clause and, therefore, nothing was left to interpretation. He wrote, "The more radical and inciting my propaganda was, the more it frightened off weaklings and irresolute characters and prevented their pushing into the first nucleus of the [Nazi] organization."

The heroic style was not exclusively a tool of dictatorships—during the Spanish Civil War, both the fascist insurgents and the supporters of the Popular Front effectively imbued their printed propaganda with heroic imagery. And not all heroic imagery has been used in the service of politics. Advertising and editorial illustration in Western industrial democracies has often employed romantic realism as a timeworn means of enhancing a product or idea in the consumer's eye. Yet heroic realism has never really been elevated to a national style in Western democracies, except during wartime, and then only for very specific needs. Even during World War II, Modernist approaches brought to the United States and England by European immigrants characterized certain wartime propaganda, thus planting the seeds of postwar graphic endeavor. Heroic realism as an official graphic style still prevails in Soviet countries.

177

DEUTSCHE LUFTHANSA

470

When it finally came, the decision as to what was true Soviet revolutionary art did not favor the avant-garde. Stalin's imposition of his Socialist Realism decrees in 1932 suppressed most of Russia's most creative and committed artists. Although a few, like Alexander Rodchenko, continued to create propaganda consistent with the official style, many others were forbidden to practice their art. Stalin effectively revived academic painting, which one critic called the "worst academics in the world," and established a sanctioned graphic language that left nothing to the imagination. For Hitler the avant-garde symbolized Bolshevism and the debasement of *Kultur.* By 1933, virtually all traces of modern German design were eliminated from public view and replaced by Teutonic models from the past.

470. Ludwig Holwein. *Deutsche Lufthansa.* Poster, 1936. Library of Congress, Washington, D.C. Poster Collection

471. Victor Borisovich Koretski. *Hello, Great Soviet Union.* Poster, photomontage, c. 1960

472. Ludwig Holwein. *Sammelt Euch im NS Reichskreigerbund.* Postcard, c. 1940

473. Victor Borisovich Koretski. *We Want Peace.* Poster, photomontage, c. 1945

474. Victor Borisovich Koretski. *Peace, Friendship, Solidarity, No to Fascism.* Poster, c. 1978

ПРИВЕТ ВЕЛИКОМУ СОЮЗУ ССР!

471

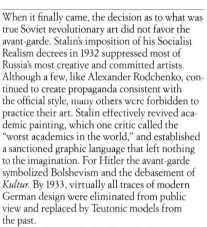

Sammelt Euch im

NS·Reichskriegerbund

472

473

НЕТ-ФАШИЗМУ!

FASCHISMUS-NEIN! NO TO FASCISM! NON AU FASCISME! NO AL FASCISMO!

474

Since war demands extraordinary sacrifice, it is often as difficult to arouse people to fight as it is to win a battle strategically. War is a difficult theme to abstract, and therefore realism is the logical and most effective means to visually sell a war. Yet the realism must not portray the savage horrors of war but rather an idealized truth. The task of illustrators in the wartime United States, Spain, and elsewhere was to mythologize through paint. The Chinese brand of Heroic Realism (usually produced as poster or book illustration by collectives of artists and printers) was employed for both political haranguing and commercial advertising, but always conveyed a message with the least possible ambiguity.

475. Illustrator unknown. *Daring Detective.* Magazine cover, May 1938

476. Herrn. *Salvad la Produccion (Safeguard Production).* Poster for the General Union of Workers during the Spanish Civil War, 1938

477. Designer unknown. *To Have and to Hold.* Propaganda poster for U.S. war bonds, 1944

478. Designer unknown. *Win a Good Harvest—Increase Grain Production.* Chinese poster printed at Shanghai People's Publishing House, 1973

479. Designer unknown. *Resolutely Support the Anti-imperialist Struggles of the People of Asia, Africa and Latin America.* Political poster, 1960

475

476

477

夺丰收 广积粮

478

Resolutely Support the Anti-imperialist Struggles of the People of Asia, Africa and Latin America.
Soutenir fermement la lutte anti-impérialiste des peuples d'Asie, d'Afrique et d'Amérique latine
Firme apoyo a la lucha antiimperialista de los pueblos de Asia, Africa y América Latina

479

480. Herbert Matter. *Pontresina*. Travel poster, 1936. Kunstgewerbemuseum, Zurich

Despite its detractors, classical Modernism exerted an immense influence on advertising and graphic design in most consumer societies immediately before and following World War II. Its iconoclastic practitioners developed a functional vocabulary that was supported by certain mainstream critics and eventually adopted by many important corporations. Some progressive government agencies even commissioned Modernist designers for various communications projects—from railway signage in Britain to postal information in Holland to wartime survival manuals in the United States. Art Deco notwithstanding, functionalism in design retained currency in those nations which, although hard hit by economic crises, relied on an industrial renaissance for renewed prosperity. While the repressive decrees of Stalin and Hitler ensured an abrupt end to Modernism in most of Europe, the industrial enterprise on which the style was predicated continued and would continue for decades to follow. Machine age graphic design was destined to endure—although somewhat altered by the new communications requirements of business in the postwar era.

In the United States, where Modernist techniques were not at first warmly accepted by conservative advertisers, marketing surveys surprisingly concluded that consumers equated Modernist design with what one style manual at the time called "the promise of the future." The American advertising pioneer, Ernest Caulkins, who championed the idea that advertising should be an equal marriage of text and image, extolled the virtues of Modernism, stating that it "offered the opportunity of expressing the inexpressible…expressing not so much a motor car, but speed; not so much a gown, but style." Simplicity was the designer's watchword, and style, therefore, would not be presented through wordy texts or literal pictures but through the association of a product with the most appropriate graphic forms.

In Late Modern, classical Modernist techniques were popularly accepted and widely applied, but the dogma associated with the orthodox schools and movements was jettisoned. Late Modern encompasses a number of distinct stylistic periods, spanning more than fifty years. The first period—immediately following Stalin's and Hitler's initial repressions of Modernist art in the early 1930s—witnessed a diaspora of Modernists, at first to the Eastern European countries and then to England, Switzerland, and the United States, where they profoundly affected prevailing design theory and practice. The second period, after the war, was one of business realignment in which emerging international corporations, needing identity systems and strategic communications, fostered a new rationalist design approach in the International Style. Then, beginning in the mid-1950s and continuing to the present, a revived interest in the design styles of the *fin de siècle* and in the artifacts of material prosperity made itself felt in contemporary layout and typography for magazines, advertising, and posters. Concurrently, advancements in photographic and computer technologies applied to typography and printing began to change not only the look but the methodology of graphic design.

The kindred spirits in the postwar design centers (London, Chicago, New York, Zurich, Basel, Ulm, Stuttgart) all began with the same prewar methods in developing their new styles. Yet Late Modern is not about conformity. Its stylistic diversity arose as much from the rejection of unworkable or unappealing ideas as from the development of new ones. Moreover—with another devastating world war over and the promised "World of Tomorrow" finally at hand—designers sought with great purpose to make styles that responded to the character of their time, although there was scant international consensus on what this was. It was viewed quite differently, for example, by the Swiss designers Max Bill, Josef Müller-Brockmann, and Armin Hofmann—who saw graphic design as systematized and architecturally constructed on a grid—and by the New York–based principals of Push Pin Studios, who preferred a provocative interplay of historical styles and forms.

Although classical Modernist designers often had utopian goals, Late Modernists held conflicting opinions about such universal aims. The period was, perhaps, more one of personal reevaluation than overriding public concern. Jan Tschichold, for instance, renounced the Prussian rigidity of the rules set forth in his Modernist bible, *New Typography,* in favor of a return to classical typography and symmetry. Other notable postwar designers, among them, Paul Rand, Alvin Lustig, Alexey Brodovitch, and Lester Beall, took certain truths from Modernism and incorporated them into distinctly personal languages. Rand's identity systems and collateral materials for major American corporations like IBM and Westinghouse are imbued with his distinctive wit and logic yet totally devoid of personal indulgences. Brodovitch's design for *Harper's Bazaar* was an outstanding example of personal style and taste in a mass-market magazine.

Narrative illustration was also redefined in the Late Modern period. Often used in a literal, unimaginative manner for editorial or advertising purposes, figurative illustration was generally regarded as a sentimental throwback to the past. While orthodox Modernists rejected narrative completely in favor of what Muller-Brockmann called the "objective illustration" of photography and photomontage, others found new means of integrating figure drawing with design in the style of turn-of-the-century posterists. Most notable among these were the Polish poster artists who, influenced by the Symbolists and Surrealists, developed a painterly graphic style with a lexicon of powerful, eerie images. The Poles, in turn, inspired the American psychedelic artists of the sixties, who went on to invent a new style of illustration by pairing comic-strip and historical references with East Indian motifs.

Japanese design is a highly imaginative synthesis of the most compelling Late Modern Western forms with traditional Japanese ones, abetted by an abundance of high-tech materials with which to visualize the future. Japan's distinctive Late Modern style has had a significant impact on the eighties' Post-Modern and New Wave designs.

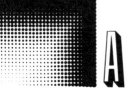

## SWISS

The Swiss object poster was distinct from the Berlin *sachplakat* in that the Swiss replaced the reductive flatness of the typical German image with a boldly rendered lithographic design. Known for his hyperrealism, Niklaus Stoecklin became a leader of what one historian calls "illustrative advertising design," in which the drawn or painted image includes the sole product identification, without any other type or lettering. Posters here by the illustrators Charles Kuhn and Herbert Leupin followed in this objective tradition. Influenced by the early phototypographic designs of the German-born Anton Stankowski, Herbert Matter created startling photomontage travel posters that defined a new style called object photography. During the thirties, Walter Herdeg designed all the publicity for the St. Moritz resort, using photomontage and hand-colored photography. In 1944, Herdeg founded *Graphis*, the Zurich-based design magazine that championed a renewed internationalism in the applied arts.

481. Charles Kuhn. *Taxi Winterhalder.* Poster, 1937. Kunstgewerbemuseum, Zurich

482. Niklaus Stoecklin. *PKZ.* Poster, 1934. Kunstgewerbemuseum, Zurich

483. Niklaus Stoecklin. *Binaca.* Poster, 1934

484. Walter Herdeg. *Graphis.* Magazine cover, 1947

485. Herbert Leupin. *Steinfels.* Poster for soap, c. 1944

481

482

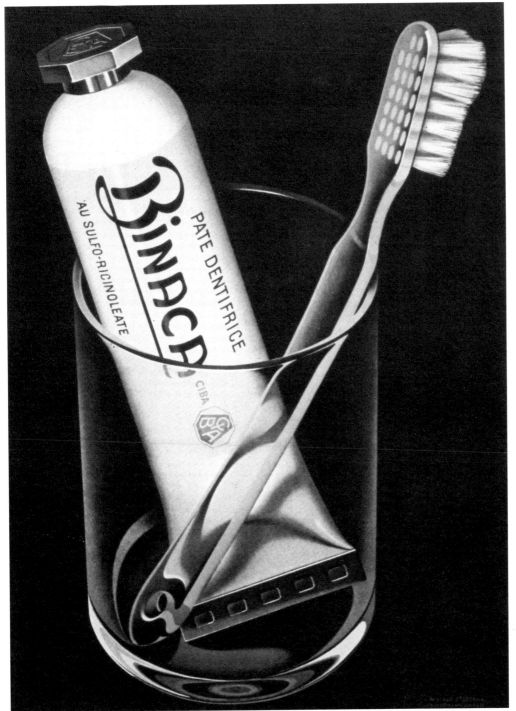

483

484

485

# A

## ENGLISH

Frank Pick, London Transport's innovative creative director, set and maintained a standard of artistic achievement unprecedented in England before the mid-twenties. In his desire to raise the level of efficiency and safety of London's Underground, Pick sought out the most up-to-date artforms (like Man Ray's delightfully futuristic poster) to leave a positive impression on the commuting public. Advertising pioneers like Pick and his successor, William Crawford, deserve credit for opening the public's mind not only to the virtues of the service they promoted but also to the modern design vocabulary. Their efforts allowed E. McKnight Kauffer, F. H. K. Henrion, and Tom Eckersley, among others, to improve the quality of print communications and, by extension, of the entire visual landscape. Describing this new methodology, Ashley Havinden writes, "The modern point of view …is to design *inside out,* as opposed to the traditional, which is a tendency to impose a preconceived solution to a problem by designing from the *outside in.*"

486. Frank Pick and Edward Johnston. *London Underground.* Trademark for London Transport, 1920

487. Man Ray. *Keeps London Going.* Poster for London Transport, 1932. The Museum of Modern Art, New York. Gift of Bernard Davis

488. F. H. K. Henrion. *Here Comes the Sun.* Poster, 1948. Courtesy the designer

489. E. McKnight Kauffer. *Empire Telegrams.* Poster for telegrams, 1941

490. Tom Eckersley. *Graphis 31.* Cover of magazine edited and art-directed by Walter Herdeg, 1950. Courtesy the designer

486

-KEEPS LONDON GOING

487

488

489

490

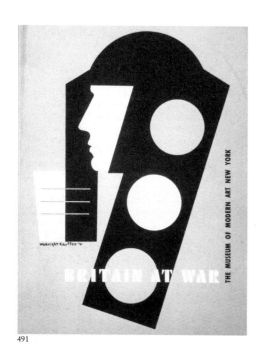

491

492

493

494

495

Despite the shift in emphasis from advertising commercial products to promulgating war-related messages, World War II expanded opportunities for British advertising designers. In the poster field, the government realized that the conventional strident patriotic and cautionary messages would not have sufficient urgency to attract the public's attention. The Ministry of Information therefore commissioned some of the leading Modernists, including Abram Games, Tom Eckersley, and F. H. K. Henrion, to produce a series of decidedly contemporary designs. These designers often combined painting and collage to transmit the government's life-saving injunctions clearly and effectively. Perhaps the most important use of good design by the Ministry of Information was their development of the public exhibition as a potent technique of social communication. Such exhibitions ranged from small shows to full-scale displays of posters and other visual aids, employed to inform and educate the public about Britain's various war needs.

491. E. McKnight Kauffer. *Britain at War.* Cover for The Museum of Modern Art exhibition catalogue, 1941

492. Abram Games. *Your Britain, Fight for It Now.* Poster for the War Office, 1943. Courtesy the designer

493. Abram Games. *Join the ATS.* Poster for the War Office, 1941. Courtesy the designer

494. Tom Eckersley. *Saving Is Everybody's War Job.* Poster for the Post Office Savings Bank of England, 1943. Courtesy the designer

495. Abram Games. *The Emergency Blood Transfusion Service Needs Blood Donors.* Poster for the War Office, c. 1942. Library of Congress, Washington, D.C. Poster Collection

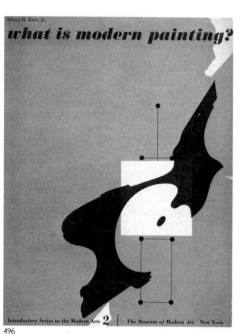

496

497

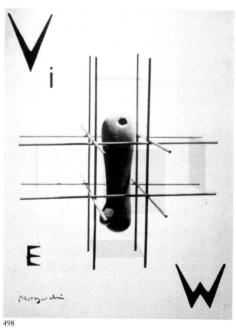

498

499

500

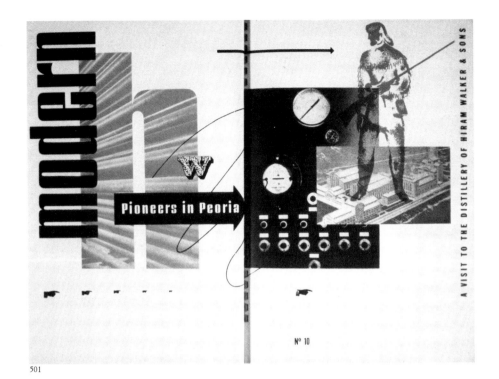

501

502

## AMERICAN

In a 1941 issue of *PM* magazine, László Moholy-Nagy wrote somewhat disappointedly about American design: "The Constructivist movement in Europe originated in countries with undeveloped industry....The message about American organization, production processes, life standards, created a Utopian picture in the mind of these young European artists. Their imaginative picture of America governed their thinking and their work. They admired exactness and precision...the skyscraper, the highways, the immense span of bridges....They tried to be the children of a new age as they believed Americans to be.

"When I came to this country I was greatly surprised to find that we Europeans were, to a certain extent, more American than the Americans. I found that our imagination went too far. [The Americans] created their high civilization by instinct, introducing invention after invention into their daily routine. However, they did not attach any philosophy to it as we did in Europe. For them the nostalgia remained for the good old traditional art.

"...It took me a long time to understand the Victorian dwellings and the imitations of Colonial architecture or the old-fashioned advertising. Fortunately I soon saw that a new generation was rising with the potentiality and discipline of that America imagined by us in Europe."

Among these young Americans, wrote Moholy-Nagy, Paul Rand was "one of the best and most capable representatives." These members of the first wave of American Modernists were influenced by other recent European émigrés besides Moholy-Nagy, including the Hungarian Gyorgy Kepes, the Czechoslovak Ladislav Sutnar, and Bauhaus master Herbert Bayer. Joining Rand were Lester Beall, who was dubbed the Midwest Modernist, and Alex Steinweiss, a New Yorker who pioneered in album-cover design.

496. Gyorgy Kepes. *What Is Modern Painting?* Exhibition catalogue cover for The Museum of Modern Art, 1952. Courtesy the designer

497. Alex Steinweiss. *AD.* Cover of professional magazine, 1941. Courtesy the designer

498. Isamu Noguchi. *View.* Cover of Surrealist art magazine, 1946

499, 500. Ladislav Sutnar. *Design and Paper.* Cover and inside pages for promotional brochure for the Marquardt Paper Co., 1941

501. Lester Beall. *Modern Pioneers in Peoria.* Pages from a promotional brochure for a printer, 1935

502. Paul Rand. *Direction.* Magazine cover, April 1940. Courtesy the designer

## AMERICAN

The United States Office of War Information employed a large staff of book and magazine designers during World War II to design cautionary and patriotic posters, survival manuals, news magazines for overseas distribution, and hundreds of other pieces of wartime propaganda. Young American Modernists had a unique opportunity to prove the viability of the new design, specifically as contrasted to the Heroic Realism of other countries' graphics. In 1942, the Austrian émigré Joseph Binder won first prize in a Museum of Modern Art competition for his iconographic recruitment poster for the United States Army Air Corps. N. W. Ayer and Son's art director, Leo Lionni, created a series of dynamic posters intended to motivate defense plant workers. In the 1930s Walter P. Paepcke, the president of Container Corporation of America, had become an early patron of Modernist design; during the war, CCA's art director, Egbert Jacobsen, commissioned designs from leading émigré and American Modernists, including Herbert Matter, Herbert Bayer, and Jean Carlu, for the company's advertising campaigns focusing on its war efforts and products. Autocar Corporation, which supplied armored trucks to the army, commissioned Paul Rand to produce a striking (and curiously timeless) visual record of its war production.

503. Ralph Eckerstrom. *CCA.* Trademark for Container Corporation of America, 1957

504. Leo Lionni. *Keep 'Em Rolling!* Poster, 1941. The Museum of Modern Art, New York. Gift of the Office for Emergency Management

505. Leo Lionni. *Container Corporation of America.* Poster, 1942. Courtesy the designer

506. Joseph Binder. *Air Corps U.S. Army.* Poster, 1941. The Museum of Modern Art, New York. Gift of the designer

507. Herbert Matter. *Container Corporation of America.* Poster, 1943. Courtesy Ex Libris, New York

508. Paul Rand. *Mechanized Mules of Victory.* Cover and pages of a truck catalogue for Autocar Corporation, 1942. Courtesy the designer

503

504

505

506

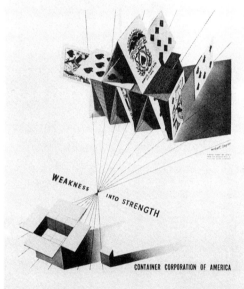
507

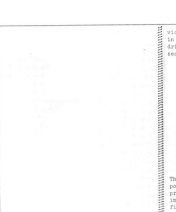

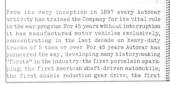

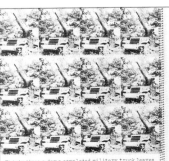

victory
in the
driver's
seat...

The U. S. Army has called upon Autocar to build big, powerful vehicles...speedy vehicles, for hauling a precious human cargo of American soldiers...sturdy impregnable vehicles, to safeguard that cargo... fighting vehicles, to conquer the forces of ill-will. Autocar immediately entered this as order Number 1 on its books, and made the order-of-the-day "production"! For the duration of the emergency Victory is in the driver's seat at Autocar, guiding an all-out effort that refuses to recognize the "impossible".

for victory

From its very inception in 1897 every Autocar activity has trained the Company for its vital role in the war program. For 45 years without interruption it has manufactured motor vehicles exclusively, concentrating in the last decade on heavy-duty trucks of 5 tons or over. For 45 years Autocar has pioneered the way, developing many history-making "firsts" in the industry: the first porcelain spark-plug; the first American shaft-driven automobile; the first double reduction gear drive; the first

circulating oil system. For 45 years Autocar insistence on mechanical perfection has wrought a tradition of precision that is honored by every one of its master workers. These are achievements that only time can win. The harvest of these years, of this vast experience, is at the service of our government. Autocar is meeting its tremendous responsibility to national defense by putting its 45 years' experience to work in helping to build for America a motorized armada such as the world has never seen.

Autocar was among the first in 1940 to receive Defense orders. Today those orders have grown to a huge backlog of many millions representing a sum proportionately higher than Autocar's already high share of the heavy-duty market and, therefore, high tribute to the quality of its product. Autocar is now producing diversified types of military vehicles: an anti-tank vehicle; Personnel Carrier; Scout Car; and Troop Carrier. Highlights from one of these assembly lines are illustrated on the following pages:

Enemy bullets shot from the usual small weapons are not likely to pierce the heavy armor plate of this body, assembled in Autocar's plant. So that delay might not pierce Autocar's high production schedule, the company perfected this special body-assembly line in the same new two-story building that houses the chassis assembly. The two assembly lines ..chassis on the first floor and body on the second   travel their own Autocar-engineered routes to one junction where they are joined into a Rolling Fortress.

The men who work on the vitals of these vehicles are unexcelled in their mechanical skill. Their hands move with the swiftness and sureness of a surgeon's, darting decisively from tool box to point of work. Armed with tremendous resources of skill and experience, the army of men at Autocar wages a relentless and victorious war against time. These men are in the front ranks in the battle of production. They are doing all in their power to supply America with an ever mounting number of military trucks.

What the artisans of Autocar production are doing now for America's military forces they have done countless times for American industry. They have built every kind of hauling vehicle from the light delivery truck to huge motorized transports for oil and gasoline. Now, for their Number 1 customer, Uncle Sam, they have increased their plant by 93,000 square feet and have added 1,500 employees to the staff, all within little more than a year's time. They permit nothing to stand in the way of production for victory.

Military strategy need not restrict the use of these vehicles to modern, smooth highways. The tractor treads used in place of rear wheels will carry them swiftly over uneven terrain...they never lose their grip. Caterpillar-like, they climb out of the deepest holes. Teamed with the rolling front bumper they keep our motorized infantry moving resistlessly forward. Despite their huge weight and powerful armor, these Autocar manufactured vehicles can cover ground at a speed of 50 miles an hour.

To save time, Autocar, the only heavy-duty truck company to do so, ingeniously combines the body and chassis assembly lines under one roof. The assembly routes were engineered and coordinated by Autocar experts so that the armor-plated body is completed simultaneously with the chassis, at a spot directly above the location of the latter. Strong cables then lower the body over the chassis, and experts set to work to fit the two major sections together with waste time and excess motion completely eliminated

Thirty times a day a completed military truck leaves the Autocar assembly line ready to roll into action. Among these is the powerful anti-tank weapon pictured on this page. Mounted on this vehicle, in addition to a machine gun, is a tank-smashing .75 mm gun. Autocar is the only company assembling these units that actually handles the installation of the guns. These superb rolling weapons of defense were engineered by the Autocar Company, working in close collaboration with government Ordnance engineers.

In executing its supreme obligation to our country, Autocar has strengthened its position for operations in post-emergency America. The heightened facilities added in behalf of defense, will be necessary to fulfill a commercial demand that had been steadily mounting before the emergency. When the war is won and liberty is secure, the stage will be set at Autocar to steer its products of peace and free enterprise to every corner of our great nation... in numbers greater than ever before in its history.

508

193

The enemy wants to know what you know...

Keep it under your
STETSON

509

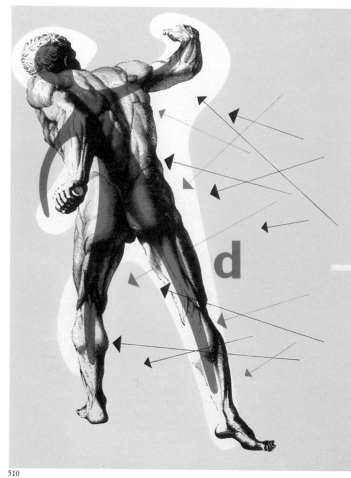

510

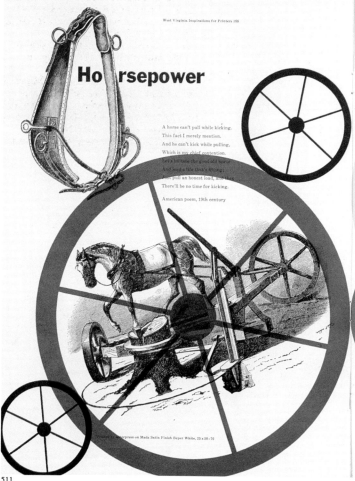

West Virginia Inspirations for Printers 158

Horsepower

A horse can't pull while kicking.
This fact I merely mention.
And he can't kick while pulling,
Which is my chief contention.
Let's imitate the good old horse
And lead a life that's fitting;
Just pull an honest load, and then
There'll be no time for kicking.

American poem, 19th century

511

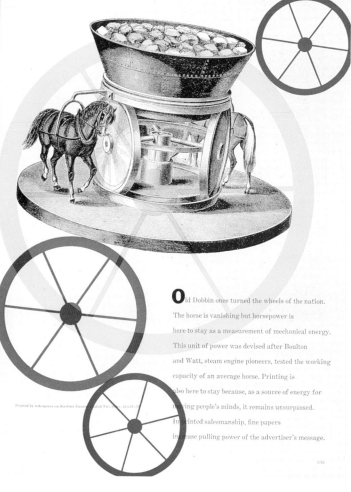

**O**ld Dobbin once turned the wheels of the nation.
The horse is vanishing but horsepower is
here to stay as a measurement of mechanical energy.
This unit of power was devised after Boulton
and Watt, steam engine pioneers, tested the working
capacity of an average horse. Printing is
also here to stay because, as a source of energy for
moving people's minds, it remains unsurpassed.
In printed salesmanship, fine papers
increase pulling power of the advertiser's message.

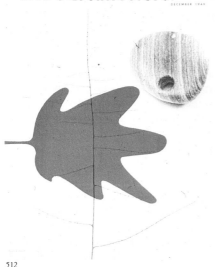

512

513

## AMERICAN

With the war over, graphic designers returned to the business of selling commercial products and ideas with a host of modern methods now fully integrated into the advertising and publishing industries. Ashley Havinden in his book *Advertising and the Artist* characterizes this modern aesthetic: "The aim of the good designer is never to show off his erudition or his modernity. He must never intrude a personal or private preoccupation with any design form. His sole intention is to put whatever talents he has for inventive construction, simplicity and understanding of the medium to...the service of expressing the idea, or complex of ideas, with utmost clarity, force and conviction." Combining European ideas of abstraction, dynamism, and asymmetry with a particularly American directness, the new design provided a viable alternative to the blatant and often vulgar style of mass-market design. Among its most successful practitioners were E. McKnight Kauffer, Mathew Leibowitz, Bradbury Thompson, John Follis, Alvin Lustig, and Herbert Matter.

509. E. McKnight Kauffer. *Keep It Under Your Stetson.* Advertisement in *Life* magazine, 1947

510. Mathew Leibowitz. *Male Torso.* Brochure cover for Sharp & Dohme, c. 1945

511. Bradbury Thompson. *Westvaco Inspirations 152.* Inside spread, 1952. Courtesy the designer

512. John Follis. *Arts & Architecture.* Magazine cover, December 1949. Courtesy the designer

513. Alvin Lustig. *A Season in Hell.* Jacket for a book by Arthur Rimbaud, 1945. Courtesy of Elaine Lustig Cohen, Ex Libris, New York

514. Herbert Matter. *Fortune.* Magazine cover, July 1948

514

515

516

## SWISS INTERNATIONAL STYLE

Their country's neutrality enabled Swiss graphic designers to continue their work during the war. Max Bill, a former Bauhaus student and a pioneer of the Swiss style, based his methodology on Constructivism. His colleague Josef Müller-Brockmann describes the process: "Copy and a picture are arranged and related in accordance with objective and functional criteria. The areas are sensitively organized with an assured touch in mathematical proportions, and due attention is paid to the rules of typography." After the war, Bill became director of the influential Hochschule für Gestaltung in Ulm, and his rationalist design ethic spread throughout Europe. The Swiss School, or International Style of Typography, was further elaborated by younger designers, from Zurich and Basel, like Müller-Brockmann, Richard P. Lohse, Hans Neuburg, Carlo L. Vivarelli, and Karl Gerstner, all of whom saw design as a vital means of communicating objective facts. Object photography, sans-serif typography, lack of ornamentation, and strict composition on the basis of the grid system are characteristic of this style. Although its inventor is not known, the grid became the most significant design tool of the postwar era. Used for prospectuses, brochures, books, and exhibition catalogues, it was perfectly adaptable to the requirements of international business. The periodical *Neue Grafik (New Graphic Design),* founded in 1958 by Lohse, Müller-Brockmann, Vivarelli, and Neuburg, reported on, analyzed, and championed this systematic approach.

515. Josef Müller-Brockmann. *Beethoven.* Concert poster, 1955. Courtesy the designer

516. *Neue Grafik 9.* Magazine cover of an international review of graphic design, March 1961. Edited by Richard P. Lohse, Josef Müller-Brockmann, Hans Neuburg, Carlo L. Vivarelli. Courtesy Josef Müller-Brockmann

517. Karl Gerstner. *You, Too, Are Liberal.* Poster, 1956. Courtesy Moore College of Art, Philadelphia. Goldie Paley Gallery

518. Max Bill. *Kunsthaus Zürich.* Exhibition poster, 1936. Kunstgewerbemuseum, Zurich

519. Carlo L. Vivarelli. *Für das Alter (For the Elderly).* Poster, 1949. Kunstgewerbemuseum, Zurich

520. Fridolin Muller. *Für das Alter (For the Elderly).* Poster, 1964. Courtesy Moore College of Art, Philadelphia. Goldie Paley Gallery

521. Various designers. Entries in a trademark design competition for Electrolux, from *Neue Grafik 13,* 1962. Permission of Josef Müller-Brockmann

517

518

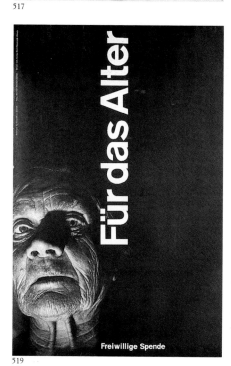

519

520

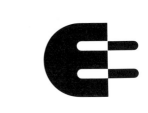
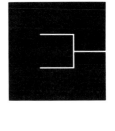

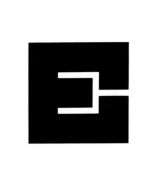
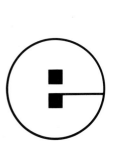

521

mittwoch, den 4. juni 1969
leitung/ erich leinsdorf
solist/ isaac stern, violine
c. m. v. weber/ freischütz-ouvertüre
l. van beethoven/ violinkonzert in d-dur, op. 61
igor strawinsky/ le sacre du printemps

sonntag, den 8. juni 1969
isaac stern, violine
alexander zakin, klavier
werke von  bach
brahms
prokofieff
bartok

dienstag, den 10. juni 1969
leitung/ antal dorati
solist/ claudio arrau, klavier
joseph haydn/ sinfonie in b-dur, nr. 98
richard strauss/ till eulenspiegels lustige streiche, op. 28
johannes brahms/ klavierkonzert in d-moll, op. 15

dienstag, den 12. juni 1969
duo alfons und aloys kontarsky, klavier
christoph caskel, schlagzeug
werke von bernd a. zimmermann
earl brown
karlheinz stockhausen
pierre boulez

konzerte
junifestwochen     1969
tonhalle—
gesellschaft
zürich

dienstag, den 17. juni 1969
leitung/ rudolf kempe
solist/ zino francescatti, violine
karl amadeus hartmann/
kammerkonzert für klarinette, streichquartett
und streichorchester (uraufführung)
felix mendelssohn/ violinkonzert in e-moll, op. 64
l. van beethoven/ siebente sinfonie in a-dur, op. 92

donnerstag, den 19. juni 1969
arturo benedetti michelangeli
werke von  clementi
schumann
ravel

dienstag, den 24. juni 1969
leitung/ wolfgang sawallisch
solist/ arthur rubinstein, klavier
arthur honegger/ monopartita
peter tschaikowsky/ klavierkonzert in b-moll, op. 23
robert schumann/ zweite sinfonie in c-dur, op. 61

dienstag, den 1. juli 1969
leitung/ rudolf kempe
solisten/ christa ludwig, alt
waldemar kmentt, tenor
w. a. mozart/ sinfonie in b-dur, kv 319
gustav mahler/ das lied von der erde

vorverkauf

tonhallekasse
musikhaus hug
pianohaus jecklin
reisebureau kuoni
filiale oerlikon kreditanstalt

preise

fr. 10.- bis 35.- orchesterkonzerte
fr. 10.- bis 30.- extrakonzerte
fr. 5.- bis 11.- musica viva-konzert

522

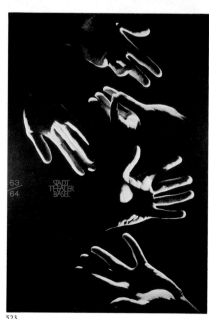

523

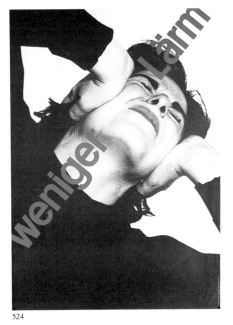

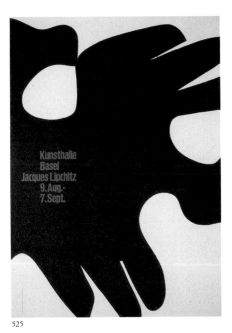

524

525

## SWISS INTERNATIONAL STYLE

The Swiss design philosophy is actually propagated through two major schools, one in Zurich, the other in Basel. Josef Müller-Brockmann typifies the former's approach, Armin Hofmann the latter's. According to Kenneth Hiebert, a Basel School alumnus, that school's methodology derives from the idea that "abstract structure is the vehicle for communication. It relies on an analysis that rigorously questions and accounts for all parts of a message. The act of searching for an appropriate structure forces the designer to make the most basic inquiry about a message, to isolate its primary essence from considerations of surface style." Communication, not seduction, is Basel's primary goal, one that dictates the need for symbols appropriate to the content of the message. Ideally, the method results in a metaphor and message that have universal appeal. As Hiebert writes, the Swiss School is concerned that design be more than "a frivolous cluttering of the environment."

522. Armin Hofmann. *Konzerte Tonhalle–Gesellschaft.* Concert poster, 1969. Courtesy the designer

523. Armin Hofmann. *Basel Municipal Theater.* Poster, 1963. Courtesy the designer

524. Josef Müller-Brockmann. *Weniger Lärm (Less Noise).* Poster against noise pollution, 1960. Courtesy the designer

525. Armin Hofmann. *Kunsthalle Basel.* Exhibition poster, 1958. Courtesy the designer

526. Josef Müller-Brockmann. *Schützt das Kind! (Protect the Child!).* Poster for the Swiss automobile club, 1955. Courtesy the designer

526

529

## CORPORATE STYLE

By the early 1950s, television and computers had begun to usher in the Information Age, and the more refined term *corporate communications* replaced the somewhat pedestrian *commercial art*. The job of the corporate communications designer was to create and maintain consistent identities and advertising campaigns. Those American designers schooled in or influenced by European Modernism had created a distinctive period methodology. Free from many of the dogmatic European strictures, their work shared certain common traits like unadorned, economical graphics and kinetic photographic accents.

527. William Golden. *CBS.* Trademark, 1951

528. Paul Rand. *IBM.* Trademark, 1956

529. Brownjohn, Chermayeff and Geismar Associates. *About U.S.: Experimental Typography by American Designers.* Pages from a booklet produced for the Composing Room, 1960

530. Gene Federico. *Woman's Day.* Advertisement for the magazine, 1953. Courtesy the designer

531. Rudolph De Harak. *The Siege of Leningrad.* Book cover, 1963. Courtesy the designer

532. Lou Dorfsman. *The Rocket's Red Glare.* Advertisement for CBS television, appearing in *The New York Times,* 1962. Courtesy the designer

533. Louis Silverstein. *Where Else but New York? Where Else but The New York Times?* Promotional advertisement, c. 1962. Courtesy the designer

534. Alexey Brodovitch. *Portfolio.* Cover for a graphic arts magazine, 1951. Permission Frank Zachary

535. Saul Bass. *Anatomy of a Murder.* Movie poster, 1959. Courtesy the designer

530

527

IBM

528

531

532

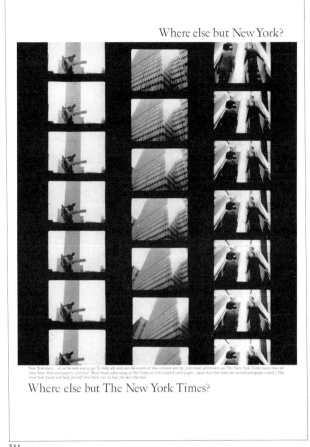

Where else but New York?

Where else but The New York Times?

533

534

535

536

CHEZ PANISSE
SECOND BIRTHDAY
CELEBRATION
TUESDAY AUGUST 28
SIX PM TO MIDNIGHT
CASSOULET
½ LITRE OF WINE
& SALAD ☷ $5²⁵
ALSO UN FILM DE
MARCEL PAGNOL

537

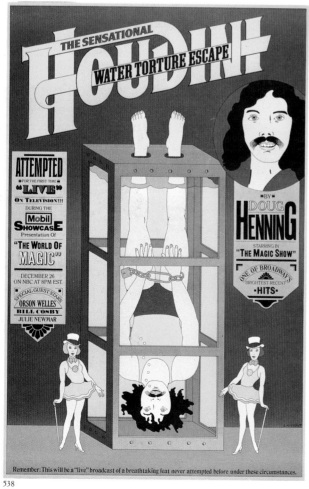

538

539

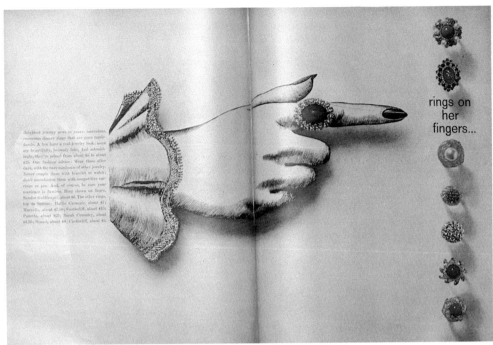

540

541

## REVIVAL

In the mid-1950s, certain designers and illustrators discovered an alternative to classical Modernism when they began to reprise vintage graphic approaches in a move that prefigured Post-Modernism. Previously considered obsolete and therefore thrown into the wastebin of popular culture, primitive painting, Victoriana, Art Nouveau, and Art Deco graphic motifs were taken up again as fresh sources of inspiration. Painterly and drawn images were reunited with typography as a total design. In addition, the revival of nineteenth-century wood types and the subsequent reissues of early twentieth-century display faces on film contributed to a renewed enthusiasm among designers for retro forms. While not suited for multinational business communications, the usually playful application of historical mannerisms was perfect for certain editorial and book designs, record albums, cultural posters, and packaging.

536. Paul Davis. *Plunkitt of Tammany Hall.* Illustration for book jacket, 1962. Courtesy the designer

537. David Lance Goines. *Chez Panisse.* Poster, 1973. Courtesy the designer

538. Seymour Chwast. *The Sensational Houdini.* Poster, 1973. Courtesy the designer

539. Milton Glaser. *Geometric Landscape.* Poster for Stuttgart bank, 1975. Courtesy the designer

540. Otto Storch. *Rings on Her Fingers.* Pages from *McCall's* magazine, 1961. Courtesy *McCall's* magazine

541. Barry Zaid. *Mata Hari.* Drawings published in *The Push Pin Graphic,* 1973. Courtesy the designer

542. Milton Glaser. *Holiday.* Magazine cover, 1967. Courtesy the designer

542

203

## ECLECTIC

By the 1960s, a design consciousness had become ingrained in every commerce-oriented, industrial society. With the proliferation of design schools, greater access to phototechnologies, and such a big store of graphic design approaches to choose from, no one style dominated. Although the leading individual stylists were copied, the lack of any guiding spiritual, political, or aesthetic force encouraged the eclectic sensibility, in works as diverse as James McMullan's realist watercolors and R. Crumb's irreverent comic strips. Herb Lubalin, with his so-called "smashed-type" and provocative word/image concoctions, exerted a huge influence, not only on American advertising and editorial design but on schools in Eastern Europe, where copies of *Avant Garde* and other publications featuring his work were rare and expensive. Also influential were art directors Henry Wolf and Willi Fleckhaus, who masterfully orchestrated both the look and contents of their respective magazines. And in London, Pentagram Studios developed a freewheeling approach to corporate and commercial communications and imbued otherwise pedestrian business communications with a characteristic wry wit, as in their alphabet employing found objects.

543. Herb Lubalin. *Avant Garde.* Magazine cover, January 1968. Courtesy Tony DiSpigna

544. James McMullan. *Paul Desmond: Late Lament.* Album cover, 1987. Courtesy the designer

545. R. Crumb (artist), Bob Cato and John Berg (art directors). *Cheap Thrills.* Album cover for Big Brother & The Holding Company (Columbia Records), 1968. Courtesy the artist

546. Michael Salisbury. *West.* Magazine cover for Sunday supplement of the *Los Angeles Times,* December 26, 1971. Courtesy the designer

547. Mervyn Kurlansky. Alphabet using found studio objects, designed for a special issue on typography for Preston Polytechnic's own design publication, 1977. Courtesy Pentagram, London

548. Henry Wolf. *Show.* Magazine cover, February 1964. Courtesy the designer

549. Willi Fleckhaus. *Twen.* Magazine contents page, 1970. Courtesy Bob Ciano

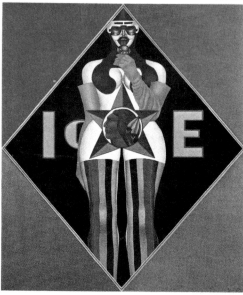

543

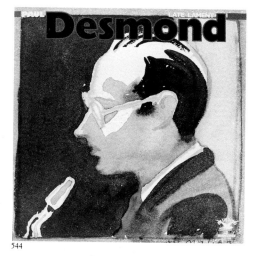

544

545

west

DECEMBER 26, 1971

Cheer up, Charlie. All is forgiven.

546

547

SHOW

THE
MAGAZINE
OF
THE
ARTS
75 CENTS
FEBRUARY 1964

Will the Real William Shakespeare Step Forward:    A special report on the Bard today

548

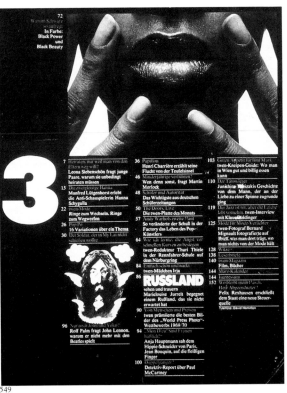

549

## POLISH

The contemporary Polish school of posters arose after World War II as a spirited attempt to rebuild the wartorn nation. Without television, with few radios, and short on newspapers, the new Communist government recognized the power of posters as a form of communication and instituted a state-supported agency to commission and publish them on a broad spectrum of themes. Although some were political and educational, most announced cultural events. Film posters were the first fertile ground in which the distinctly bizarre Polish style flowered. Scenes from the film were rarely shown; instead, the artists captured the film's essence, often through visual metaphor. Cultural posters became a significant outlet for individual artistic expression, as artists aimed to establish their own artistic styles and identities. Rather than a coherent movement, the Polish school was a wildly diverse community of painters and graphic designers.

550. Franciszek Starowieyski. *Oni (They)*. Theatre poster, c. 1983. Courtesy the designer

551. Jan Lenica. *Lebensbilder-Zeitbilder*. Poster for an opening exhibition of the Postermuseum in Essen, West Germany, 1984. Courtesy the designer

552. Roman Cieslewicz. *Liberté-Wolnosc (Polish Liberty)*. Political poster, 1981. Courtesy the designer

553. Andrzej Pagowski and Krystyna Hofmann. *Wojna Swiatow (The War of the Worlds)*. Film poster, 1982. Courtesy the designers

554. Andrzej Czeczot. *Szewcy (Shoemakers)*. Poster for a play by Witkacy, 1985. Courtesy the designer

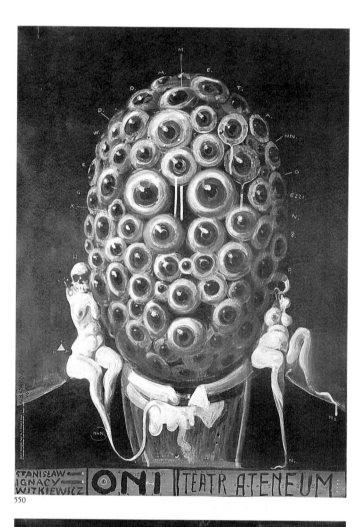

550

551

552

553

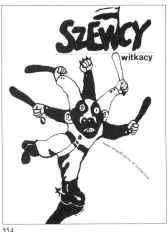

554

555

556

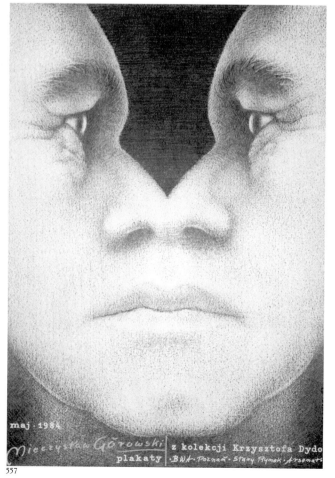

557

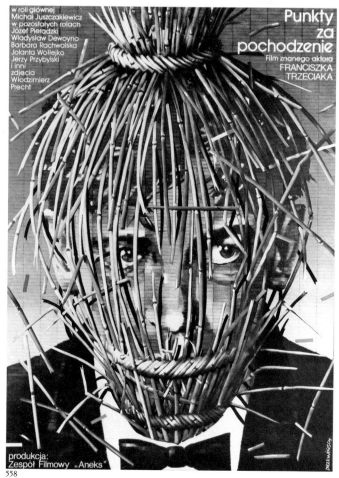

558

TOMASZ ZALIWSKI, PIOTR ŁYSEK i HENRYK BISTA
W FILMIE TADEUSZA CHMIELEWSKIEGO
WŚRÓD NOCNEJ CISZY
PRODUKCJA:
ZESPÓŁ FILMOWY "X"

559

## POLISH

The 1950s through the 1970s are regarded by critics as the golden age of Polish posters. While considered advertising art, the Polish work was unlike anything ever seen in Western commerce. Its typically strange, idiosyncratic world view developed through innovative applications of Western styles like Art Nouveau, Surrealism, and Pop Art. Unencumbered by the rules of Western design, Polish designers used painting, photography, and hand-lettering in unprecedented, often discordant, combinations. Among the leading stylists were Franciszek Starowieyski, who built upon the Surrealist vocabulary, and Jan Lenica, whose haunting imagery drew upon Jugendstil. The proliferation of design clichés eventually contributed to a creative malaise in the late seventies. When the Solidarity Movement emerged in the early eighties, the need for exciting visual communications was briefly reestablished.

555. Franciszek Starowieyski. *Breda.* Poster, c. 1984. Courtesy the designer

556. Edward Dwurnik. *Teatr Narodowy (National Theater).* Poster, c. 1985. Courtesy the designer

557. Mieczyslaw Gorowski. *Z Kolekcji Krzysztofa Dydo (From the Collection of Christopher Dydo).* Poster, 1983. Courtesy the designer

558. Leszek Drzewinski. *Punkty za Pochodzenie (Point of Origin).* Antiwar poster, 1985. Courtesy the designer

559. Jerzy Czerniawski. *Wśród Nocnej Ciszy (Stillness of Night).* Poster, c. 1984. Courtesy the designer

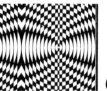 

## PSYCHEDELIC

For a very brief period, Psychedelia was an honest reflection of the 1960s American youth culture; then it was usurped as a marketable fashion by trendsetters in the merchandising business. Curiously, Psychedelia is best defined by Otto Wagner's term *gesamtkunstwerk* (the total work of art), for it connotes the hippie movement's return to communal living, its attempts at arts and crafts production, and its union of art, music, and literature. In its purest form, the Psychedelic style was applied to the design of newspapers, broadsides, posters, clothing, jewelry, furniture, and automobiles (many of its early proponents in California decorated hot rods for a living before turning to rock and roll). Psychedelia was a visual code; those who could pierce the layers of symbolism to read the message, either with the naked eye or with the aid of hallucinogens, became members of the "underground" family. Although Psychedelia reused Austrian Secessionist lettering, Art Nouveau ornament, East Indian symbols, and Victorian typography, its drug-inspired palette and comic-book iconography mark it as a distinctly American graphic style. The most innovative Psychedelic artists were the underground cartoonists Wes Wilson, Rick Griffin, Stanley Mouse, and Victor Moscoso, who all together produced hundreds of posters for West Coast rock concerts.

560. Gerald Holtom. Nuclear disarmament symbol, 1956

561. David King and Roger Law. *The Jimi Hendrix Experience/Axis: Bold as Love.* Record album cover, 1967

562. Wes Wilson. *The Association: Concert at the Fillmore Auditorium.* Concert poster, 1966. Courtesy the designer

563. Wes Wilson. *The Byrds at the Fillmore.* Poster, 1967

564. Victor Moscoso. *The Miller Blues Band.* Concert poster, 1966. Courtesy the designer

565. Victor Moscoso. *Otis Rush.* Concert poster, 1967. Courtesy the designer

566. Victor Moscoso. *Big Brother & the Holding Company.* Concert poster, 1967. Courtesy the designer

560

561

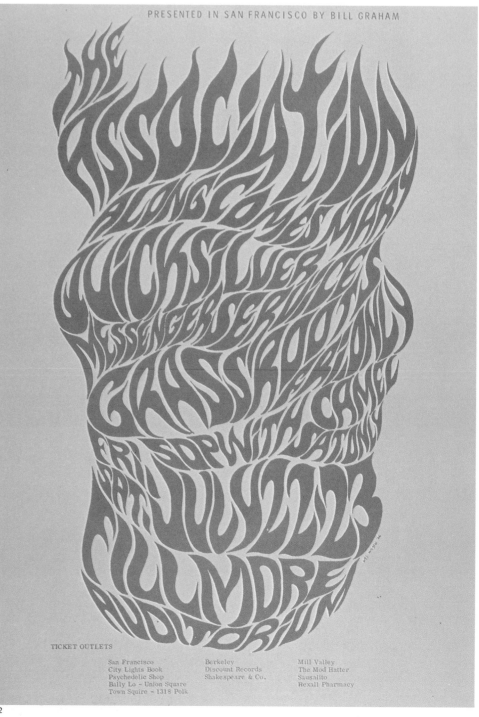

562

563

564

565

566

211

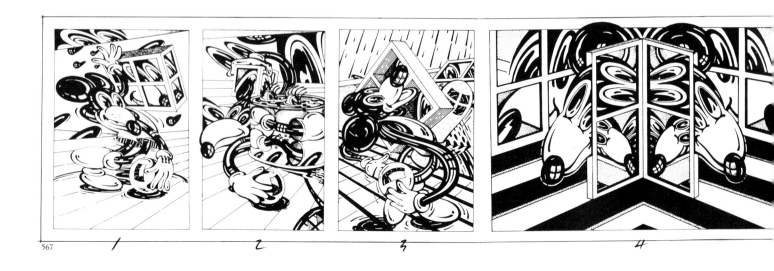

567    1     2     3     4

# ALPHA PSYCHEDELITYPE

# PSYCHEDELITYPES!

568

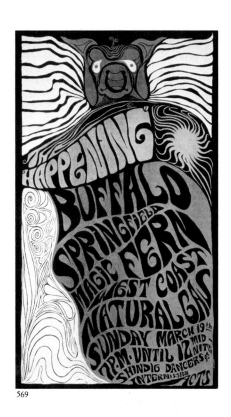

569

570

571

5                    6                    7

BILL GRAHAM PRESENTS IN SAN FRANCISCO

TICKETS  **SAN FRANCISCO:** City Lights Bookstore; S.F. State College (Hut T-1); The Town Squire (1318 Polk); Kelley Galleries (3681A Sacramento); Wild Colors (1418 Haight); Bally Lo (Union Square); **BERKELEY:** Discount Records; Shakespeare & Co.; **SAN MATEO:** Town & Country Records; **REDWOOD CITY:** Redwood House of Music; **PALO ALTO:** Dana Morgan Music; **SAN RAFAEL:** Record King; **SAUSALITO:** The Tides Bookstore

572

## PSYCHEDELIC

A capital of the beat movement in the fifties, San Francisco was also the birthplace of the hippie and Psychedelic movements. Yet variants of the Psychedelic style spread throughout the United States and eventually Europe. During the late sixties, John Van Hamersveld, whose graphic style varied from typographical illustration to fluid cartoon imagery, was an inventive proponent in Los Angeles. Since Psychedelic image making could be rather simple (hand-lettering, for instance, required only a rapidograph) and printing costs were low (the split-fountain color technique needed only one pass through a press), Psychedelic posters were ubiquitous. In Seattle, called "a city of posters" by one critic, a prolific community of poster and handbill artists established itself. New York City was known for its underground newspapers and the original Psychedelicatessen, while other centers of Psychedelic activity were found in Atlanta, Chicago, and Dallas. One contributing factor to Psychedelia's demise was Photolettering Inc.'s issuance in 1969 of its Psychedelitype catalogue, which made it possible for anyone to set type in a Psychedelic style.

567. John Van Hamersveld. *Psychedelic Solutions.* Drawing, 1969. Courtesy the designer

568. Designer unknown. *Psychedelitypes!* Alphabets from Photolettering Inc., 1969

569. Designer unknown. *Buffalo Springfield.* Concert poster, 1967. Courtesy Art Chantry

570. Tom Robbins and Ray Collins. *Loving Sunday.* Poster for a love-in, 1967. Courtesy Art Chantry

571. John R. Moenring. *Donovan.* Concert poster, 1962. Courtesy Art Chantry

572. Wes Wilson. *Buffalo Springfield/Steve Miller Blues Band.* Concert poster, 1967. Library of Congress. Washington, D.C. Poster Collection

573. Rick Griffin. *The Oracle.* Magazine cover, 1968

573

213

## JAPANESE

Influenced by the European avant-garde, a concurrent Modernist movement began in Tokyo around 1910 but was squelched in the mid-thirties, during Japan's age of militarism. It took nearly two more decades before that spirit could be recovered. As the channel for influence shifted from Europe to the United States, historian James Fraser noted that "in the post–World War II period, Japanese graphic design has given as much as it has absorbed." In his capacity as managing director of the Japan Design Center in 1960, Yusaka Kamekura brought Japan's innovative new designers together with its booming postwar industry, and the results were remarkable. Tadanori Yokoo broke from the International Style to pursue a more intuitive and anarchic approach that emphasized the Japanese fascination with past, present, and future cultural icons, both Eastern and Western.

574. Kenji Itoh. *Kataoka Bussan Co., Ltd.* Package design for tea, 1986. Courtesy the designer

575. Takashi Nomura (designer) and Seitaro Kuroda (illustrator). *Mosquito on the 10th Floor.* Film poster, 1982. Courtesy Keisuke Nagatomo

576. Shigeo Okamoto. *Life and Pottery.* Poster for the 21st Pottery Test and Research Center Exhibition, 1986. Courtesy the designer

577. Tadanori Yokoo. *Science Fiction Movies.* Film festival poster, 1975. Courtesy the designer

578. Tadanori Yokoo. *The Wonders of Life on Earth.* Poster for a book by Isamu Kurita, 1965. Courtesy the designer

579. Tadanori Yokoo. *John Silver.* Theater poster, 1967. Courtesy the designer

575

576

574

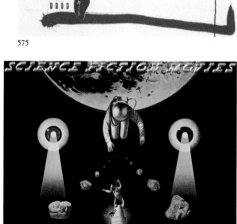

577

578

581

582

## JAPANESE

The 1970 Osaka World Exposition, with seventy-six participating countries, marked a turning point for Japanese designers. Associating with so many foreign visitors stimulated them to reexamine their own cultural roots and to apply them to their architecture, arts and crafts, and graphic design. Although most contemporary Japanese advertising designers adopted Western images from Pop Art, comic strips, television, and film, they transformed them into evocations of the emerging contemporary, high-tech Japanese society. In moving from an essentially Constructivist- and Bauhaus-inspired methodology to a more culturally eclectic visual lexicon, Japanese designers prefigured New Wave and Post-Modern tendencies in America and Europe. This change of emphasis did not occur in an organized manner, however, but separately evolved in the work of individual designers. Prominent among Japan's leading individualists is Shigeo Fukuda. Stylistically distinct from other Japanese designers, his simple, emblematic imagery combines the Japanese taste for economy with a witty, ironic sensibility.

580. Yusaku Kamekura. *Hiroshima Appeals.* Poster, 1983. Courtesy the designer

581. Shigeo Fukuda. Poster for an exhibition of the designer's work, 1984. Courtesy the designer

582. Shigeo Fukuda. Poster for a private exhibition, 1986. Courtesy the designer

583. Shigeo Fukuda. Poster for a one-man exhibition, 1986. Courtesy the designer

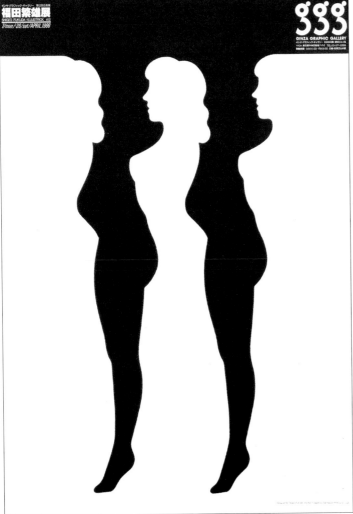

583

217

## JAPANESE

Though not easily codified or defined, Japanese graphic style is recognizable—and not merely by its typography or the occasional Japanese visual reference. Called upon to advertise products and disseminate ideas, both to their compatriots and to the world, Japanese designers speak in a curiously national yet international voice. By employing the full range of photographic and computer communication-arts tools available today, they are able to transform the poster's two-dimensional surface. Their newly created three-dimensional playgrounds may bear either typically elegant harmonies or discordant colors, random shapes, and explosive images. Kazumasa Nagai and Ikko Tanaka are two pioneers of contemporary design, each having made a distinct contribution to Japanese graphic style.

584. Kazumasa Nagai. Poster for Japanese graphic art exhibition in Paris, 1984. Courtesy the designer

585. Kazumasa Nagai. *Zero Nuclear Weapons.* Poster for the Hiroshima-Nagasaki Publishing Committee, 1982. Courtesy the designer

586. Ikko Tanaka. *Asian Performing Arts Institute, UCLA.* Theater poster, 1981. Courtesy the designer

587. Ikko Tanaka. *Noh.* Performance poster, 1981. Courtesy the designer

584

585

Nihon Buyo

UCLA
Asian Ien Performing Arts
Institute 1981
Los Angeles
Washington, D.C.
New York

586

587

# BLACK SABBATH

# TECHNICAL ECSTASY

588. George Hardie and Richard Manning (Hipgnossis). *Black Sabbath: Technical Ecstasy.* Record album cover, 1976. Courtesy the designers

Within the basically eclectic design environment of the eighties, the term *Post-Modern* has come to apply to a distinctive international style based not on dogma but on the somewhat haphazard confluence of various theories and practices of individual designers worldwide. In current architectural criticism, the term formally and effectively describes the rejection of orthodox Modernist purity in favor of an updated Neo-classical ornamentation; in contemporary design, it is less precise, perhaps only a temporary rubric. The most general interpretation of the term for design purposes would include all contemporary practitioners who are not strict Bauhausians and would embrace such eighties' substyles as Neo-Dada, Neo-Expressionism, Punk, and Pacific Modern.

Like Art Deco, the last major international style, Post-Modern blends art history and new technology with a decorative tendency to achieve a broad-based, commercially acceptable look. Linking its various substyles are certain distinctive visual, if not philosophical, characteristics: a playful kinetic geometry featuring floating forms, sawtooth rules, and randomly placed blips and lines; multiple layered and fragmented images; pleasant pastel harmonies; discordant, letter-spaced typography; and frequent references to art and design history.

The Post-Modern design aesthetic was in the wind long before the name was coined. In the late fifties and the sixties, certain premature Post-Modernisms appeared in the Art Nouveau and Art Deco mannerisms reprised in the work of Push Pin Studios. Even earlier, in 1947, Ettore Sottsass, Jr., had executed a series of graphics combining Constructivist forms and gaily colored geometric debris in a prefiguration of his influential yet short-lived Memphis Style. When he realized, in the early 1980s, that he had little chance of significantly improving the broader urban environment, Sottsass decided to focus on redesign of the home, the last domain of individual freedom. His cartoon-like, pastel-colored Memphis furniture, textiles, and accessories were at

once playful, irreverent, and critical of rigid functionalism. Their nature as three-dimensional collage/assemblages strongly affected the look of graphic design in Milan, Barcelona, Los Angeles, San Francisco, and Tokyo. And it continues today to define how graphic design is applied to consumer durable products.

The earliest Swiss contributions to Post-Modernism can be traced to Basel, where Wolfgang Weingart joined the faculty of the Basel Allegemeine Gewerbeschule in 1968. Rejecting the order and cleanliness of the Swiss grid-locked design and typography, Weingart mixed type weights within the same word, created grids and then violated them, and arranged type into images. Though drawing from Swiss formalism, Weingart's Basel Style provided a kind of computer-age liberation from two-dimensional space. Numerous European and American students who studied with Weingart expanded his creative approach to create a distinct look for the eighties.

The New York designer Dan Friedman, a Basel graduate and later a teacher at Yale and SUNY Purchase, was one of the most effective teachers of the new style. Friedman devised various stimulating student projects that tested the relationship between avant-garde and practical design applications. In 1973, he wrote: "Legibility (a quality of efficient, clear, and simple reading) is often in conflict with readability (a quality which promotes interest, pleasure, and challenge in reading). To what degree can a typographic statement be both functional and at the same time aesthetically unconventional?" Friedman's approach was to ricochet through American design education. In Los Angeles, designer April Greiman and photographer Jayme Odgers took the new language further by using kinetic photography. They combined Basel precepts with California Pop/Funk in what might be termed an image overload, similar in texture to the work of Hipgnosis, the British album-cover design studio, and the Japanese poster artist Tadanori Yoko. Greiman later expanded the boundaries of legibility even more through the use of abstract computer imagery. Concurrently, a group of San Francisco designers, influenced by the

architects Robert Venturi and Michael Graves, developed Post-Modern decorative motifs characterized by a streamlined Neo-classicism. Teachers at the Cranbrook Academy in Bloomfield Hills, Michigan, formulated an analytical design approach based on the theory of deconstruction: the limits of abstract visual communication are tested by finding how many levels of meaning can be expressed through complex typographic configurations. While essentially decorative, this theory is best applied in the functional design work of the contemporary Dutch firms Studio Dumbar and Total Design.

Along with such analytical explorations of graphic design, there were the more expressive, serendipitous approaches. Like Psychedelia almost a decade before, Punk (also known as Neo-Expressionism and Neo-Dada) was the spiritual offspring of the sixties' underground press and its anti-design aesthetic. Originating in England as an offshoot of the rock music scene, Punk developed in the context of various local cultures, particularly in London, New York, Los Angeles, and Seattle. Its design was governed by speed and economy, and its posters and tabloid newspapers were characterized by the use of raw-edged torn paper and ruling tape and by a "ransom-note" approach to type and image. As with the underground press, comics played an important role in Punk's overall visual image. Swiss Punk represented a more refined use of type and image—a more violent high-tech attack on the grid—and eventually deteriorated into the more commercially oriented New Wave. As cartoonist Gary Panter laments, "Punk was an honest expression, while New Wave is a packaging term."

Despite the Post-Modern label, design style in the eighties must be defined as the sum of its various parts. Evidence definitely exists of a common period vocabulary, or at least a kindred aesthetic sensibility and artistic cross-pollination, visible in all media and applied to diverse products. Yet the aesthetic continues to evolve primarily from the styles of specific designers and to be propagated through the media as popular fashion. Only time will reveal its true nature and significance.  221

## MEMPHIS/BASEL/ZURICH

Founded in Milan in 1980, Memphis developed from the freewheeling creativity and conscious rejection of functional design in Italy during the seventies. The term became synonymous with cartoon-like furniture and textiles that, as Emilo Ambasz says, "have made peace with the ephemeral." In Basel, during the late sixties, Wolfgang Weingart violated the traditional Swiss rules of order and cleanliness with his free-form typography characterized by step rules, wide letterspacing, and the mixing of type weights. In Zurich, Odermatt and Tissi developed a method of typographic collage that intersperses surface forms with strips of lettering and creates a sense of spontaneity that gives the viewer the illusion of involvement in the design process.

589. Ettore Sottsass. *Casablanca.* Furniture piece, 1981. Courtesy Artemide Inc., New York

590. Nathalie Du Pasquier. *Cerchio.* Memphis pattern, 1983. From *Memphis: Una Questione di Stile,* published by Istituto Mides

591. Nathalie Du Pasquier. *Arizona.* Memphis pattern, 1983. From *Memphis: Una Questione di Stile,* published by Istituto Mides

592. Memphis logos

593. Wolfgang Weingart. *18 Didacta Eurodidac.* Poster, 1979. Courtesy Reinhold Brown Gallery, New York

594. Wolfgang Weingart. *Das Schweizer Plakat 1900–1983.* Poster to promote the book by Bruno Margadant, 1983. Courtesy the designer

595. Siegfried Odermatt. *Design aus den Niederlanden.* Exhibition poster, 1982. Courtesy the designer

596. Rosmarie Tissi. *Englersatz.* Poster for a typesetting company, 1983. Courtesy the designer

589

590

591

592

593

594

595

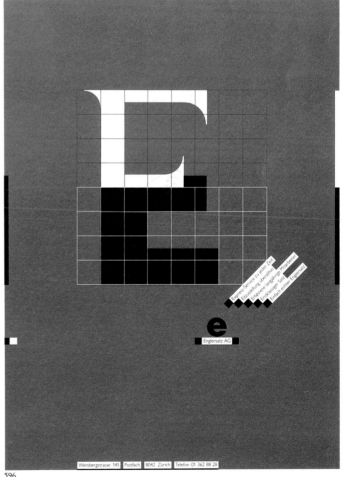

596

597

598

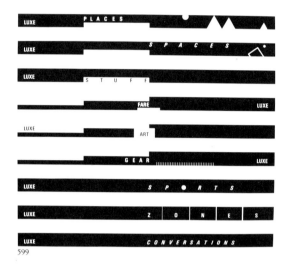

599

600

601

602

603

604

## AMERICAN NEW WAVE

Many designers who studied in Switzerland during the late sixties and the seventies returned to the United States to practice what they had learned. Their activities, however, did not reflect the rational design influence of an earlier generation but instead constituted a zealous assault on the fundamental principle of legibility and, thereby, an attempt to define a current graphic vocabulary. Experiments with new optics and computers resulted in the kinetic quality of their designs. The work here answers Dan Friedman's question: "To what degree can a typographic statement be both functional and at the same time aesthetically unconventional?"

597. Hans-U. Allemann. *Package Design.* Poster, 1979. Courtesy the designer

598. Michael Zender. *Cincinnati Symphony Orchestra.* Program cover, 1979. Courtesy the designer

599. April Greiman. *Luxe Magazine.* Magazine headers, 1979. Courtesy the designer

600. Dan Friedman. *Idea.* Cover of *Typography Today,* 1981. Courtesy the designer

601. Inge Druckrey. *Yale Symphony Orchestra.* Poster, 1979. Courtesy the designer

602. April Greiman/Jayme Odgers. *CalArts.* Poster, 1978. Courtesy the designers

603. William Longhauser. *The Language of Michael Graves.* Exhibition poster, 1983. Courtesy the designer

604. Nancy Skolos. *AIGA of Boston.* Poster, 1985. Courtesy the designer

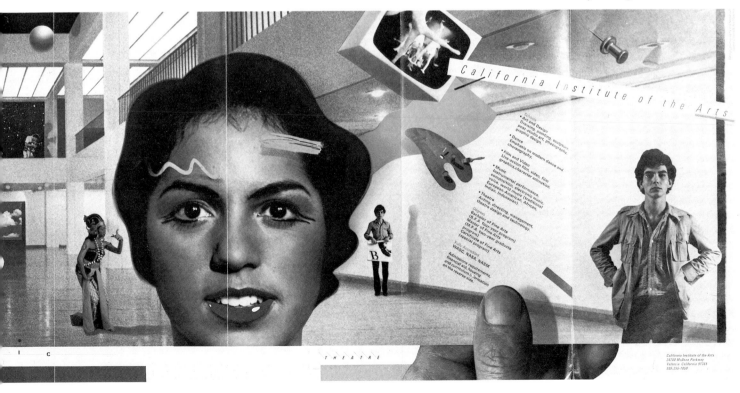

## AMERICAN NEW WAVE

A playful eclecticism underlies eighties design of all kinds. Graphic imagery reflects the contemporary fetish for products of the material, commercial, and high-tech culture. Some designers have cleverly updated the typographic and illustration styles of the twenties and reapplied them to various commercial durables, from watchfaces to shopping bags. Others have drawn on computer technology to change the look, if not the substance, of books and magazines.

605. Swatch watches, c. 1987

606. John Jay. *New Year 1983.* Shopping bag for Bloomingdale's, 1982. Richard Hsu (art director) and Melanie Marder Parks (artist). Courtesy Bloomingdale's, New York

607. John Jay. *New Year 1984.* Shopping bag for Bloomingdale's, 1983. Richard Hsu (art director) and Gene Greif (artist). Courtesy Bloomingdale's, New York

608. Carol Bokuniewicz, Maira Kalman, and Tibor Kalman. *David Byrne: Three Big Songs.* Record album cover, 1983. Courtesy M & Co., New York

609. Charles Spencer Anderson and Joe Duffy. *Partners in Performance.* Cover of an invitation to a conference, 1986. Courtesy Duffy Design Group

610. Jane Kosstrin and David Sterling. *Fetish.* Magazine cover, Fall 1980. Courtesy Doublespace, New York

611. Jane Kosstrin and David Sterling. *Fetish.* Magazine pages, Fall 1980. Courtesy Doublespace, New York

612. Rudy Vanderlans. *Emigre, The Magazine That Ignores Boundaries.* Magazine cover, 1986. Courtesy Emigre Graphics, Berkeley

613. Warren Leherer. *French Fries.* Pages from a book published by Ear/Say, 1984. Courtesy the designer

614. Rudy Vanderlans. *Magritte's Hat.* Trademark designed on the Macintosh computer, 1987. Courtesy Emigre Graphics, Berkeley

606

607

605

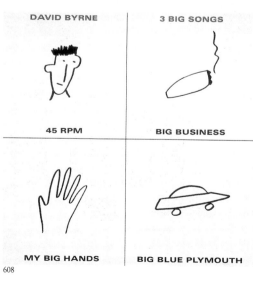

DAVID BYRNE     3 BIG SONGS

45 RPM     BIG BUSINESS

MY BIG HANDS     BIG BLUE PLYMOUTH

608

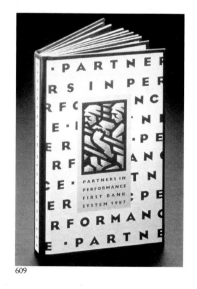

609

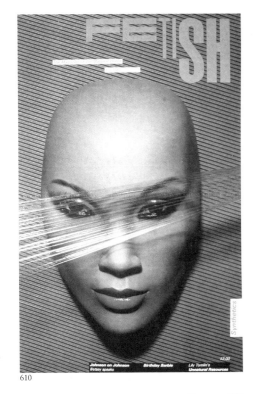

610

611

612

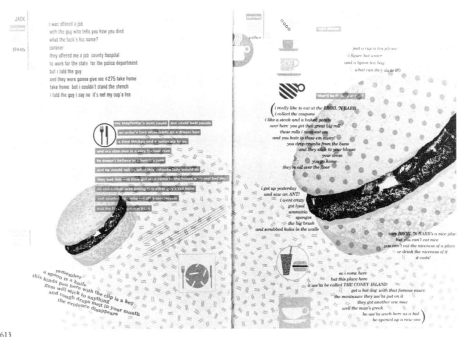

613

# Magritte's Hat

614

615

616

617

618

## AMERICAN PUNK

Like other twentieth-century youth movements, current youth culture has invented its own dominant design language. As signals of rebellion, comics are mainstays of the new style, and the basic primitivism of the collage technique helped to express an essential rawness. Collage was therefore the preferred artistic method during the early stages of Punk, and it was ultimately refined as a mainstream design technique.

615. Art Chantry. *Give Peace a Dance.* Poster, 1987. Courtesy the designer

616. Designer unknown. *Fiorucci.* Poster, date unknown. Courtesy Fiorucci, New York

617. Christopher Garland. *Boraxx.* Newspaper cover, 1981. Courtesy the designer

618. Louis Fishauf. Unpublished collage, 1981. Courtesy the designer

619. Gary Panter (artist), Art Spiegelman and Françoise Mouly (designers/editors). *Raw #3.* Magazine cover, 1981. Courtesy Raw Books, New York

620. Sue Huntley and Donna Muir (artists); Susan Hochbaum and Peter Harrison (designers). *Annual Report for Warner Communications.* Spread, 1986. Courtesy Pentagram, New York

621. Mark Marek. *New Wave Comics.* Book cover, 1984. Courtesy the designer

619

621

620

A

## AMERICAN POST-MODERN

Prevailing trends in architecture have traditionally influenced typographic and pictorial styles. In light of the increased creative interplay today between architects and interior and graphic designers, it is not surprising that an architectonic style of graphics has come to typify the American Post-Modern style.

622. Michael Manwaring. Hanna wine label, 1986. Courtesy the designer

623. Seth Jaben. *E. G. Smith Color Institute.* Advertisement, 1987. Courtesy the designer

624. Sussman/Prejza & Company, Inc. Designs for the 1984 Olympics. *Above:* Environmental graphics for the Arts Festival at Exposition Park; *below:* Entry to track and field events at the Los Angeles Memorial Coliseum. Courtesy Sussman/Prejza & Company, Inc., Los Angeles

625. Woody Pirtle and Alan Colvin. *Houston —A Celebration of Architecture.* Poster, 1983. Courtesy the designers

626. Michael R. Orr, Donna Bagley, and Rachel Schreiber Levitan. *16th Annual Exhibition of the Rochester Society of Communicating Arts.* Catalogue cover, 1985. Courtesy the designers

627. Michael Vanderbyl. *Sources.* Lecture series announcement, 1984. Courtesy the designer

628. Steve Snider. *Zipper Hospital.* Trademark, 1985. Courtesy the designer

629. Woody Pirtle. *Aubrey Hair.* Trademark, 1973. Courtesy the designer

630. John Casado. *Sir Cecil Beaton.* Exhibition invitation, 1974. Courtesy the designer

631. Susan Johnson. *The Current Thing.* Trademark, 1979. Courtesy the designer

622

623

624

625

626

# S O U R C E S

628

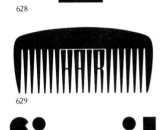

629

630

627

631

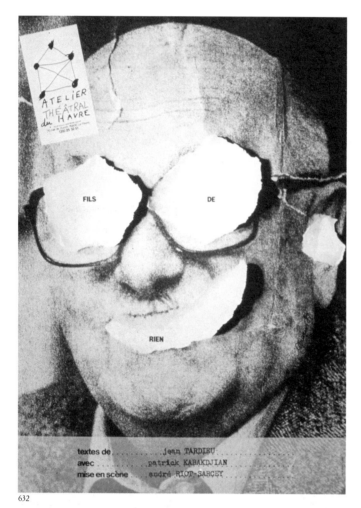

textes de . . . . . . . . . jean TARDIEU
avec . . . . . . . . . patrick KABAKDJIAN
mise en scène . . . . . andré RIOT-SARCEY . . . . .

632

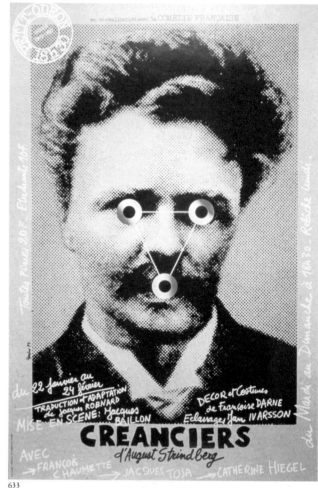

633

634

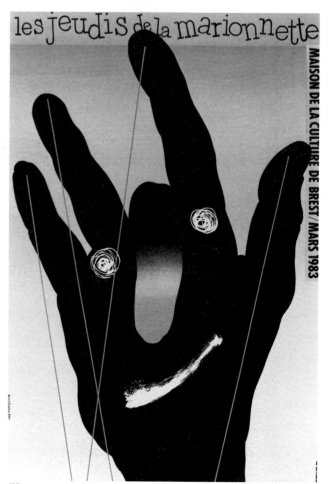

635

636

637

638

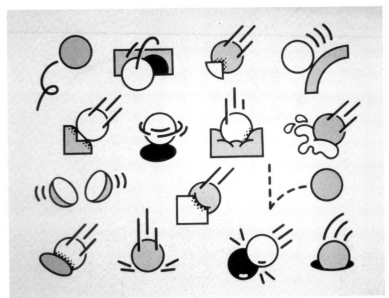

639

## EUROPEAN NEW WAVE

Responding to the need to communicate forcefully with participants in the 1968 general strike, French graphic designers developed an effective visual language of solid graphic forms and unadorned hand-lettering. The vocabulary of the design collective Grapus has become more sophisticated over the years—with layered photography, intricate typographical and pictorial designs, and unique color and black and white experiments. The posterist Alain Le Quernec has fine-tuned the permutations of the type and image combination. Studio Dumbar, one of Holland's perpetually innovative design firms, has extended the boundaries of acceptable corporate, government, and service-oriented communications. The Dutch designer Joost Swarte draws upon past cartoon masters and vintage decorative typefaces for a contemporary style that works as well in a comic book as on Dutch postage stamps. Paul Wearing's fabric print typifies the return to humorous decorative motifs in graphics and fabric design.

632. Grapus (Alexander Jordan, Garald Paris-Clavel, and Pierre Bernard). *Atelier Théâtral.* Theater poster, 1981. Courtesy Grapus, Paris

633. Grapus (Alexander Jordan, Garald Paris-Clavel, and Pierre Bernard). *Créanciers.* Theater poster, 1980. Courtesy Grapus, Paris

634. Grapus (Alexander Jordan, Garald Paris-Clavel, and Pierre Bernard). *Grapus.* Exhibition poster, 1982. Courtesy Grapus, Paris

635. Alain Le Quernec. *Thursdays of the Marionette.* Poster, 1983. Courtesy the designer

636. Gert Dumbar. *Mondrian.* Poster, 1972. Courtesy Studio Dumbar, The Hague

637. Joost Swarte. Postage stamps, 1986. Courtesy the designer

638–39. Studio Dumbar. Floor-identification system in a hospital, using bouncing balls, 1979–80. Courtesy Studio Dumbar, The Hague

640. Paul Wearing. Crocodile fabric print, 1985. Courtesy the designer

640

233

## SELECTED BIBLIOGRAPHY

Abdy, Jane. *The French Poster.* New York: Graphiques, 1977.

Ades, Dawn. *Photomontage.* New York: Pantheon, 1976.

———. *Posters: The 20th-Century Poster: Design of the Avant-Garde.* New York: Abbeville, 1986.

Anikst, Mikhail, ed. *Soviet Commercial Design of the Twenties.* New York: Abbeville, 1987.

Anscombe, Isabelle, and Gere, Charlotte. *The Arts and Crafts Movement in England and America.* New York: Rizzoli, 1978.

*Art Deco Trends in Design.* Chicago: The Bergman Gallery and University of Chicago, 1973.

Arnheim, Rudolf. *Art and Visual Perception: A Psychology of the Creative Eye.* Berkeley, Calif.: University of California Press, 1974.

Arwas, Victor. *Art Deco.* New York: Harry N. Abrams, 1980.

Ashwin, Clive. *A History of Graphic Design and Communication: A Source Book.* London: Penbridge, 1983.

Aslin, Elizabeth. *The Aesthetic Movement: Prelude to Art Nouveau.* New York: Praeger, 1969.

Baljev, Joost. *Theo van Doesburg.* New York: Macmillan, 1975.

Banham, Reyner. *Theory and Design in the First Machine Age.* New York: Praeger, 1967.

Barnicoat, John. *A Concise History of Posters: 1870–1970.* New York: Oxford University Press, 1980.

Battersby, Martin. *The Decorative Thirties.* New York: Walker, 1971.

———. *The Decorative Twenties.* New York: Walker, 1969.

Bayer, Herbert. *Bauhaus 1919–1928.* New York: The Museum of Modern Art, 1972.

———. *Herbert Bayer: Painter, Designer, Architect.* New York: Van Nostrand Reinhold, 1967.

Billcliffe, Roger. *Mackintosh Textile Designs.* New York: Taplinger, 1982.

Bing, Samuel. *Artistic America, Tiffany Glass and Art Nouveau.* Reprint. Cambridge, Mass.: M.I.T. Press, 1970.

Black, Mary. *American Advertising Posters of the Nineteenth Century.* New York: Dover, 1976.

Boe, Alf. *From Gothic Revival to Functional Form: A Study in Victorian Theories of Design.* Oslo: Oslo University Press; Oxford: Blackwell's, 1957.

Bojko, Szymon. *New Graphic Design in Revolutionary Russia.* New York: Praeger, 1972.

Bolin, Brent C. *Flight of Fancy.* New York: St. Martin's, 1985.

Branzi, Andrea. *The Hot House: Italian New Wave Design.* Cambridge, Mass.: M.I.T. Press, 1986.

Briggs, Asa, ed. *William Morris: Selected Writings and Designs.* Harmondsworth, England: Penguin, 1962.

Broos, Kees. *Piet Zwart 1885–1977.* The Hague: Gemeentemuseum, 1973.

Brown, Robert K., and Reinhold, Susan. *The Poster Art of A. M. Cassandre.* New York: E. P. Dutton, 1979.

Brunhammer, Yvonne. *The Nineteen Twenties Style.* London: Paul Hamlyn, 1969.

Burckhardt, Lucius. *The Werkbund: History and Ideology, 1907–1933.* New York: Barron's, 1977.

Busch, Donald. *The Streamlined Decade.* New York: George Braziller, 1968.

Cabarga, Leslie. *A Treasury of German Trademarks.* New York: Art Direction Book Co., 1985.

Callen, Anthea. *Women Artists of the Arts and Crafts Movement, 1870–1914.* New York: Pantheon, 1980.

Campbell, Joan. *The German Werkbund: The Politics of Reform in the Applied Arts.* Princeton: Princeton University Press, 1978.

Carter, Rob; Day, Ben; and Meggs, Philip. *Typographic Design: Form and Communication.* New York: Van Nostrand Reinhold, 1985.

Carter, Sebastian. *Twentieth Century Type Designer.* New York: Taplinger, 1987.

Clark, Robert J. *Arts and Crafts Movement in America.* Princeton: Princeton University Press, 1972.

Constantine, Mildred, and Fern, Alan. *Revolutionary Soviet Film Posters.* Baltimore: Johns Hopkins University Press, 1974.

———. *Word and Image.* New York: The Museum of Modern Art, 1968.

Cooper, Austin. *Making a Poster.* London: The Studio, 1949.

Cooper, Douglas. *The Cubist Epoch.* London: Phaidon, 1970.

Crane, Walter. *Of the Decorative Illustration of Books Old and New.* London: George Bell, 1896.

———. *William Morris to Whistler.* London: George Bell, 1911.

Delhaye, Jean. *Art Deco Posters and Graphics.* New York: Rizzoli, 1978.

Delpire, Robert. *Paris 1925.* Paris: Gallimard, 1957.

*Design in America: The Cranbrook Vision 1925–1950.* New York: Harry N. Abrams, 1983.

Deslandres, Yvonne, with Lalanne, Dorothea. *Poiret.* New York: Rizzoli, 1987.

Dewey, John. *Art as Experience.* Reprint. New York: Wideview/Perigee, 1980.

Dorfles, Gillo. *Kitsch: The World of Bad Taste.* New York: Universe, 1969.

Downey, Fairfax. *Portrait of an Era as Drawn by Charles Dana Gibson: A Biography.* New York: Charles Scribner & Sons, 1936.

Elliott, David, ed. *Alexander Rodchenko and the Arts of Revolutionary Russia.* New York: Pantheon, 1979.

Ferebee, Ann. *A History of Design from the Victorian Era to the Present.* New York: Van Nostrand Reinhold, 1970.

Fortz, Adrian. *Objects of Desire: Design and Society from Wedgwood to IBM.* New York: Pantheon, 1986.

Fraser, James, and Heller, Steven. *The Malik Verlag 1916–1947, Berlin, Prague, New York.* New York: Goethe House; Madison, N.J.: Fairleigh Dickinson University, 1985.

Friedman, Mildred, ed. *DeStijl: 1917–1931, Visions of Utopia.* New York: Abbeville, 1982.

Frutiger, Adrian. *Type, Sign, Symbol.* Zurich: ABC Verlag, 1980.

Fuld, James J. *A Pictorial Bibliography of the First Editions of Stephen C. Foster.* Philadelphia: Musical Americana, 1957.

Gallo, Max. *The Poster in History.* New York: American Heritage, 1974.

Garner, Philip. *Contemporary Decorative Arts from 1940 to the Present.* New York: Facts on File, 1980.

Gerstner, Karl, and Kutler, Marcus. *Die Neue Graphik/The New Graphic Art.* New York: Hastings House, 1959.

Glaser, Milton. *Milton Glaser Graphic Design.* Woodstock, N.Y.: Overlook, 1974.

Gluck, Felix, ed. *World Graphic Design: Fifty Years of Advertising Art.* New York: Watson-Guptill, 1969.

Gombrich, E. H. *Art and Illusion.* 2nd edition. Princeton: Princeton University Press, Bollingen Series, 1961.

Grannis, Chandler B., ed. *Heritage of the Graphic Arts: A Selection of Lectures Delivered at Gallery 303, New York City.* New York and London: R. R. Bowker, 1972.

Gray, Camilla. *The Russian Experiment in Art 1863–1922.* New York: Charles Scribner & Sons, 1973.

Gray, Nicolette. *A History of Lettering: Creative Experiment and Letter Identity.* Oxford, 1986.

———. *Nineteenth Century Ornamented Typefaces.* Berkeley: University of California Press, 1977.

Greif, Martin. *Depression Modern: The Thirties Style in America.* New York: Universe, 1977.

Hageney, Wolfgang. *Paris, 1928–1929.* Rome and Milan: Edition Belvedere, 1985.

Hammond, Wayne G., and Volz, Robert L. *Book Decoration in America, 1890–1910.* Revision. Williamstown, Mass.: Chapin Library, Williams College, 1979.

Havinden, Ashley. *Advertising and the Artist.* London: The Studio, 1956.

Heartfield, John. *Photomontages of the Nazi Period.* New York: Universe, 1977.

Henderson, Sally, and Landau, Robert. *Billboard Art.* San Francisco: Chronicle, 1979.

Hillier, Bevis. *Art Deco of the 20s and 30s.* London: Studio Vista; New York: Dutton, 1968.

235

———. *The Decorative Arts of the Forties and Fifties: Austerity Binge.* London: Studio Vista, 1970.

———. *The Style of the Century 1900–1980.* New York: E. P. Dutton, 1983.

———. *The World of Art Deco.* New York: E. P. Dutton, 1971.

Hine, Thomas. *Populuxe.* New York: Alfred A. Knopf, 1986.

Hipgnossis and Hardie, George. *The Work of Hipgnossis.* New York: A & W Visual Library, 1978.

Hlavsa, Oldruich. *A Book of Type and Design.* New York: Tudor, 1960.

Hofmann, Armin. *Graphic Design Manual: Principles and Practice.* New York: Van Nostrand Reinhold, 1965.

Horn, Richard. *Memphis: Objects, Furniture, and Patterns.* Philadelphia: Running Press, 1986.

Hornung, Clarence P., and Johnson, Fridolf. *200 Years of American Graphic Art: A Retrospective Survey of the Printing Arts and Advertising Since the Colonial Period.* New York: George Braziller, 1976.

Howarth, Thomas. *Charles Rennie Mackintosh and the Modern Movement.* London: Routledge and Kegan Paul, 1952.

Hulten, Pontus, organizer. *Futurismo, Futurism and Futurisms.* New York: Abbeville, 1986.

Hurlburt, Allen. *The Design Concept.* New York: Watson-Guptill, 1981.

———. *The Grid.* New York: Van Nostrand Reinhold, 1978.

Huszar, Vilmos. *Schilder en Ontwerper 1884–1960, De Grote Onbekende Van de Stijl.* Utrecht: Sjarel Ex, Els Hoek, 1985.

Igarashi, Takenobu, ed. *World Trademarks and Logotypes II.* Tokyo: Graphic-sha, 1987.

*Jan Tschichold: Leben und Werk des Typographen.* With an introduction by Werner Klemke. Dresden: VEB Verlag der Kunst, 1977.

Japan Package Design Association, ed. *Package Design in Japan: Its History, Its Faces.* Tokyo: Rikuyo-sha, 1976.

Johnson, Diana Chalmers. *American Art Nouveau.* New York: Harry N. Abrams, 1980.

Johnson, Douglas and Madeleine. *The Age of Illusion: Art and Politics in France 1918–1940.* New York: Rizzoli, 1987.

Jones, Owen. *The Grammar of Ornament.* Reprint. New York: Portland House, 1986.

Jubb, Michael. *Cocoa & Corsets.* London: Public Record Office, Her Majesty's Stationery Office, 1984.

Kahn, Douglas. *John Heartfield: Art and Mass Media.* New York: Tanam, 1985.

Kallir, Jane. *Viennese Design and the Wiener Werkstätte.* New York: Galerie St. Etienne/George Braziller, 1986.

Karginov, German. *Rodchenko.* New York: Pantheon, 1980.

Kelly, Rob Roy. *American Wood Type, 1828–1900: Notes on the Evolution of Decorated and Large Types.* New York: Da Capo, 1969.

Kepes, Gyorgy. *Language of Vision.* Chicago: Paul Theobald, 1945.

———. *The New Landscape.* Chicago: Paul Theobald, 1956.

Khan-Magomedov, Selim O. *Alexander Rodchenko: The Complete Work.* Cambridge, Mass.: M.I.T. Press, 1987.

———. *Alexander Vesnin and Russian Constructivism.* New York: Rizzoli, 1987.

Kimura, Katsu. *Art Deco Package Collection.* Tokyo: Rikuyo-sha, 1985.

Kostelanetz, Richard, ed. *Moholy-Nagy.* New York and Washington: Praeger, 1970.

Koretski, Victor Borisovich. *Comrade Poster.* Moscow, 1978.

Koumenhoven, John A. *Made in America: The Arts in Modern Civilization.* New York: Doubleday, 1948.

Kunzle, David. *The Early Comic Strip.* Berkeley: University of California Press, 1973.

Lang, Lothar. *Expressionist Book Illustration in Germany, 1907–1927.* Boston: New York Graphic Society, 1976.

Larner, Gerald and Celia. *The Glasgow Style.* London: Astragal, 1980.

Lewis, John. *Anatomy of Printing: The Influences of Art and History on Design.* New York: Watson-Guptill, 1970.

———. *The Twentieth Century Book.* New York: Van Nostrand Reinhold, 1967.

Lewis, John, and Brinkley, John. *Graphic Design.* London: Routledge & Kegan Paul, 1954.

Lindsay, Jack. *William Morris: His Life and Work.* New York: Taplinger, 1980.

Lippard, Lucy R. *Dadas on Art.* Englewood Cliffs, N.J.: Prentice-Hall, 1971.

Lissitzky-Kuppers, Sophie. *El Lissitzky: Life, Letters, Text.* London and New York: Thames & Hudson, 1980.

Lista, Giovanni. *Le Livre Futuriste.* Modena, Italy: Editions Panini, 1986.

Lois, George, and Pitts, Bill. *The Art of Advertising: George Lois on Mass Communication.* New York: Harry N. Abrams, Inc., 1977.

Lodder, Christina. *Russian Constructivism.* New Haven: Yale University Press, 1987.

Lucie-Smith, Edward. *Cultural Calendar of the 20th Century.* London: Phaidon, 1981.

McCarthy, Fiona. *A History of British Design, 1830–1970.* London and Boston: George Allen & Unwin, 1979.

McClelland, Gordon. *Rick Griffin.* New York: Putnam and Perigee Paper Tiger, 1980.

McDermott, Catherine. *Street Style: British Design in the 80s.* New York: Rizzoli, 1987.

Macfall, Haldane. *Aubrey Beardsley: The Man and His Work.* London: John Lane, 1928.

McLean, Ruari. *Jan Tschichold: Typographer.* Boston: David R. Godine, 1975.

———. *Modern Book Design.* New York: Faber & Faber, 1958.

———. *Victorian Book Design.* New York: Faber & Faber, 1963.

McLuhan, Marshall, and Fiore, Quentin. *War and Peace in the Global Village.* New York: Bantam, 1968.

Madsen, Stephen Tschudi. *Sources of Art Nouveau.* New York: Da Capo, 1976.

Marchand, Roland. *Advertising the American Dream: Making Way for Modernity 1920–40.* Berkeley: University of California Press, 1985.

Margolin, Victor. *American Poster Renaissance: The Great Age of Poster Design, 1890–1900.* New York: Watson-Guptill, 1975.

Marzio, Peter. *The Democratic Art: Pictures for a 19th Century America.* Boston: David Godine, 1979.

Mayor, A. Hyatt. *Popular Prints of the Americas.* New York: Crown, 1973.

Meggs, Philip B. *A History of Graphic Design.* New York: Van Nostrand Reinhold, 1983.

Meikle, Jeffrey L. *Twentieth Century Limited: Industrial Design in America, 1925–1939.* Philadelphia: Temple University Press, 1979.

Metzl, Ervine. *The Poster: Its History and Its Art.* New York: Watson-Guptill, 1963.

Moholy-Nagy, László. *Vision in Motion.* Chicago: Paul Theobald, 1947.

Morison, Stanley. *First Principles of Typography.* Cambridge, England: Cambridge University Press, 1957.

Mouron, Henri. *A. M. Cassandre.* New York: Rizzoli, 1985.

Müller-Brockmann, Josef. *The Graphic Artist and His Design Problems.* New York: Hastings House, 1961.

———. *A History of Visual Communication.* New York: Hastings House, 1967.

Müller-Brockmann, Josef, and Müller-Brockmann, Shizuka. *A History of the Poster.* New York: Hastings House, 1961.

Murgatroyd, Keith. *Modern Graphics.* London: Studio Vista, 1969.

Naylor, Gillian. *The Arts and Crafts Movement: A Study of Its Sources, Ideals, and Influence on Design.* Cambridge, Mass.: M.I.T. Press, 1975.

Neuwmann, Eckhard. *Bauhaus and Bauhaus People.* New York: Van Nostrand Reinhold, 1970.

———. *Functional Graphic Design in the 20s.* New York: Reinhold, 1967.

Ozenfant, Amédée. *Foundations of Modern Art.* New York: Dover, 1953.

Packer, William. *The Art of Vogue Covers 1919–1940.* New York: Bonanza, 1980.

Passuth, Kristina. *Moholy-Nagy.* London and New York: Thames & Hudson, 1984.

Pentagram. *Ideas on Design.* New York: Faber & Faber, 1986.

———. *Living by Design.* New York: Whitney Library of Design, 1978.

Peterson, Theodore. *Magazines in the Twentieth Century.* Champaign-Urbana, Ill.: University of Illinois Press, 1964.

Pevsner, Nikolaus. *Pioneers of Modern Design: From William Morris to Walter Gropius.* Harmondsworth, England: Penguin, 1960.

Pitz, Henry C. *The Practice of Illustration.* New York: Watson-Guptill, 1947.

Prokopoff, Stephen. *The Modern Dutch Poster.* Champaign-Urbana, Ill.: University of Illinois, Krannert Art Museum, 1987.

Pulous, Arthur J. *The American Design Ethic: A History of Industrial Design to 1940.* Cambridge, Mass.: M.I.T. Press, 1986.

Quilici, Vieri, ed. *Rodchenko, the Complete Work.* Cambridge, Mass.: M.I.T. Press, 1987.

Radice, Barbara. *Memphis: Research, Experiences, Results, Failures and Successes of New Design.* New York: Rizzoli, 1984.

Rand, Paul. *A Designer's Art.* New Haven: Yale University Press, 1985.

———. *Thoughts on Design.* New York: Van Nostrand Reinhold, 1971.

Read, Herbert. *Art and Industry.* New York: Horizon, 1961.

Reed, Orrel P., Jr. *German Expressionist Art: The Robert Gore Rifkind Collection.* Los Angeles: University of California, Frederick S. Wright Art Gallery, 1977.

Rennert, Jack. *Timeless Images.* Tokyo: Isetan Museum of Art, 1984.

Rhodes, Anthony. *Propaganda: The Art of Persuasion, World War II.* Victor Margolin, ed. New York: Chelsea House, 1976.

Rowland, Kurt. *History of the Modern Movement.* New York: Van Nostrand Reinhold, 1974.

Rubin, William S. *Dada, Surrealism, and Their Heritage.* New York: The Museum of Modern Art, 1968.

Rublowsky, John, and Heyman, Ken. *Pop Art.* New York: Basic Books, 1965.

Sanders, Barry. *The Craftsman: An Anthology.* Santa Barbara: Peregrine Smith, 1978.

Sartogo, Piero. *Italian Re-Evolution: Design in Italian Society in the Eighties.* La Jolla, Calif.: La Jolla Museum of Contemporary Art, 1986.

Schau, Michael. *All American Girl: The Art of Coles Phillips.* New York: Watson-Guptill, 1975.

Schmidt, Joost. *Lehre und Arbeit am Bauhaus 1919–32.* Düsseldorf: Edition Marzona, 1984.

Schweiger, Werner J. *Wiener Werkstätte: Design in Vienna, 1903–1932.* New York: Abbeville, 1984.

Selz, Peter, and Constantine, Mildred. *Art Nouveau.* New York: The Museum of Modern Art, 1976.

———. *Art Nouveau: Art and Design at the Turn of the Century.* New York: The Museum of Modern Art, 1959.

Sembach, Klaus-Jurgen. *Exactitude: Style 1930.* New York: Universe, 1986.

Shahn, Ben. *The Shape of Content.* Cambridge, Mass.: Harvard University Press, 1957.

Snyder, Gertrude, and Peckolick, Alan. *Herb Lubalin: Art Director, Graphic Designer and Typographer.* New York: American Showcase, 1985.

Sparke, Penny. *An Introduction to Design and Culture in the Twentieth Century.* London: Allen & Unwin, 1986.

Sparke, Penny; Hodges, Felice; Coad, Emma Dent; and Stone, Anne. *Design Source Book.* Secaucus, N.J.: Chartwell, 1986.

Sparling, H. Halliday. *The Kelmscott Press and William Morris, Master-Craftsman.* New York: Macmillan, 1924.

Spencer, Herbert. *Pioneers of Modern Typography.* New York: Hastings House, 1970.

———. *The Liberated Page: A Typographical Anthology.* San Francisco: Bedford, 1987.

Spencer, Isobel. *Walter Crane.* New York: Macmillan, 1975.

Spiegelman, Art, and Mauly, Françoise, eds. *Read Yourself Raw.* New York: Pantheon, 1987.

Sutnar, Ladislav. *Package Design: The Force of Visual Selling.* New York: Arts, 1953.

Taylor, Joshua C. *Futurism.* New York: The Museum of Modern Art, 1961.

Thorgerson, Storm, and Dean, Roger, eds. *Album Cover Album: A Book of Record Jackets.* New York: Dragon's World Book, 1977.

Tichi, Cecelia. *Shifting Gears: Technology, Literature, Culture in Modernist America.* Chapel Hill, N.C.: University of North Carolina Press, 1987.

Tolmer, A. *Mise en Page: The Theory and Practice of Layout.* London: The Studio, 1930.

Tracy, Walter. *Letters of Credit: A View of Type Design.* Boston: David Godine, 1987.

Twyman, Michael. *Printing, 1770–1970: An Illustrated History of Its Development and Uses in England.* London: Eyer & Spottiswoode, 1970.

Updike, Daniel Berkeley. *Printing Types, Their History, Forms and Use: A Study in Survivals.* New York: Dover, 1980.

Vallance, Aymer. *William Morris: His Art, His Writings and His Public Life.* London: Studio Editions, 1986.

Van Doesburg, Theodore. *Principles of Neo-Plastic Art.* London: Lund Humphries, 1969.

Varnedoe, Kirk. *Vienna 1900: Art, Architecture and Design.* New York: The Museum of Modern Art, 1986.

Veronesi, Guilia. *Style & Design 1909–1929.* New York: George Braziller, 1968.

Watkinson, Raymond. *Pre-Raphaelite Art and Design.* New York, 1970.

Weber, Eva. *Art Deco in America.* New York: Bison, 1985.

Weill, Alain. *The Poster: A Worldwide Survey and History.* Boston: G. K. Hall, 1985.

Weisberg, Gabriel P. *Art Nouveau Bing, Paris Style 1900.* New York: Harry N. Abrams, in Association with the Smithsonian Institution Traveling Service, 1986.

Welo, Samuel. *Trademark and Monogram Suggestions.* New York: Pitman, 1937.

Wember, Paul. *Johan Thorn Prikker.* Krefeld, Germany: Scherpe Verlag, 1966.

Wingler, Hans M. *The Bauhaus: Weimar, Dessau, Berlin, Chicago.* Cambridge, Mass.: M.I.T. Press, 1969.

Wornum, Ralph N. *Analysis of Ornament.* London: Chapman & Hall, 1879.

Yasinskaya, I. *Revolutionary Textile Design: Russia in the 1920s and 1930s.* New York: Viking, 1983.

Young, Frank H. *Advertising Layout.* New York: Pascal Covici, 1928.

## ANNUALS

American Institute of Graphic Arts. *AIGA Graphic Design, USA.* New York: Watson-Guptill, 1980.

Art Directors Club. *Annual of Advertising and Editorial Art.* New York: 1921–present.

Coyne, Richard. *CA Annual of Design and Advertising.* Palo Alto: Communications Arts Books, 1958.

Herdeg, Walter. *Graphis Annual.* Zurich: Graphis Press; New York: Hastings House, 1952.

*Print Casebooks.* Three six-volume editions of the best in graphic design from 1975 to 1980. Bethesda, Md.: R. C. Publications.

"The Society of Illustrators." *The Illustrators Annual.* New York: Hastings House, 1959.

*Typography: The Annual of the Type Directors Club.* New York: Watson-Guptill, 1985.

# INDEX

The name of every designer of an illustrated work is listed below, by the page number on which the work appears.

1/24/00 Midwest 23.20 (27.95) 76545.